AF600476

THE CATHOLIC UNIVERSITY OF AMERICA
CANON LAW STUDIES
No. 349

THE DISCRETIONARY AUTHORITY OF THE ECCLESIASTICAL JUDGE IN MATRIMONIAL TRIALS OF THE FIRST INSTANCE

A DISSERTATION

Submitted to the Faculty of the School of Canon Law of the Catholic University of America, in Partial Fulfillment of the Requirements for the Degree of Doctor of Canon Law

by the

REVEREND ARCHIBALD M. BOTTOMS, J.C.L.
Priest of the Diocese of Amarillo, Texas

THE CATHOLIC UNIVERSITY OF AMERICA PRESS
WASHINGTON, D. C.
1955

NIHIL OBSTAT:
John Rogg Schmidt, J.C.D.
Censor Deputatus

Washingtonii, D.C., die 19 maii 1954

IMPRIMATUR:
✠ Laurence Julius FitzSimon, D.D.
Episcopus Amarillensis

Amarillensi, die 23 maii, 1954

COPYRIGHT 1955 BY
THE CATHOLIC UNIVERSITY OF AMERICA PRESS, INC.

Printed by The Abbey Press, St. Meinrad, Indiana, U.S.A.

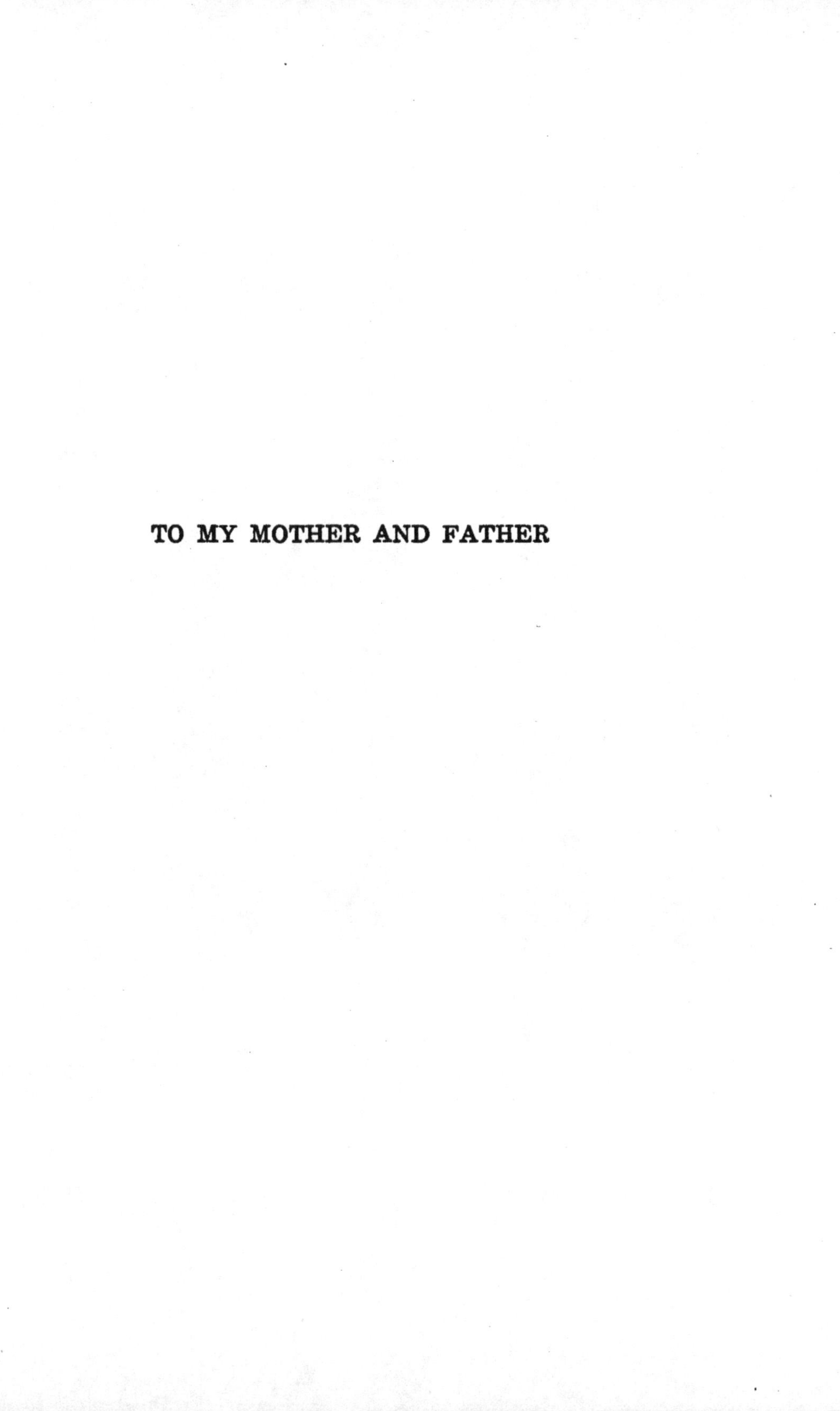

TO MY MOTHER AND FATHER

FOREWORD

THE purpose of this study is to provide the historical background for, and a commentary on, the discretionary authority of the ecclesiastical judge in matrimonial trials of the first instance. By discretion is meant the freedom to decide or to act—the exercise or choice of will. In its application to the ecclesiastical judge, discretionary authority may be defined as the right to exercise judgment in the presiding over and the directing of court procedure, and in the arriving at a decision. It is evident that in every trial the judge has the leading rôle, and although the norms of procedure are well defined, much is left to his discretion. His obligation is, therefore, to direct the trial and to pronounce what is conformable to established right and equity.[1]

In the early centuries, matrimonial questions were decided by the bishop. Such causes were relatively few and simple, and causes involving nullity of marriage were not brought before an ecclesiastical judge for trial in the early ages of the Church. By the eighth and ninth centuries, however, with the increase in the number of diriment impediments and other factors, questions concerning the nullity of marriage had become relatively frequent in ecclesiastical courts. For the first twelve centuries, matrimonial procedure was not different from the procedure in other matters. Over a period of time, the circumstances and difficulties peculiar to marriage causes brought about specific legislation regarding marriage trials. The basis of our modern canonical procedure in matrimonial causes was formed by Benedict XIV when he established norms of judgment in his Constitution *Dei miseratione*, of Nov. 3, 1741.

This dissertation will be divided into three sections, as follows:

[1] Cf. Can. 1577, §2.

Section I. The Development of the Discretionary Power of the Judge in the Pre-Code Era.

Section II. The Discretionary Authority of the Judge in Presiding over and Directing Court Procedure.

Section III. The Discretionary Authority of the Judge in Evaluating the Judicial Evidence.

The writer wishes to take this occasion to thank all who assisted him in any way. Particularly, he wishes to express his gratitude to the Most Reverend Laurence J. FitzSimon, D.D., Bishop of Amarillo, for the opportunity of advanced study; he also wishes to acknowledge his deepest appreciation for the invaluable assistance and suggestions given him by the Faculty of the School of Canon Law.

TABLE OF CONTENTS

SECTION I.

THE DEVELOPMENT OF THE DISCRETIONARY POWER OF THE JUDGE IN THE PRE-CODE ERA

CHAPTER ONE

THE JUDGE IN ROMAN LAW

The procedural regulations of Roman law exerted a strong influence on the formation and development of canonical procedure,[1] to such an extent that there arose the maxim, *"Ecclesia vivit lege Romana,"* "The Church lives by Roman law."

During the first eight centuries the use of Roman law was not very frequent, and the Church went to Roman law during this period as the existing state law, not as to law which it had accepted and canonized, as it were. The practice of using Roman law as a subsidiary source, first recognized by Pope Gregory I in 603,[2] was given its strongest confirmation by Pope Lucius III (1181-1185). Lucius openly declared that just as civil law did not disdain to imitate canon law, so too canon law was helped by civil law.[3]

In the modern period of canon law history, Pope Benedict XIV (1740-1758) in his private work, *De Synodo Dioecesana,* stated that Roman law provisions which had been expressly approved by the Church could and should be ad-

[1] Schmalzgrueber, *Ius Ecclesiasticum Universum* (5 vols. in 12, Romae, 1843-1845) lib. II, tit. I, n. 4; Devoti, *Institutionum Canonicarum Libri IV* (4 ed. Romana, Leodii, 1874), lib. III, tit. I, n. 26; Wernz, *Ius Decretalium* (6 vols., vol. V, Prati, 1914), V, *De Iudiciis Ecclesiasticis,* Lib. I, p. 7 (Hereafter cited *De Iudiciis*); Cicognani, *Canon Law* (2. ed., authorized English version by J. O'Hara and F. Brennan, Philadelphia, 1935), pp. 47-51; Bouix, *Tractatus de Judiciis Ecclesiasticis* (2 vols., Parisiis, 1855) I, pp. 19-23; Noval, *Commentarium Codicis Iuris Canonici,* lib. IV, *De Processibus,* pars I, *De Iudiciis* (Romae, 1920), p. 13; Roberti, *De Processibus* (2 vols., Romae; Vol. I, ed. altera, 1941, Vol. II, 1926), I, 1.

[2] C. 7, C. II, q. 1; c. 38, C. XI, q. 1; c. 2, C. XVI, q. 6.—Jaffé, *Regesta Pontificum Romanorum* (2. ed. by F. Kaltenbrunner. 33-590; by P. Ewald: 590-882; and by S. Löwenfeld: 882-1198, referred to as JK, JE, JL, Lipsiae, 1885-1888), JE, n. 1912.

[3] C. 1, X, *de novi operis nunciatione,* V, 32.—JL, n. 15189.

duced in ecclesiastical legislation, and that at times it would also be useful and praiseworthy to adduce certain other provisions of Roman law which the Church had neither expressly approved nor condemned.[4]

The Roman civil procedure, which was very slowly developed, readily admits of division into three distinctive periods: 1. The *legis actio,* from the beginning of Rome until about 150 B.C.; 2. the formulary or ordinary procedure, from 150 B.C. until about A.D. 300; 3. The extraordinary procedure, or the *cognitio extra ordinem,* from about the year 300 until post-Justinian times. The first two periods are also classed together as one system, the *ordo iudiciorum privatorum,* in distinction to the third period of the bureaucratic *cognitio.*[5]

Art. I. The Judge In The Legis Actio

Under the *ordo iudiciorum* there was no one person acting in the capacity of the judge according to the present day conception of a judge. Instead, two parties, the magistrate and the *iudex* (here so termed to distinguish him from the judge with full capacity to act), performed the judicial functions. Thus, during the period of the *legis actio* and likewise during the times of the subsequent formulary procedure, there were regularly two phases or parts to a lawsuit. The first was the proceedings *in iure;* the second, the proceedings *in iudicio,* or *apud iudicem.*

In the proceedings *in iure,* the matter was brought before the magistrate by a fixed ritual, each party and the magistrate himself going through a series of acts and declarations, prescribed by statute and interpretations of statute.

[4] De Synodo Dioecesana—*Opera Omnia,* Tom. XI (Prati, 1844), lib. IX, cap. 10, n. 1.

[5] Wenger, *Institutes of the Roman Law of Civil Procedure* (rev. ed., translated by Fisk: New York, Veritas Press, 1940), pp. 256-334; Jolowicz, *Historical Introduction to the Study of Roman Law* (Cambridge, University Press, 1932), p. 179; Amos, *The History and Principles of the Civil Law of Rome* (London, 1883), pp. 341-342; Buckland, *A Textbook of Roman Law from Augustus to Justinian* (2. ed., Cambridge: University Press, 1932), pp. 607-608.

The ceremonies completed, the matter was *in iudicio* and referred for trial and decision to the *iudex*, not an official but a private person, chosen by the parties from a list. If the decision was against the defendant, it was enforced by seizure of him by the plaintiff, and, in the last resort, sale into slavery.

Originally the judicial office was not thus partitioned, but in ordinary litigation the king not only decided whether there was a relevant case averred, but himself heard and considered the merits and pronounced a final judgment.[6]

Being a finder of facts and an adjudicator, the *iudex* might be compared with a modern judge who hears a case without a jury. However, the *iudex* stood in a peculiar relationship with the parties and with the judicial magistrate, and was a private citizen, not a professional judge. The nearest approach today to the *iudex* would be a referee with authority to render final judgment. But "referee" seems rather a lame translation of "*iudex*."

As might be expected under a system where there were no professional judges, the proceedings *in iudicio* were in the earliest times free from restrictions of form, and the *iudex* was quite at liberty in weighing the evidence presented to him and in reaching a decision.

ART. II. THE JUDGE IN THE FORMULARY SYSTEM

The second period of civil procedure in the Roman law is known as the formulary period because of the written statement or formula drawn up by the praetor for the purpose of instructing the *iudex*, who was to try the case. It was a brief, concise statement setting out the claim of the plaintiff and the duty of the *iudex* to find either for the plaintiff or for the defendant according to the evidence presented.

In the formulary system, dominant in the classical age, the main lines of the procedure were unchanged. As in the

[6] Cicero, *De Rep.*, V, 2, 3; cf. Muirhead—Goudy—Grant, *Historical Introduction to the Private Law of Rome* (3. ed., London, 1916), p. 168.

first period, the fundamental character of the system was the proceedings *in iure* before the magistrate, and *in iudicio* before the *iudex*. To begin, the parties being in court, the plaintiff stated the nature of his claim and evidence, and asked of the praetor or magistrate the formula he wanted.[7] The possible variety of defenses and answers thereto made the matter *in iure* much more complex than under the old system. Ultimately the issues were embodied in the formula approved by the praetor. It was issued under his authority, but it was not his duty to see that it stated the dispute correctly; that was for the parties.

The function of the magistrate was very different from his part in the *legis actio*: he had to decide difficult points and exercise a wide discretion, and so it is not surprising that he habitually acted with a council of advisors. There were many matters which the praetor did not refer to the *iudex*, but decided himself, a practice which tended to increase. If on the agreed facts the praetor held that there was no case, he could refuse the action, but if he held that there was a claim, then the admission of the facts probably amounted to a confession.[8]

The *iudex* in the formulary procedure, chosen as in the *legis actio*, received instructions on the law in the formula. They were terse and highly technical in import, and limited judgment for the plaintiff to a certain action, if it was proved to exist; if not so proved, there had to be judgment for the defendant. All that the so-called instructions as to the law really accomplished was to require the *iudex* to render judgment for the plaintiff if the facts required for the laying of an action were shown to exist, no matter how unjust it might have seemed to him upon the merits. The *iudex* had no power to amend, alter or depart from the formula.[9] The question was disputed whether a *iudex* could weigh in his judgment the private knowledge which he might happen to have concerning the case.

[7] Cicero, *in Verr.*, 2.3.65.152; Cod. (3.9)1; Cod. (2.57) rubr.
[8] Buckland, *A Textbook of Roman Law*, p. 635.
[9] Wenger, *Institutes*, p. 192.

A decision not authorized by the formula was not thereby null. However, an action was available against a *iudex* who from carelessness or unfairness gave a wrong decision, or neglected his duty. A judgment once given could not be corrected.[10]

ART. III. THE JUDGE IN THE EXTRAORDINARY PROCEDURE

The third and last procedural system of Roman law, known as the *cognitio extra ordinem,* was the system in use at the time when the Church was emerging from the persecutions and feeling the need of a more definite procedure. It was called "extraordinary" because it was a procedure outside of the regular order of the formulary procedure, and was otherwise called libellary by reason of the notice of suit (*libellus conventionis*) served upon a defendant.

The procedure *extra ordinem* did not come into existence by any one definite act of legislation, and there is no positive date that can be assigned for its adoption. Step by step the new procedure took the place of the formulary procedure, until in time a complete transition was made. The offices of magistrate and *iudex* became one, and the arbitral nature of the judgment was lost. Even during the time of the formulary procedure, certain cases had been heard and decided by the praetor alone, no reference being made to the *iudex.*[11] This convenient and more expeditious way of disposing of various matters had great influence in bringing to pass a more general practice of the same kind in all questions.

The *iudex,* or folk-judge, was abolished by Diocletian in 294, and again in 334 by Constantine.[12] Administrative and judicial functions were in many cases united, and there was a hierarchy of courts surmounted by that of the emperor.

By the fifth century there had evolved and developed

[10] D. (44.7)5.4; D. (42.1)55.

[11] Burdick, *Principles of Roman Law and Their Relation to Modern Law* (Rochester, N. Y., 1938), p. 666.

[12] Cod. (3.3)2; (3.14)1.

through practice and legislation the *libellus* proceedings,[13] the final Justinian preliminaries of litigation. The proceeding began with the delivery of a bill of complaint in an original and a copy to the competent judge. The judge examined summarily the bill of complaint submitted to him, and could at once, if it was insufficient on its face, proceed to rejection. Otherwise and normally there resulted the issuance of a decree providing that the complaint was to be served upon the defendant, and the latter to be summoned.

At first, in the *cognitio* system, the judge had an increased influence on the proceedings. This is indicated by the fact that in reaching his decision the judge needed no longer to be limited to the proofs produced by the parties, but he could intervene officially in the ascertainment of truth. However, the bureaucracy and absolutism of the *cognitio* period gradually came to be reflected in the encroachments made on the judge's freedom of appraising the value of proof.[14] Not trusting the free consideration of the judge, the bureaucratic system set up rules of law to guide the judge in evaluating proofs and in reaching a decision. The rules provided for externalities, which even the non-learned man could easily establish, as the standard for whether or not a fact was to be considered proved. Such rules could be applied without regard for the judge's subjective opinion.

[13] Nov. (53.3); Inst. (4.6)24.
[14] Wenger, *op. cit.*, pp. 261; 275; 334.

CHAPTER II

THE JUDGE IN GERMANIC LAW

From the barbarian invasions to the revival of Roman law in the twelfth century, ecclesiastical procedure, while remaining basically Roman, felt the influence of the Germanic laws of processes. However, the Church never accepted the Germanic laws or the laws of barbarian tribes in general as supplementary sources of its law.[1] The office of the ecclesiastical judge was less affected by Germanic influence than was the general court procedure itself.

In Germanic law the judge appraised the proofs in a purely legal method, in which it was the law and not his discretion which determined what efficacy the various arguments should have; in the classical period of Roman law the judge appraised the proofs by the method of free appraisal, in which it was left entirely to the prudence of the judge to make of the proofs what he would, the law in no way limiting his discretion.[2] Elements of both methods are found in present day ecclesiastical procedure, with the system of free appraisal as found in Roman law having the more influence, especially in marriage causes, where it is incumbent upon the judge to evaluate for himself such proofs as the confession and the oath of the parties, and the reports of the experts.[3]

The idea of the increased activity of the parties, lessening somewhat the power of the judge, was derived from Germanic law; but for the most part Germanic customs were

[1] Van Hove, *Commentarium Lovaniense in Codicem Iuris Canonici*, Vol. I, tom. I. *Prolegomena* (2. ed., Mechliniae, Romae: H. Dessain, 1945), pp. 261-262; Cicognani, *Canon Law*, p. 51.

[2] Roberti, *De Processibus*, II, p. 31; Noval, *De Iudiciis*, p. 308; Wanenmacher, *Canonical Evidence in Marriage Cases* (Philadelphia, 1935), n. 139.

[3] Wanenmacher, *loc. cit.*

rejected in connection with the judge.[4] In the Germanic system of procedure, the judge was reduced to the position of a referee in the probative period of the trial—a position very similar to the *iudex* of the formulary period of Roman law. In the Carolingian period the formalism and rigor of the earlier Germanic procedure was modified, chiefly as a result of the Christian influence.[5]

[4] C. 3, X, *de consuetudine*, I, 4; Roberti, *op. cit.*, II, 4.

[5] Cf. Glasson, *Histoire du Droit et des Institutions de la France*, (Paris, 1889), III, 468, 493-494.

CHAPTER III

THE JUDGE IN THE *IUS ANTIQUUM*

ART. I. THE JUDGE IN *APOSTOLIC* TIMES

From the very beginning there existed in the Church a canonical procedure which the ecclesiastical authorities employed to carry out the Church's God-given power of judging over the faithful.[1] In the New Testament, the essential elements of a trial are outlined by Our Lord Himself: the judge in the external forum, the plaintiff and the defendant, the consideration of the case, the judgment, and finally the penalty.[2]

The power of the judge asserted itself in the Apostles' immediate correction of unlawful acts. The immediate successors of the Apostles did not fail to claim and exercise this same prerogative, judging unlawful acts and pronouncing sentence in the external forum.[3]

The exercise of judicial power by the bishops was at first a quite simple form of procedure, which gradually evolved and developed. The chief consideration in regard to judicial procedure that occupied the early bishops with their manifold labors was a simple administration of strict justice for the body of the faithful. Hearings were expedited with a minimum of the technicalities and solemnities which frequently trammeled and delayed the administration of justice in the secular courts.[4]

[1] Acts, V, 9. Cf. Roberti, *De Processibus,* I, 1.

[2] Matt., XVIII, 15; Cf. Bouix, *Tractatus de Judiciis Ecclesiasticis* I, 30.

[3] Devoti, *Institutionum Canonicarum Libri IV,* lib. III, tit. I, n. 13; Wernz, *De Iudiciis,* lib. I, p. 69.

[4] Devoti, *op. cit.,* lib. III, tit. I, n. 25. Cf. *Didascalia et Constitutiones Apostolorum* (ed. F. X. Funk, Paderborn, 1905), lib. II, cap. 11, 12, 37, 38, 42, 43, 46, 47, 48, 49.

Art. II. The Judge In Post-Apostolic Times

In the first centuries the Apostles and their successors, the early bishops, were free to act as sole judges, without having to use advisors, or to act in collegiate tribunals.[5] However, almost from the beginning the Roman Pontiff had his council of advisors *(presbyterium),* and usually called together a synod to decide the more serious questions.[6]

As the number and kind of causes increased, a more detailed system of ecclesiastical procedure was developed. Much of this development was accomplished in the Councils of Africa.[7] There the custom was gradually introduced that bishops would decide serious questions especially such as pertained to the sacrament of matrimony, in provincial councils. In line with this, bishops gathered around them clerics as an advisory board in judging lesser questions.[8] Thus it came about that very often marriage causes were adjudged by colleges of judges assembled in provincial councils. When only a single judge was used, marriage causes were judged by bishops alone, seldom by archdeacons.[9]

During this period the outstanding figure in the judiciary —next to the bishop—gradually became the archdeacon. Originally the archdeacon was appointed by the bishop to administer the temporalities of the Church, but the transformation of the archdeaconship into a benefice endowed with income from the districts as set up by the synodal assembly, and the coupling of ordinary jurisdiction with the

[5] Wernz, *De Iudiciis,* Lib. I, p. 83.

[6] "Qui antiquitatis monumenta pervolverit, . . . reperiet omnino certa: Presbyterium, seu (quod idem est) cathedrale capitulum, de facto et de jure fuisse consilium Episcopi (per quinque priora saecula)."—Bouix, *De Judiciis,* I, 343; Wernz, *op. cit.* Lib. I, p. 72.

[7] Cf. I Council of Carthage (348), c. 11—Bruns, *Canones Apostolorum et Conciliorum IV—VII* (2 vols., Berolini, 1839), I, 115; II Council of Carthage (393), c. 10—Bruns, *op. cit.,* I, 121.

[8] Wernz, *De Iudiciis,* Lib. I, p. 83; Bouix, *op. cit.,* I, 342.

[9] Perrone, *De Matrimonio Christiano,* (3 vols., Romae: Typis S. Congr. de Prop. Fide, 1858) II, 351.

benefice, in time gave the archdeacon ordinary power as a judge.[10]

ART. III. CHARACTERISTICS OF PRE-GRATIAN JUDICIAL POWER

There being as yet no iron-clad rules of procedure, the judge enjoyed quite a wide discretionary power in directing the unfolding of the process. Matrimonial cases played a comparatively small part of court procedure, and there was no distinct matrimonial procedure. The system of proof remained basically Roman, the decision of the case depending upon the conviction of the judge; the testimony of witnesses seems to have been by far the most prominent means of proof during this period.[11]

Documentary proof was used, but after the division of the Carolingian monarchy there was a return to the original Germanic distrust for documents.[12] Oaths were admitted as supplementary proof, becoming common in the ninth, tenth and eleventh centuries.[13]

In estimating the value of these various proofs and in reaching a decision, the judge was free. However, he was frequently admonished not to allow himself to be influenced

[10] Thomassinus, *Vetus et Nova Ecclesiae Disciplina circa Beneficia et Beneficiarios* (Lucae, 1728), Pars I, Lib. 1-2, cap. 17; Wernz, *De Iudiciis*, Lib. I, p. 83.

[11] John VIII, 17; II Cor., XIII, 1; S. Ambrosius, *Epistola V*—Migne, *Patrologiae Cursus Completus, Series Latina*, 221 Vols., Parisiis, 1844-1855, (hereafter referred to as *MPL*), XVI, 892; II Council of Braga (572)—Bruns, II, 41; *Capitula Angilramni*, XIII—Hinschius, *Decretales Pseudo-Isidorianae et Capitula Angilramni* (Lipsiae, 1863), p. 768; Leo IV, *Epistola ad Episcopos Brittaniae*—*MPL* CXV, 667. Cf. Devoti, *Institutionum Canonicarum Libri IV*, lib. III, tit. IX, n. 9.

[12] Willett, *The Probative Value of Documents in Ecclesiastical Trials*, The Catholic University of America Canon Law Studies, n. 171 (Washington, D.C., the Catholic University of America Press, 1942), pp. 27-28.

[13] Moriarity, *Oaths in Ecclesiastical Courts*, The Catholic University of America Canon Law Studies, n. 110 (Washington, D.C., Catholic University of America, 1937), p. 17.

by favor, hatred, anger, levity, money, etc., in making his judgment.[14] The judge was instructed to conduct the trial according to the strict prescriptions of law, considering the cause fully and carefully before passing a sentence. Gregory I (†604) said that it was a grave and unseemly matter to give a certain and definite sentence in a dubious case.[15] Abuses crept in, however, and there is evidence that judges allowed their decisions to be influenced wrongly, despite the regard for truth and justice revealed in the amount and detail of procedural legislation.[16]

Pervading the entire concept of the exercise of judicial power was the idea of equity—christian equity based on the New Testament.[17] The Fathers frequently reiterated this ideal—that there could be no real justice without equity.[18] As the number of invalidating laws grew in the matrimonial procedure, equity became more limited in application to the substantive law itself, for equity could not be applied in causes involving nullity because of diriment impediments, except in a restricted sense.

[14] S. Ambrosius, *Comment. in Psalm. 118*, v. 156: "Iudicet ille, qui ad pronunciandum nullo odio, nulla offensione, nulla levitate ducatur." —*MPL*, XXXIV, 1494-1495; S. Gregorius I, *Registrum Epistolarum*: "Restringenda sub ratione potestas est, nec quid agendum prius, quam concitata ad tranquillitatem mens redeat."—*MGH*, *Epistolae*, Tom. II, pars II (ed. L. M. Hartmann, Berolini, 1899), p. 240.

[15] *MGH*, *ibid.*, p. 246.

[16] E.g., Council of Seville (419): "... multi sunt, qui indiscussos potestate tiranica, non auctoritate canonica dampnant. Et sicut nonnulos gratia favoris sublimant, ita quosdam odio invidiaque humiliant, et levi opinionis aura condemnant quorum crimen non approbant." —Bruns, II, 70.

[17] Wohlhaupter, *Aequitas Canonica*: *Eine Studie aus dem Kanonischen Recht* (Paderborn, 1931) pp. 27-32.

[18] E.g., Lactantius (d. 325), *Divinae Institutiones*, 5, 14: "Altera est iustitiae pars aequitas."—*MPL*, VI, 598; S. Ambrosius (334-397), *De officiis ministrorum*, Lib. III, C. 5, n. 31: "Iustus habet legem mentis suae et aequitatis et iustitiae suae normam."—*MPL*, XVI, 163; S. Petrus Chrysologus (406-450): "Aequitas sine bonitate et sensu coelesti saevitia est."—*MPL*, III, 743.

CHAPTER IV

THE *DECRETUM* OF GRATIAN

Gratian's treatment of procedure was limited principally to criminal processes—usually one or both of the parties in the cause being clerics.[1] Matrimonial causes as yet did not occupy much of the ecclesiastical procedure. It is apparent from Gratian's manner of speaking that it was only in the twelfth century that the necessity of having recourse to an ecclesiastical judge to obtain a separation was acknowledged.[2] Gratian held to the severity of Roman law in stating that only the husband had the right of accusation in the case of adultery.[3]

It was the duty of the judge to appraise the evidence. A confession made by the accused was recognized as one of the most compelling means of proof. The testimony of witnesses as a means of proof still held a very prominent place in the *Decretum*, and in many of the quoted texts it is referred to as the only means of proof other than confession.[4] However, Gratian warned the judge that he should not be swayed by the number of witnesses as much as by the reliability of the testimony given.[5]

Gratian frequently referred to the care with which a judge should hear a case, giving minute instructions for estimating the probative value of the testimony, and reminding the judge of the grave obligation he had before God, the final Judge, to render a just sentence. Commenting on the situation which called for the furnishing of proof regarding the existence of a clandestine marriage, Gratian

[1] Van Hove, *Prolegomena*, pp. 306-346.

[2] C. 1, 3, 4, C. XXXIII, q. 2; De Becker, *De Sponsalibus et Matrimonio* (Lovanii, 1913), p. 440.

[3] C. 10, C. XXXII, q. 1.

[4] Cc. 1, 2, 5, 10, C. II, q. 1; cc. 1, 2, C. XV, q. 5.

[5] (C.3), C. IV, q. 2-3.

remarked that a certain and definite sentence was not to be given in a doubtful matter. In confirmation of this statement he quoted a pseudo-Isidorian canon, ascribed to Pope Evaristus (97-105), stating that no one should be judged or condemned without true and just proof, that evil things heard should move no one, and that without certain proof no one should ever believe them when they are rumored about, but first should inquire carefully and do nothing hastily.[6]

Gratian used a text from the Capitularies of Angilram, ascribed to Pope Eleutherius (175-189), admonishing the judge to search into the cause thoroughly by means of a full inquiry, freely permitting of questioning, responding and objecting, so that the action of both parties might be made altogether clear.[7] In a pseudo-Isidorian canon ascribed to Pope Melchiades (311-314), the bishops of Spain were warned to judge by a decision based not on suspicion but on proof.[8]

Gratian also referred to a letter of St. Augustine, in which the Bishop of Hippo declined to pass judgment in a doubt. Just as a secular court when referring a doubtful cause to a higher tribunal did not give a decision, so he in leaving a doubtful cause to God would not pass judgment.[9]

Gratian insisted that the judge could not pass sentence without submitting the case to the due procedure of a court trial.[10] Even though the judge knew certain things to be true, he could not accept them in court unless they were demonstrated by way of certain evidence.[11]

Gratian carefully instructed the judge how to evaluate the testimony of a witness. If all witnesses agreed, and if the nature of the matter being judged and the inclination

[6] Cc. 10, 11, C. XXX, q. 5—JK, n. 127.
[7] C. 11, c. XXX, q. 5; Hinschius, *Decretales*, p. 763.
[8] C. 13, C. II, q. 1—JK, n. 334.
[9] C. 12, C. II, q. 1; also *Ep. 78*, n. 4, in *MPL*, XXXIII, 269.
[10] Cc. 1-3, 5, 10-13, 18, 20, C. II, q. 1.
[11] C. 75, C. XI, q. 3.

warranted it, the testimony was to be followed. But if some of the witnesses, even though fewer in number, said some thing else, then the judge should believe what fitted the nature of the cause and lacked suspicion of enmity or favor, and should confirm the inclination of his mind from the arguments and testimony which he found to be more apt. For he was to look, not for numbers, but for the sincerity and credibility of the testimony and for testimony which would assist in reflecting the light of truth. He was to have regard for the truthfulness, dignity, habits and stability of the witnesses, and was to give careful scrutiny to those who vacillated in their own testimony. He was carefully to examine the credibility of a witness by checking his condition in life—whether he was a senator or a plebeian, whether his life was honorable and unimpeachable, or notorious and blameworthy, and whether he was testifying against an enemy or in favor of a friend.[12]

Certain qualifications were required of the judge: he could not be infamous; in order to judge rightly, he himself had to be blameless and free of that which he judged in others; in passing judgment he could not allow himself to be influenced by hatred, offense, anger or levity, but had to judge according to the prescriptions of law, examining the merits of the cause, and not holding his silence when questions needed to be asked. He could not accept a fee for discharging his duties. The judge who entertained a false charge knowingly rendered himself equally guilty with the one who made it. Throughout the procedure as delineated by Gratian there was reflected the concept that the judge is morally responsible to God, the ultimate Judge.[13]

Gratian considered discretion the mother of all virtues,[14] and equity the mother of justice;[15] he adverted to the

[12] (C.3), C. IV, q. 2-3, as based on D. (22.5) in the Roman law.

[13] C. III, q. 7, in toto; cc. 58-78, C. XI, q. 3.

[14] Urban II, as quoted in c. 3, C. I, q. 5: "... ex consideratione discretionis, quae est mater omnium virtutum."

[15] C. 16, C. XXV, q. 1: "... considerata tamen rationis aequitate, ut quae est mater iustitiae."

leavening effect of equity upon justice, and his application of these principles may be summed up in his quotation from St. Isidore of Seville (560-636): "Iuste iudicans misericordiam cum iustitia servat."[16]

[16] C. 10, D. XLV.

CHAPTER V

THE JUDGE IN THE *IUS NOVUM*

The Decretals of Gregory IX, among the first authentic canonical collections, were made up chiefly of previous legislation as finally assembled in a body of law. So relatively complete was the treatment of procedural regulations in the second book of this collection, that Boniface VIII and Clement V introduced no far-reaching additions or variations regarding it in their later collections.[1] The Decretals, together with the *Liber Sextus* and the *Clementinae,* remained in force until the Code of Canon Law became effective in 1918, and consequently existed as the authentic and classical source of procedural legislation through seven centuries.

In general, the procedure of the decretal period was similar to what had somewhat confusedly been represented in the *Decretum.* It represented a development of, not a change in the previous procedural law. The judge directed the unfolding of the trial, and appraised the proofs. The principles governing the burden of proof were retained from the pre-Decretal legislation: the burden of proof rested on the party who asserted the affirmative of the issue. However, the burden of the prosecution, by the inquisitorial method, was shifted from the plaintiff to the court.

The principal forms of proof employed were witnesses, documents, evidence of fact, presumptions, oaths offered and taken, confession, and official inspection. To have the value of a full proof, documents had to be either public documents, or authenticated private documents; they could not, in the opinion of the judge be susceptible to the suspicion of fraud or deceit.[2] In private suits of minor importance, when only partial proofs were available, the judge could

[1] Wernz, *De Iudiciis,* Lib. I, pp. 8-9.

[2] Willett, *The Probative Value of Documents in Ecclesiastical Trials,* pp. 30-32.

permit the litigants to settle their controversy by means of a decisory oath, or command them to take a supplementary oath.[3]

Celestine III (1191-1198) declared that a valid confession relieved the plaintiff of the burden of proof and justified the immediate pronouncement of sentence.[4] To have this effect, however, the confession had to be made during the trial, before a competent judge, freely and deliberately, from certain knowledge, and concerning a thing which, while being likely, was adverse to the confessing party.[5]

In reaching his decision the judge could take counsel with jurists without being bound by their opinions.[6] Innocent III (1198-1216) ruled that the judge was forbidden, however, to render a decision by way of taking a vote of the ones present at the hearings.[7]

While the judge was quite free to evaluate the evidence presented to him, he was not at liberty to render justice arbitrarily. When the trial was finished, and the defense heard, it was the duty of the judge to scrutinize all the alleged facts for the purpose of pronouncing the sentence. Celestine III[8] and Innocent III[9] declared that the judge had to study *all* the evidence—depositions, confessions, allegations, and all other evidence presented—and then make up his mind *(formet animi sui motum)*.[10] Gregory I (590-604) had long before decreed that the sentence had to conform to

[3] Moriarity says such oaths were seldom used. Cf. *Oaths in Ecclesiastical Courts*, pp. 23-35.

[4] C. 10, X, *de transactionibus*, I, 36; JL, n. 17675; Schmalzgrueber, *Ius Ecclesiasticum Universum* lib. II, tit. XVIII, n. 18.

[5] Schmalzgrueber, *op. cit.* lib. II, tit. XVIII, nn. 11-16.

[6] *Glossa* ad c. 4, C. III, q. 7; Durandus, *Speculum Iuris* (Venetiis, 1566), Lib. II, partic. II, *de requisitione concilii.*

[7] C. 3, X, *de consuetudine*, I, 4; Potthast, *Regesta Pontificum Romanorum inde ab anno post Christum natum MCXCVIII ad annum MCCCIV* (2 vols. Berolini, 1874-1875), n. 604.

[8] C. 27, X, *de testibus et attestationibus*, II, 20; JL, n. 17649.

[9] C. 6, X, *de renunciatione*, I, 9; Potthast, n. 1695; c. 10, X, *de fide instrumentorum*, II, 22; Potthast, n. 3872.

[10] Cf. Wernz-Vidal, *Ius Canonicum*, VI, *De Processibus*, n. 586 (hereafter cited *De Processibus*).

the law and legitimate custom; if it was opposed to certain and evident ecclesiastical laws or customs, it was not valid.[11]

The Decretalists clearly illustrated the idea that the discretionary power of the judge was to be based upon justice *and* equity, and that in his procedure the judge needed to follow equity.[12] Pope Innocent III stated clearly and precisely that the judge should be both merciful and rigorous, and that he should be guided by equity, especially in the absence of explicit law.[13] Pope Boniface VIII (1294-1303) summed up the law by declaring that the judge should maintain a mean between extremes.[14]

The power of the judge in directing the trial was augmented through the introduction of the summary procedure —an introduction brought about by the increased lengthiness of ecclesiastical procedure.[15] Clement V (1305-1314) decreed that for certain causes, notably matrimonial, the judge could conduct the trial simply and without the usual formalities.[16] This rather indefinite instruction left confusion as to just what limitations in the procedure were intended. To clarify this, Clement issued his celebrated constitution *Saepe* in 1306, in which he determined the nature of this new and summary process: the judge could proceed without the introductory *libellus* or the subsequent *litis contestatio,* he could himself undertake the inspection in the cause, and entirely at his own discretion direct the unfolding of the trial.[17] Thus, although the judicial acts were limited,

[11] Cc. 1, 3, X, *de sententia et re iudicata,* II, 27; JE, nn. 1210, 1212.

[12] Alexander III: "Judex debet procedere secundum aequitatem iuris."—c. 13, X, *de officio et potestate iudicis delegati,* I, 29; JL, n. 13877; Innocentius IV: "Iudex debet in procedendo servare aequitatem."—c. 1, *de restitutione spoliatorum,* II, 5, in VI°

[13] C. 10, X, *de purgatione canonica,* V, 34; Potthast, n. 693; c. 5, X, *de dolo et contumacia,* II, 14; Potthast, n. 1324; c. 5, X, *de causa possessionis et proprietatis,* II, 12; Potthast n. 1683.

[14] C. 2, *de sepulturis,* III, 6, in Extravag. com.

[15] Roberti, *De Processibus,* I, 8-9.

[16] "... simpliciter et de plano ac sine strepitu iudicii et figura." —c. 2, *de iudiciis,* II, 1, in Clem.

[17] C. 2, *de verborum significatione,* V, 11, in Clem.

the judge's active cognizance of the cause was not diminished. This summary process as set up by Clement V continued almost unchanged until the introduction of the Code.

SCHOLION. THE OFFICIALIS

The *officialis* has his origin in the twelfth and thirteenth centuries;[18] however, no definite time can be assigned for the origin of the *officialis* as a universal figure in the Church, since from diocese to diocese there were different circumstances, and the needs of the bishops were divergent.

The *officialis* in his origin did not reflect the same office as the vicar general. In the beginning the vicars general were procurators who substituted for the bishop in his absence, and in the course of time came to perform these duties even while the bishop was present. However, although their origin and office were different, the *officialis* and the vicar general were often identified, for in the smaller dioceses the vicar general was usually the *officialis* as well.[19] The point to be noted here is that the *officialis,* either as a distinct official or in the person of the vicar general, was an ordinary judge, and thus had much wider discretionary powers than the usual delegated judge.

[18] Bouix, *De Judiciis,* I, 347-348; Wernz, *Ius Decretalium,* Tom. II, pars II, pp. 635-636; Tobin, *De Officiali Curiae Dioecesanae* (Romae: Apud Aedes Pontificiae Universitatis Gregorianae, 1936), pp. 49-50.

[19] E. Fournier, *Les Origines du Vicaire Général* (Paris, 1922), pp. 65-66; Tobin, *De Officiali,* nn. 187-194.

CHAPTER VI

THE JUDGE IN THE *IUS NOVISSIMUM*

ART. 1. THE PERIOD OF DECLINE: TO THE *Dei Miseratione* (1741).

There was little legislative change affecting the discretionary power of the judge during the two hundred years that followed the Council of Trent. The Council of Trent had withdrawn all matrimonial causes from the courts of deacons, archdeacons and other persons subordinate to the bishop.[1] Despite the fact, however, that the Council of Trent had clearly determined that the court of first instance was exclusively to be that of the ordinary of the place, authors soon sought to vindicate the competency of subordinate judges to judge matrimonial causes;[2] it was not until the reforms of Benedict XIV (1740-1758) in the constitution *Dei miseratione* that this erroneous opinion was conquered.

Canonists, in commenting on the Decretals, had divided proofs by reason of their probative value into full *(plena)* and half *(semi-plena)* proofs. This helped to bring about a mechanical system of judging, in which the judge reached his decision by a mere mathematical combination of fractions of proof to add up to a full proof.[3] The judge's dis-

[1] Conc. Trident., sess. XXIV, *de ref.*, c. 20; cf. also Benedictus XIV, const. *Dei miseratione*, 3 Nov. 1741, § 4—*Codicis Iuris Canonici Fontes* (9 vols., Romae [postea Civitate Vaticana]: Typis Polyglottis Vaticanis, 1923-1939), n. 318 (hereafter cited *Fontes*); S.C.C., 11 sept. 1762, § *Haec—Collectio omnium Conclusionum et Resolutionum S. C. Concilii ab anno 1564 ad annum 1860*, ed. S. Pallottini, 18 vols., Romae, 1868-1895, Vol. XI, p. 78, n. 74; S.C.C., instr., 22 aug. 1840, § *Cum itaque—Fontes*, n. 4069.

[2] Mansella, *De Impedimentis Matrimonium Dirimentibus ac de Processu Judiciali in Causis Matrimonialibus*, (Romae, 1881), p. 171 (hereafter cited *De Processu Iudiciali in Causis Matrimonialibus*).

[3] Lega, *Praelectiones in Textum Iuris Canonici de Iudiciis Ecclesiasticis: De Iudiciis Ecclesiasticis Civilibus*, (Romae 1905) Lib. I, Vol. I, 461.

cretionary power to appraise proofs suffered as a natural consequence.

Diocesan courts struggled to function with old machinery in an era noted chiefly for a constant decline in procedural efficiency. So widespread was the laxity and deterioration during the early eighteenth century that Pope Benedict XIV was forced to speak several times against the corruption and injustice of these courts.[4]

In 1655, the Holy Office condemned the proposition which said that if the litigants had equal arguments, the judge could accept money for pronouncing sentence in favor of one and against the other.[5] This gives some indication of the trend. Individual judges, through intent or lack of knowledge, far exceeded the legitimate bounds of their power; the judge's discretionary power was often stretched to a point of deciding whether he should pass judgment contrary to truth.

Benedict XIV gave a description of the judge in the era preceding him. Ecclesiastical judges too hastily and with insufficient reason declared marriages null. As a result of this some parties had passed on to third and fourth marriages while the first consorts still lived. These judges acted with little or no examination of the cause, either through sheer ignorance or in consequence of positive malice. Oftentimes judges were delegated though they lacked the necessary knowledge of law and the required uprightness of character.[6] The advent of Benedict XIV marked the beginning of a procedural reform and the gradual ending of these abuses.

Art. II. The Period Of Reform

In this last period before the Code, the judge reached his highest degree of efficiency in matrimonial procedure dur-

[4] Ep. encycl., *Matrimonii,* 11 apr. 1741, Introduction—*Fontes* n. 307; ep. encycl. *Quamvis Paternae,* 26 aug. 1741, § 1—*Fontes* n. 315; const. *Dei miseratione,* 3 nov. 1741, §§ 1, 2, 3—*Fontes,* n. 318.

[5] S.C.S. Off., decr. 24 sept. 1665, prop. 26 damn.—*Fontes,* n. 734.

[6] Const. *Dei miseratione,* §§ 1-4—*Fontes,* n. 318.

ing the pre-code era. In the beginning, the decrees of the Council of Trent concerning the court of the first instance were repeated and emphasized. Thenceforth for all practical purposes there was but one court in the diocese, the bishop's court.[7] In this court the bishop himself was *ex officio* the ordinary judge of the first instance.[8] During the vacancy of the see, the vicar capitular (administrator) possessed this power *ex officio*.[9]

Sometimes the bishop reserved to himself the privilege of presiding as head of his court. More often he exercised his authority through another. Regularly the vicar general assumed the bishop's place in the tribunal.[10] If so, he formed one court with the bishop and no appeal could be made from him to the bishop.[11] The instruction *Causae matrimoniales* implied that the vicar general could not act as judge without a mandate.[12] Bouix (1808-1870) held that he needed a mandate for criminal but not for matrimonial causes. The majority of the canonists however held that he acted as judge by virtue of his office.[13] The vicar general could not delegate his power.[14] The confusion between the

[7] S.C.C. instr. 22 aug. 1840, § *Praeterea—Fontes,* n. 4069.

[8] Conc. Trident., sess. XXIV, *de ref.*, c. 20; S.C.C., instr., 22 aug. 1840, § *Cum itaque—Fontes,* n. 4069.

[9] S.C.C., instr., 30 ian. 1768, § *Demum—Thesaurus Resolutionum S. C. Concilii,* (167 Vols., Vols. I-V, Urbini, 1739-1740; Vols. VI-CLXVIII. 1741-1909), Tom. XXXVII, pp. 32-33.

[10] Benedictus XIV, const. *Dei miseratione,* 3 nov. 1741, § 4;—*Fontes,* n. 318; S.C.Ep. et Reg., instr., 11 iun. 1880, n. 34.—*Fontes,* n. 2005; S. C. de Prop. Fide, instr., a. 1883, n. XXXIV—*Fontes,* n. 4900; S. C. de Prop. Fide, instr. *Causae matrimoniales,* a. 1883, n. 6—*Fontes,* n. 4901 (Hereafter referred to as *Causae Matrimoniales*).

[11] S.C.C., *Ostunen.*, 12 iul. 1823—*Fontes,* n. 3984.

[12] S.C. de Prop. Fide instr. a. 1883, § 6: "Accusatione sic recepta, munus moderatoris actorum episcopus vel ipse sibi assumet, vel suum vicarium generalem, aut alium probum et expertum virum e clero ad illud delegabit."—*Fontes* n. 4901.

[13] Bouix, *De Judiciis,* I, 415 and 431; Mansella, *De Processu Iudiciali in Causis Matrimonialibus,* p. 173.

[14] Bouix, *op. cit.*, I, p. 121; Smith, *Elements of Ecclesiastical Law* (3 vols., Vol. II 2. ed., New York, 1887), p. 20, n. 714.

offices of vicar general and *officialis* thus continued. Even just prior to the Code there was not a universal judicial official distinct from the vicar general like the present day *officialis*. Attempts were made, especially in France, to have all court work assigned to a priest other than the vicar general. This man was at times spoken of as the *officialis*, and he received general delegation to be judge in all causes.[15]

The bishop was also empowered to act through other delegated judges. These delegated judges needed mandates from the bishop to act.[16] Although not necessarily so, delegated judges, whether acting individually or as a college, were generally taken from the synodal judges mentioned by the Council of Trent and concerning whom Pope Benedict XIV had issued his encyclical letter *Quamvis Paternae*.[17] At least four of these were to be named in each diocese, each evincing the proper qualities of sound doctrine, prudence and zeal for justice. If possible, a judge holding some ecclesiastical dignity was to be sought. Custom gradually excluded laymen as judges in ecclesiastical causes.[18]

While the bishop was not compelled by law during this period to employ at any time a collegiate court, such a practice was strongly recommended for the more difficult causes, and was in conformity with the practice of the Roman Rota.[19] Thus Cardinal Rauscher, 1797-1875), in formulating his highly practical Austrian Instruction of 1855, commanded that a collegiate tribunal be set up for matrimonial causes, which was to consist of a president and from four to six judges.[20]

[15] Bouix, *op. cit.*, I, 348; Bassibey, *Le Mariage devant les Tribunaux Ecclesiastiques; Procédure Matrimoniale Générale* (Paris, 1899), n. 4 and n. 28 (hereafter cited *Le Mariage*).

[16] *Causae matrimoniales,—Fontes*, n. 4901; Cf. Bouix, *op. cit.* I, 348.

[17] Conc. Trident., sess XXV, *de ref.*, c. 10; Benedictus XIV, ep. encycl. *Quamvis Paternae*, 26 aug. 1741—*Fontes*, n. 315.

[18] Bouix, *op. cit.*, I, 462; Bassibey, *Le Mariage*, n. 28. Cf. also *Quamvis Paternae*, § 6—*Fontes*, n. 315.

[19] Wernz, *De Iudiciis*, Lib. I, p. 75; p. 85; Smith, *Elements of Ecclesiastical Law*, II, p. 375, n. 1415.

[20] *Instructio pro Iudicis Ecclesiasticis quoad causas Matrimoniales*,

Appointed to assist the judge in various ways were the auditors. Auditors gathered evidence for criminal trials as well as for matrimonial causes.[21] The auditor could draw up the abstract of the trial after the informative process was concluded.[22] Similar to the auditors were the assessors. Technically these were advisors to the judge in conducting and deciding the more difficult causes. They were appointed by either the bishop or the judge. Their appointment was of a character not compulsory but highly recommended.[23]

A new official in the matrimonial procedure—the great instrument of reform and possibly the greatest single bit of new legislation for procedure in this period—was the defender of the marriage bond. Pope Benedict XIV made the establishment of this office compulsory in every diocesan court.[24] This office he created to protect the marriage bond against unlearned, easy-going and malicious judges, and against collusion on the side of the parties and of other persons.

In causes of public interest, the judge could proceed *ex officio* in the gathering of evidence. He assisted the *defensor* in this official investigation in matrimonial causes.[25] It was the judge's duty to convoke the tribunal for the taking cognizance of even an individual cause; he presided at all the sessions, issued the decrees and orders, and cited the parties and the witnesses.[26] If there was a collegiate court and if the many judges of the curia had a general delegation,

§ 97—*Acta et Decreta Sacrorum Conciliorum Recentiorum, Collectio Lacensis* (7 vols., Friburgi Brisgoviae, 1870-1892), V, 1305, (hereafter cited as *Instructio Austriaca*).

[21] S. C. Ep. et Reg., instr., 11 iun. 1880, n. 12—*Fontes*, n. 2005; S. C. de Prop. Fide, instr., a. 1883, n. XII—*Fontes*, n. 4900; *Causae Matrimoniales*, n. 15; Wernz, *De Iudiciis*, Lib. I, p. 122.

[22] S. C. Ep. et Reg., instr., 11 iun. 1880, n. 29—*Fontes*, n. 2005.

[23] *Causae matrimoniales*, n. 24; Wernz, *De Iudiciis*, Lib. I, p. 127.

[24] Const. *Dei miseratione*, 3 nov. 1741—*Fontes*, n. 318.

[25] *Instructio Austriaca*, § 177; S. C. de Prop. Fide, instr., a. 1883, n. XI—*Fontes*, n. 4900; S. C. de Prop. Fide, instr., 20 iul. 1878, § *Commissionis*—Smith, *op. cit.*, Vol. II, Appendices I & II.

[26] *Causae matrimoniales*, n. 9—*Fontes*, n. 4901.

the president *(praeses)* distributed the causes among these judges, unless the Bishop made other arrangements. Nothing was said about how this was to be done except that men endowed with proper qualifications and subject to no suspicion in relation to the parties were to be chosen.[27]

The judge decided all exceptions in a cause other than the one of suspicion raised against himself. Little change is noted in the solemn procedure in actions and exceptions throughout the period, although Benedict XIV had striven to restore many of these solemnities in his constitution *Dei miseratione*. One reason for this was the widespread use of the Clementine privilege, which had brought about the disregard of solemn procedure.[28]

The judge rendered the decision regarding the competence of his own court. If the parties wished to question the decision in favor of competence, they did so within ten days of the reception of the citation. If their claim of incompetence was denied, they were free to appeal this to a higher court. If the lower court was declared competent by the higher court, the cause was returned to the lower court.[29]

The citation of the parties and of the witnesses was made by the judge *(moderator)*. The citations were necessarily set down in writing and were preserved in the acts.[30] Ordinarily accusations were stated in detail in the citation to the accused party, but when prudence demanded otherwise the accusations were not to be contained in the citation itself.[31] The use of registered mail was allowed in the presenting of citations, because of the assurance that was to be gained regarding the presentation, the acceptance, or the refusal through the returned postal certificate.[32] A sen-

[27] *Instructio Austriaca*, § 99.

[28] S.C.C., *Turritana*, 13 ian. 1725—*Fontes*, n. 3292; ; Lega, *De Iudiciis Ecclesiasticis*, Lib. I, Vol. I, p. 543, n. 548.

[29] *Instructio Austriaca*, §§ 103, 104.

[30] *Causae matrimoniales*, n. 9—*Fontes*, n. 4901.

[31] S.C. Ep. et Reg., instr. 11 iun. 1880, nn. 22 and 23—*Fontes*, n. 2005.

[32] *Ibidem*, n. 14—*Fontes*, n. 2005.

tence rendered after a defective citation of the parties was null and void; it could not be sanated in any manner.[33]

If the work of investigation could not be completed at one sitting (e.g., the examination of an individual witness or expert), the judge had power to suspend the session and to designate the day and hour for resuming the interrupted period.[34] Persevering throughout this period was the Tridentine requirement that a cause be finished in two years at the latest.[35] If the cause was not completed within this time, the parties could have recourse to a superior competent judge, provided it was not they who were at fault in the delay.[36] This law did not apply if the quality of the cause was such as to require a longer time; the general rule was that each cause was to be finished "*quamprimum,*" and it remained for the judge to see that this was done.[37]

The notary or the chancellor kept the acts of the court. The acts were of primary importance: "*Quod non est in actis, non est in mundo,*" and a record of all actions had to be kept in writing in these acts.[38] The acts were kept in the archives of the court, and the notaries could not give copies of the judicial acts and documents without a mandate of the judge, to whose discretion this was left.[39]

Witnesses were heard separately. If the witnesses consented and the judges deemed it prudent, the testimony could be repeated in the presence of the defendant—the so-called confrontation of witnesses.[40]

Prior to testifying, there was the oath to tell the truth.

[33] S.C.C., 23 apr. 1768, § *Nullam*—Pallottini, Vol. II, p. 71, n. 8; Wernz, *De Iudiciis*, Lib. 1, p. 320.

[34] S.C.C., instr., 22 aug. 1840, § *Si examen*—*Fontes*, n. 4069.

[35] Conc. Trident., sess. XXIV, *de ref.*, c. 20.

[36] S.C.C., *Umbriaticen.*, 26 apr. 1659—*Fontes*, n. 2758.

[37] Wernz, *De Iudiciis*, Lib. I, p. 268; Ferrari, *Summa Institutionum Canonicarum* (4. ed., 2 vols., Genuae, 1889), II, n. 733.

[38] Wernz, *De Iudiciis*, Lib. I, p. 289; p. 285. Cf. S.C.C., instr., 22 aug. 1840—*Fontes*, n. 4069.

[39] S.C. Ep. et Reg., decr., 16 oct. 1600, n. 11—*Fontes*, n. 1586.

[40] S.C.S. Off., instr., a. 1858, § *Testes*—*Fontes*, n. 946; *Causae matrimoniales*, n. 11—*Fontes*, n. 4901.

The judge could exact, if necessary, an oath of secrecy, and at the end of the testimony the oath of veracity and of secrecy (concerning the questions and answers) might be renewed. The judge could first give a sermon on the seriousness of the oath, if he deemed it necessary.[41]

Questions were asked in court by the judge only[42] or by his auditor.[43] The defender of the bond had the right and duty of making out the questionnaires; however, the judge could propose other questione *ex officio*,[44] and in special causes was given the greatest freedom in this.[45] Questions could be proposed to witnesses by the defender but only through the judge, and also by the parties through the judge.[46]

If experts were needed, the judge alone chose them.[47] Earlier these individuals were chosen either *ex officio* by the judge or by the parties themselves.[48] The judge likewise set the time limits for obtaining their testimony, and fixed the day and the hour for the presenting of this testimony.[49]

Interlocutory sentences and decrees could be issued at the discretion of the judge. They were given in legitimate form, and a record thereof was preserved in the acts, even if given *viva voce*.[50]

The publication of the process took place after the judge and the defender declared that the probatory process was

[41] *Causae matrimoniales*, n. 12; S.C.C., instr., 22 aug. 1840, § *Cum itaque—Fontes*, n. 4069.

[42] S.C.S. Off. instr. a. 1858, § *Primus—Fonte,s* n. 946.

[43] *Instructio Austriaca*, § 161.

[44] S.C.C., instr., 22 aug. 1840, § *Praefinita—Fontes*, n. 4069; S.C. Ep. et Reg., instr., 11 iun. 1880, n. 11—*Fontes*, n. 2005; *Causae matrimoniales—Fontes*, n. 4901.

[45] S.C.S. Off., instr., a. 1858, § *Primus—Fontes* n. 946.

[46] S.C.C., instr., 22 aug. 1840, §§ *Interim* and *Poterit.* —*Fontes* n. 4069.

[47] S.C.C., instr., 22 aug. 1840, § *Exhibitis—Fontes*, n. 4069; *Instructio Austriaca*, 4 maii, 1855, n. 166.

[48] Lega, *De Iudiciis Ecclesiasticis*, Lib. I, Vol. I, p. 510, n. 497.

[49] S.C.C., instr., 22 aug. 1840, §§ *Judex* and *Designata—Fontes*, n. 4069.

[50] *Causae matrimoniales*, n. 9: Wernz, *De Iudiciis*, Lib. I, p. 297.

complete.[51] The decree of publication, which was the formal communication of evidence to the parties, was issued by the judge, and signed also by the defender and by the notary.[52]

After the formal defense, the conclusion of the cause came when the defender declared there was nothing further to be offered.[53] Prior to the pronouncing of sentence, it was recommended that a judge who functioned singly should consult two or three experts; the collegiate court was to pronounce sentence according to a majority vote.[54]

[51] *Causae matrimoniales*, n. 22—*Fontes*, n. 4901.

[52] S.C.C., instr., 22 aug. 1840, § *Quatenus*—*Fontes*, n. 4069; *Causae matrimoniales*, n. 22—*Fontes*, n. 4901.

[53] S.C. Ep. et Reg., instr., 11 iun. 1880, n. 35—*Fontes*, n. 2005; S.C.C., instr., 22 aug. 1840, § *Omnibus absolutis*—*Fontes*, n. 4069; *Causae matrimoniales*, n. 24—*Fontes*, n. 4901.

[54] S. C. de Prop. Fide, instr. *Causae matrimoniales*, a. 1883, n. 24—*Fontes* n. 4901; *Instructio Austriaca*, 4 maii, 1855, § 99.

SECTION II.

THE DISCRETIONARY AUTHORITY OF THE JUDGE IN PRESIDING OVER AND DIRECTING COURT PROCEDURE UNDER THE CODE OF CANON LAW

CHAPTER I

A SUMMARY OF THE FUNCTIONS OF THE JUDGE

At the very beginning of his pontificate, in a motu proprio of March 19, 1904, entitled *Arduum sane*,[1] Pius X (1903-1914) announced his intention of providing for the preparation of a code in which should be gathered "with order and clearness all the laws of the Church, . . . removing all that were abrogated or obsolete, adopting others as far as needed by the exigencies and the customs of the present time, and making new ones according to need and opportunity." There was little doubt that such a move was justified, as Pius X frankly conceded in the motu proprio: "the laws of the Church had so increased in number and were so separated and scattered, that many of them were unknown not only to the people, but to the most learned scholars as well."[2]

Prepared by a commission of cardinals and canonists under the leadership of Pietro Gasparri, later named a cardinal, the Code[3] was promulgated on Pentecost, May 27, 1917, by means of a constitution of Benedict XV (1914-1922) entitled *Providentissima Mater Ecclesia,* to become effective on Pentecost of the following year, May 19, 1918.[4]

Greatly instrumental in formulating the canons of the Code referring to procedure was Michael Cardinal Lega (1860-1935), one of the members of the Codification Com-

[1] *Acta Sancta Sedis* [*A.S.S.*]. (41 vols., Romae, 1865-1908). XXXVI (1903-1904), 549.

[2] Abbo-Hannon, *The Sacred Canons* (2 vols., St. Louis: B. Herder, 1952), I, pp. xviii-xix.

[3] *Codex Iuris Canonici Pii X Pontificis Maximi iussu digestus Benedicti XV auctoritate promulgatus* (Romae: Typis Polyglottis Vaticanis, 1917). Hereinafter, simply the canon will be cited.

[4] *Acta Apostolicae Sedis* [*AAS*] (Romae 1909-1929; Civitate Vaticana, 1929-), IX (1917), pars II, die 28 iunii, 1917.

mission, whose writings are frequently cited in any work touching upon ecclesiastical procedure.[5]

The laws of procedure to be observed in matrimonial trials in diocesan tribunals are prescribed in Book IV *(De Processibus)* of the Code, and elucidated in the *Instructio* of the S. Congregation of the Sacraments in 1936.[6] Also of special interest are the *Regulae servandae* for non-consummation cases issued in 1923.[7] Throughout the trial, the judge should have in mind the regulations which the Code enacts in Canon 20.[8]

Since the promulgation of the Code, causes involving the bond of marriage are reserved to the judgment of a collegiate tribunal of at least three judges,[9] except the summary

[5] V. Bartoccetti, in his preface to Lega's *Commentarius in Iudicia Ecclesiastica* (3 vols., Anonima Libraria Cattolica Italiana, Romae, 1950), Vol. I, p. xi, states: "Improbus iste labor sapientis Decessoris juris, viam stravit Codicis redactioni, quae ordinem logicum non historicum decretalium secuta est. Nam cum Michael Lega jam ab initio praeparationis Codicis adlectus sit inter Praelatos et postea transierit in Commissionem Cardinalium pro Codice redigendo, cum in re processuali facile ceteros peritia et sollertia antecederet, haud difficulter tenere possumus libros IV et V Codicis, magna saltem ex parte Nostro esse tribuendos, quod quidem comparando canones Codicis cum operibus antea a Card. Lega editis quisque facile persentit." This post-Code work of Cardinal Lega is hereinafter cited as Lega (ed. Bart.), *Commentarius;* Bartoccetti himself tells us, in the preface to the second edition, "... ne uno quidem verbo ex manuscripto clarissimi Cardinalis Lega immutato."

[6] S.C. de Sacramentis, *Instructio servanda a tribunalibus dioecesanis in pertractandis causis de nullitate matrimoniorum,* 15 aug. 1936 —*AAS,* XXVIII (1936), 313-361. This document will hereinafter be cited simply by its article numbers.

[7] S. C. de Sacramentis, decr., *De processibus in causis dispensationis super matrimonio rato et non consummato,* 7 maii 1923—*AAS,* XV (1923), 389-391; and *Regulae Servandae, ibid.,* pp. 392-413.

[8] "Si certa de re desit expressum praescriptum legis sive generalis sive particularis, norma sumenda est, nisi agatur de poenis applicandis, a legibus latis in similibus; a generalibus iuris principiis cum aequitate canonica servatis; a stylo et praxi Curiae Romanae; a communi constantique sententia doctorum."

[9] Can. 1576, § 1; § 2; art. 13.

judicial causes listed in canon 1990, and the purely administrative cases.[10]

It is the duty of the presiding judge, in general, to direct the cause and to decree whatever is necessary for the administration of justice.[11] This also applies, *congrua congruis referendo,* to the synodal or pro-synodal judges, who form the tribunal with the presiding judge, and to the auditor when participating in the trial. The presiding judge is to recall to a sense of duty all those in the trial who seriously depart from proper decorum.[12]

The functions of the judge in a marriage trial are herewith listed summarily according to the fourfold distinction of the judicial office: a) the collegiate tribunal, in which the three judges act as a single body under the guidance of the presiding judge, determining their actions by majority vote when there is any question;[13] b) the presiding judge, who may be either the bishop himself, the *officialis,* or one of the *vice-officiales;*[14] c) the auditor or *iudex instructor;*[15] and d) the recording judge or *ponens.*[16]

ART. I. FUNCTIONS RESERVED TO THE COLLEGIATE TRIBUNAL

A comparative survey of the pertinent prescripts of the Code and of the *Instructio* indicates that the following functions are to be performed only by the collegiate tribunal: to decide an exception proposed against the tribunal;[17] to admit or reject the *libellus* as soon as possible—at least within a month;[18] to determine the intervention of the

[10] Articles 226-231.

[11] Can. 1577, § 2; art. 14, § 2; cf. art. 68 for the chief duties of the judge.

[12] Can. 1640, § 2; art. 68, § 1.

[13] Can. 1577, § 1.

[14] Can. 1578; speaking of the bishop, however, the canon states: "valde expedit ut causas iudicandas relinquat tribunali ordinario..."

[15] Can. 1582; art. 24.

[16] Can. 1584; art. 22, § 1.

[17] Can. 1610, § 1; art. 9.

[18] Can. 1709, § 1; arts. 61; 62 § 2; 64; and 67. However, the *officialis* can reject the petition by means of a decree, if it is evident

promoter of justice *(promotor iustitiae)* whenever there is a question of safeguarding procedural law;[19] to dismiss, for a just and grave reason, both the attorney and the advocate;[20] to increase the punishment, if necessary, of a delinquent advocate assigned for gratuitous representation, even to suspension from the office of advocate; [21] if the bill of complaint *(libellus)* be accepted, to order the separation of the consorts if they are perchance still living together and if in the judgment of the ordinary grave scandal exists;[22] to reserve to itself, when it deems this necessary or prudent, any or all of the duties of the presiding judge outlined in § 2 of article 68;[23] to decide a recourse sought in opposition to administrative acts of the presiding judge;[24] to go contrary to the opinion of the defender of the bond that additional proofs are necessary (but only by unanimous vote);[25] if the parties disagree, to define *ex officio* the point at isssue between them;[26] to decide whether proof is to be admitted contrary to a ruling of the presiding judge or auditor;[27] to decide whether a defendant, when not answering a summons or when not putting in his appearance, is to be declared in contempt of court;[28] to decide, in order to

either that the impugnment has no juridical foundation, or that the plaintiff is incapable of impugning the marriage, or that the tribunal is without jurisdiction.—S. C. de Sacramentis, 18 ian. 1938 (private): Bouscaren, *Canon Law Digest,* II, 546.

19 Art. 16, § 1.

20 Can. 1663; art. 51.

21 Art. 240, § 1; cf. can. 1916, § 1.

22 Art. 63. However, although this article specifies the "tribunal," it could reasonably be argued that this mode of speech is of a general import, so that the presiding judge in virtue of his wide discretionary authority could order the separation of the consorts if need be.—cf. art 68, § 2; art. 69.

23 Cf. art. 68, § 2, where it is stated, "nisi collegium aliquid sibi reservaverit."

24 Art. 69.

25 Can. 1969; art. 71.

26 Art. 92, § 2.

27 Art. 95, § 2.

28 Art. 115.

avert serious harm, that certain testimonials are not to be published;[29] to reach a decision, in the face of a dispute between the judges and the parties, regarding the necessity of calling experts;[30] to decide, with the consent of the woman, in causes of impotency or non-consummation to appoint two male medical doctors for her physical examination;[31] to admit or reject the conclusions of the experts, with an expression of the reasons for this;[32] to decide what is to be done when a party refuses to present a document requested upon a decree of the auditor;[33] to decide the admission or rejection of an incidental question;[34] to decide whether an incidental question, once it is admitted, is to be decided judicially or administratively;[35] to decide upon the intervention of the promotor of justice in incidental questions;[36] to decide whether a verbal discussion *(discussio oralis)* is necessary in an incidental question;[37] to decide the incidental question in the same sentence that decides the principal cause, if it prove convenient;[38] for a just cause, to correct or to revoke an interlocutory sentence before the principal cause is completed;[39] to evaluate the judicial evidence according to their own conscience, for the pronouncement of the sentence;[40] to decide, for a serious cause, upon a longer period of time than the prescribed one-month time limit between the reaching of the decision and the publishing of the sentence;[41] to demand a supplementary investigation

[29] Art. 138, § 2; cf. art. 130, § 1.

[30] Art. 140, § 2.

[31] Can. 1979, § 2; art. 150, n. 2; S.C.S. Off., decr., 12 iun. 1942.—*AAS*, XXXIV (1942), 200. It seems, however, that the presiding judge could also do this, for § 2 of art. 68 states that the presiding judge can appoint experts unless the college reserves this to itself.

[32] Can. 1804, §§ 1-2; art. 154, §§ 1-2.

[33] Art. 167, § 2.

[34] Can. 1839; arts. 188; 189 §§ 1-2.

[35] Can. 1840; § 1; art. 190, § 1.

[36] Art. 190, § 2; cf. art. 16, § 1.

[37] Art. 192, § 2; cf. art. 186.

[38] Art. 194.

[39] Can. 1841; art. 195.

[40] Can. 1869, § 3; art. 197, § 3.

[41] Art. 200, § 1.

of the cause, even after the conclusion of the cause;[42] to decide, when proof emerges which points to non-consummation rather than to impotency, to forward the acts together with their own opinion to the Sacred Congregation of the Sacraments; or to determine that the proofs of non-consummation are insufficient and must be completed;[43] to retract and emend an invalid sentence which it has rendered;[44] if either or both consorts attempt marriage after a decision of nullity but pending an appeal, to decree a prohibition of the exercise of the marriage right until the pronouncement of the definitive sentence;[45] to determine how the expenses are to be borne by the parties;[46] to grant the plaintiff and the defendant gratuitous legal assistance commensurate with their genuine poverty;[47] to revoke the exemption or the reduction of judicial expenses if the alleged poverty or just right proves non-existent.[48]

ART. II. FUNCTIONS RESERVED TO THE PRESIDING JUDGE

This article lists only those functions which, as reserved to the presiding judge, cannot be exercised by the auditor. It is understood that the presiding judge can also perform any or all of the duties outlined for the auditor in the following article, unless a particular function has already been undertaken by a duly assigned auditor.[49] In Title IX, *De Probationibus,* the words *"praeses," "instructor,"* and *"auditor"* are used by the *Instructio* interchangeably.[50]

The functions reserved to the presiding judge are: to designate as actuary one of the court notaries;[51] to appoint

[42] Art. 201, §§ 1-2.
[43] Can. 1963, § 2; art. 206, § 1.
[44] Art. 211, § 2.
[45] Can. 1672, § 3; art. 223.
[46] Art. 236, § 1; cf. art. 234, n. 1.
[47] Art. 237, §§ 1-2.
[48] Art. 239.
[49] Cf. art. 68, § 3.
[50] Art. 96, § 1. The expression, "examining judge," when hereinafter used, will signify both the presiding judge and the auditor.
[51] Can. 1585, §§ 1-2; art. 17.

an assistant actuary, if it should become necessary;[52] to designate one of the judges of the college as recording judge *(ponens)*,[53] or himself to act as recording judge with the assent of the other two judges;[54] to appoint an advocate to aid a plaintiff or a defendant who cannot meet the requisite payment for one;[55] to remind a negligent advocate appointed for gratuitous advocacy of his duties in the matter;[56] to admit qualified procurators,[57] even one who does not reside in the locality of the tribunal;[58] to allow several procurators to be named by a party;[59] to receive the declaration of the removal of the advocate or procurator by the party;[60] to approve the cause for an advocate's or procurator's renouncement of his office;[61] to appoint an auditor for a definite case, if the bishop has not already made provision; to remove this auditor at any stage for a just reason and without prejudice to the parties;[62] to decide exceptions against the subordinate members of the court, and the auditor;[63] to assign an advocate to a party who has none, or to designate another in a special case;[64] to see that the identity of the plaintiff is established;[65] to permit reception of evidence even before the joinder of issue *(litis contestatio)*;[66] to effect the joinder of issue[67] and to approve the formulation of the mutually acknowledged points in dispute *(con-*

[52] Art. 19, § 3; cf. *infra*, p. 49.
[53] Can. 1584; art. 22, § 1.
[54] Art. 22, § 2.
[55] Art. 237, § 1; art. 53, § 2.
[56] Art. 240, § 2.
[57] Can. 1659, § 1; art. 49, § 1.
[58] Art. 47, § 4.
[59] Can. 1656, § 2; art. 47, § 2.
[60] Art. 52, § 1.
[61] Art. 54, n. 3.
[62] Can. 1583; arts. 23, § 1, and 25.
[63] Can. 1614, § 3; art. 31, § 3; art. 31, § 1; cf. can. 1580, § 2; art. 23, § 1.
[64] Art. 43, §§ 1-3; cf. can. 1655.
[65] Art. 58.
[66] Can. 1730; art. 68, § 2.
[67] Arts. 88, 92, § 1.

cordatio dubiorum);[68] to pass on the sufficiency of the excuse adduced by a defendant when he does not appear as cited;[69] and even to declare the defendant contumacious with the assent of the tribunal;[70] to declare a cause abandoned by the contumacious plaintiff,[71] or an instance quashed or renounced;[72] to decide on the necessity of admitting certain proofs;[73] to set the length of time for the offering of proofs and the presentation of defenses;[74] to compel compliance from disobedient witnesses, or to fine them;[75] to order the publication of the procedure and the communication of the acts to the parties,[76] and to set the time within which the proofs are to be completed;[77] to decree the cause concluded;[78] to permit the admission of new evidence even after the conclusion of the cause;[79] to set a time for the presentation of defenses and allegations, and to decree that they be printed if he deem it necessary;[80] to set a time within which the defender of the bond is to present his animadversions;[81] to grant the parties permission to offer more than one rebuttal;[82] to extend or, with the consent of all concerned, to curtail the time assigned for the filing of briefs, defenses, or replies;[83] to limit the undue expansion of defenses;[84] to see to it that copies of the proceedings do not fall into the hands of strangers to the

[68] Can. 1729, § 2; art. 92, § 1.
[69] Art. 89, § 1.
[70] Art. 89, § 2; art. 115.
[71] Cans. 1849; 1850 § 1; art. 91, § 1.
[72] Art. 68, § 2.
[73] Can. 1749; art. 95, §§ 1-2.
[74] Art. 68, § 2.
[75] *Loc. cit.*
[76] Art. 175, §§ 1-2.
[77] Art. 175, § 3.
[78] Art. 177, § 1.
[79] Art. 178, § 2.
[80] Can. 1862, § 1; art. 179, §§ 1-3.
[81] Art. 180, § 1; art. 71, § 1, n. 1.
[82] Art. 180, § 4.
[83] Can. 1862, § 2; art. 181.
[84] Can. 1864; art. 182.

cause;[85] to allow and to moderate an oral discussion;[86] to set the day and the hour of the decision, and to notify the parties of this;[87] to set the day and the hour for the convening of the judges to pronounce the judgment;[88] to assign, for a just reason, the writing of the sentence to some judge, other than the recording judge, who took part in the discussion;[89] if necessary, to compel the defender of the bond to see to the completion of the evidence in a cause originally presented on the grounds of impotence or for some other cause of nullity, but which now points rather to nonconsummation;[90] to fix the expenses and honoraria that are owed to the experts, the amount that is owed to witnesses, and the other judicial expenses;[91] to determine the amount to be deposited beforehand in the treasury of the tribunal for the defraying of expenses;[92] to judge whether an advocate is to be excused from rendering gratuitous representation or is to be obliged to perform this service.[93]

Art. III. Functions Which May Be Performed By The Auditor

Any or all of the functions listed in this article can be performed by the presiding judge should he so desire.[94] The auditor's duties are: to summon and hear the witnesses, and to prepare other judicial acts, according to the terms of his mandate;[95] to sign the summons, if necessary;[96] to order the court messenger to go into another diocese for the pur-

[85] Art. 184.
[86] Can. 1866; art. 186, §§ 1, 2, 4, and 5.
[87] Art. 185.
[88] Art. 198, § 1.
[89] Art. 200, § 2.
[90] Art. 206, §§ 1-2.
[91] Art. 68, § 2; art. 234, nn. 2-3.
[92] Art. 235, §§ 1-2.
[93] Can. 1916, § 1; art. 240, §§ 1-2.
[94] Can. 1577, § 2, art. 14, § 2; cf. art. 68, § 3. The auditor is also called the *instructor* of the acts (can. 1582; art. 24).
[95] Can. 1582; art. 24.
[96] Can. 1715; art. 76, § 2.

pose of serving a summons;[97] to order if necessary a summons to be served by means of registered mail,[98] or by way of an edict;[99] to repeat a summons, if it appears to be necessary;[100] to make judicial inspections, and to examine and compare the relevant documents;[101] to establish the identity of the deponents;[102] to conduct the examination of the parties, witnesses, and experts;[103] to conduct, when necessary, the confrontation of parties and witnesses, either among themselves or with each other;[104] to swear in the deponents, admonishing them of the sanctity of an oath, or, in exceptional cases, to permit unsworn depositions;[105] to compel the parties and witnesses to produce the necessary documents;[106] if they deny that they have the documents, to demand, if it be expedient, that they confirm their denial by means of an oath;[107] to demand that the entire document be produced instead of simply an excerpt, if necessary;[108] to try to bring about the appearance in court of a recalcitrant plaintiff or defendant;[109] to introduce witnesses *ex officio,*[110] and to summon necessary witnesses *ex officio* even after the examination of the parties' witnesses has been completed;[111] to guard against collusion between the parties;[112] to admit by way of a decree the unfit or suspect as witnesses;[113] to admit or reject volunteer witnesses;[114] to

[97] Art. 79, § 2.
[98] Can. 1719; art. 80.
[99] Can. 1720; art. 83.
[100] Art. 86.
[101] Cans. 1807; 1821, § 2.
[102] Art. 97.
[103] Art. 101; cf. art. 99.
[104] Arts. 114, 133.
[105] Art. 96, § 1.
[106] Art. 158.
[107] Art. 167, §§ 1, 3; cf. arts. 158, 163, § 2; 168.
[108] Art. 166.
[109] Cans. 1845; 1849; art. 115.
[110] Can. 1619, § 2; art. 123, § 1.
[111] Art. 134.
[112] Art. 113, §§ 2-3.
[113] Can. 1758; art. 120.
[114] Can. 1760; art. 124.

announce or withhold, as may be deemed prudent, the names of the witnesses before their examination;[115] to order the publication of the testimony;[116] to allow, by way of exception, the presence of the parties or of their advocates or procurators at the examination of the witnesses;[117] to see to it that the answers of the deponents are faithfully recorded by the notary;[118] to sign the written records of the testimony;[119] to place procurators and advocates under the special oath of maintaining secrecy;[120] to comply with the request of witnesses who testify on condition that their names be kept secret;[121] to extend the time allowed to the parties for the rejection of witnesses,[122] and to reject futile and dilatory petitions for the reprobation of witnesses;[123] to designate the experts [124] and interpreters;[125] to substitute other experts if necessary;[126] and to decide on an exception when it is lodged against an expert;[127] to swear in the experts;[128] to decree, if that be deemed necessary, that the experts conduct their examination collegiately with a joint report;[129] to designate a more competent expert *(peritior)*, if necessary;[130] to determine what points are to be especially looked for in the examination by the experts;[131] to fix a time,

[115] Can. 1763; art. 126, § 2.
[116] Art. 134.
[117] Art. 128.
[118] Can. 1778; arts. 103, § 2; 129.
[119] Art. 104, § 2.
[120] Art. 130, § 1.
[121] Art. 130, § 2.
[122] Can. 1764, § 4; art. 131, § 1.
[123] Art. 131, § 4.
[124] Can. 1793; arts. 68 § 2; 141; 150; 151.
[125] Art. 108.
[126] Arts. 144-145, cf. also can. 1803, §§ 1-2.
[127] Can. 1796, §§ 1-2; art. 145.
[128] Art. 146.
[129] Art. 148, § 2; can. 1802. But see can. 1980 §§ 1-2, and Reg. 93, § 2, of the *Regulae Servandae* issued on May 7, 1923—*AAS*, XV (1923), 141.
[130] Art. 153.
[131] Art. 147, § 1.

when it is deemed necessary, for the completion of examinations and the submitting of opinions by the experts;[132] to see to it that personal presumptions will be invoked only when they are supported by proper facts;[133] along with the presiding judge, carefully to consider all the judicial evidence before the publication of the process;[134] to set a time within which the parties and the defender of the bond may examine and weigh new evidence with a view to impugning it;[135] to decree, when it is deemed expedient, that an incidental question raised by the parties be presented to the tribunal for admission or rejection.[136]

Art. IV. Functions Of The Recording Judge

The recording judge *(ponens)* is to report on the cause in the meeting of the judges;[137] to write the decision in the form of an affirmative or negative reply to the petition proposed, and to affix his own signature along with the signatures of the other judges;[138] if the tribunal decrees that the decision is to be kept secret until the time of the formal publication of the sentence, then the recording judge is to establish this decision by means of his decree;[139] finally, he is to draw up the formal sentence in Latin.[140]

132 Art. 147, § 4; can. 1799, § 2.
133 Art. 174.
134 Art. 175, § 1.
135 Art. 175, § 3.
136 Art. 188, § 1.
137 Can. 1584; art. 22, § 1.
138 Art. 198, § 6.
139 Art. 199.
140 Art. 200, § 2; cf. art. 22, § 1.

CHAPTER II

THE DISCRETIONARY AUTHORITY OF THE JUDGE RESPECTING CERTAIN OTHER PARTICIPANTS IN JUDICIAL PROCEDURE

ART. I. THE JUDICIAL NOTARY

The discretionary authority of the judge concerning the judical notary is manifested in the following:

1) The judge is to designate[1] as actuary, at the beginning of the trial, one of the group of ecclesiastical notaries already appointed by the ordinary.[2] The judge may not *appoint* an ecclesiastical notary, nor may he designate as actuary one who is not already an ecclesiastical notary.[3] Moreover, the judge may not even *designate* the actuary, if the ordinary has chosen to do so himself,[4] except when an assistant notary becomes necessary.[5]

2) The judge may designate as actuary the chancellor, who is a notary by virtue of his office,[6] should circumstances warrant it.[7]

[1] The word "designate" signifies the selection of an already duly appointed notary; "appoint" signifies creating or constituting a person as an ecclesiastical notary.

[2] Can. 1585, § 2; art. 17.

[3] Cf. can. 373, § 1. Toliusis (*De Notario Curiae Dioecesanae* [Romae, 1951], p. 73) states: "Iudex qua talis personam privatam in actuarium assumere nequit. At quia munus actuarii nullam secumfert iurisdictionem, sed merum ministerium publicum, ad id iudex, persona publica, quemvis idoneum deputare potest de quolibet consensu Episcopi. Ita Officialis, constituendo tribunal collegiale, 'haud invalide eligit actuarium, qui saepius iam designatus est ab Ordinario aut certum est idoneus.' "

[4] Can. 1585, § 2; art. 17.

[5] Art. 19, § 3.

[6] Can. 372, § 3.

[7] Cf. Prince, *The Diocesan Chancellor*, The Catholic University of America Canon Law Studies, n. 167 (Washington, D..: The Catholic University of America Press, 1942), p. 80; Duerr, *The Judicial*

3) The judge may designate an assistant notary, who will help the actuary in his official duties.[8] While the *Instructio* does not so specify, it logically follows that the restrictions given in 1) above concerning the principal actuary apply also to the assistant actuary. It could hardly be presumed that the judge would have wider discretionary power concerning the assistant than concerning the principal actuary.

4) The judge may designate more than one assistant actuary, since art. 19, § 3, sets no limit; the number will then be determined, at the discretion of the judge, according to the necessity.

5) The judge may designate, when necessary, substitute actuaries—subject of course to the conditions enumerated above in 1).[9]

6) The judge may direct the actuary to record certain responses according to substance rather than verbatim, in the judicial interrogations.[10] It seems that in such a case the judge should dictate to the notary the answer which he wishes recorded merely in substance.

7) The judge is to recall the actuary to his sense of duty, if that should prove necessary,[11] and may remove the actuary from functioning in the trial, if he deems the removal necessary.[12]

Notary, The Catholic University of America Canon Law Studies, n. 312 (Washington, D.C.: The Catholic University of America Press, 1951), p. 50.

[8] Art. 19, § 3.

[9] This conclusion is simply a logical application of the judge's discretionary authority; art. 19, § 1, at first sight seems to contradict it. However, when one considers that the actuary is referred to in art. 19, § 1, in the same context with the judges, the defender of the bond, and the promoter of justice, it becomes evident that this art. refers rather to the appointing, and not the designating, of an assitant actuary. It would be unreasonable to presume that the judge could designate an actuary, but not a substitute. Cf. Reg. 18, *Regulae Servandae* (1923)—*AAS*, XV (1923), 395.

[10] Can. 1778; art. 103, § 2.

[11] Art. 68, § 1.

[12] But see also can. 1585, § 2, *in fine*: "...nisi ipse Ordinarius aliquem pro ea causa iam designaverit."

Art. 17 specifies that the presiding judge is to designate the actuary. It is to be noted that this provision has direct reference to the selection of an actuary at the *beginning* of the trial, in the constituting of the tribunal's personnel. In view of the fact that the auditor has discretionary authority equivalent to that of the presiding judge in the probatory period of the trial,[13] it seems certain that at least in this probatory period—during which practically all of the actuary's functions occur—the auditor could likewise designate substitute and assistant actuaries, freely and without reference to the presiding judge.[14] He must, of course, choose only duly appointed ecclesiastical notaries, according to the norms given above.

Art. II. The Auditor

A. The Appointment of an Auditor

Analogously to the appointment and designation of a notary,[15] a distinction should be made between the *appointment* of an auditor, and the *designation* of one for a particular case.

The bishop, and only he, can appoint several auditors permanently, forming as it were a group of duly qualified auditors similar to the group of duly appointed ecclesiastical notaries.[16] The presiding judge[17] can appoint an auditor, but

[13] Cf. Art. 96, § 1.

[14] "Item iudex delegatus ad determinatam causam, quin determinatus sit actuarius, eundem sibi valide adsciscit; cui enim delegata potestas est, ea quoque intelliguntur concessa sine quibus eadem exceri non potest (c. 200, § 1)."—Hanssen, *De Sanctione Nullitatis in Processu Canonico* (Romae: Apollinaris, 1939), p. 57.

[15] Cf. *supra*, p. 00.

[16] Art. 23, § 1: "Episcopus unum aut plures auditores seu actorum instructores, sive stabiliter, sive pro certa causa, constituere potest."

[17] Art. 23, § 1, uses the word "*Officialis*"; however, this authority is also vested in the vice-official when he acts as presiding judge. Cf. Reg. 46, R. J., in VI°: "Is, qui in ius succedit alterius, eo iure, quo ille, uti debebit." Doheny, *Canonical Procedure in Matrimonial Cases* (2 vols., Vol. I, *Formal Judicial Procedure*, 2. ed., 1948; Vol. II, *Informal Procedure*, 1944, Milwaukee: Bruce Pub. Co.), I, p. 83, seems to restrict this authority to the *Officialis* as such.

only for a determined case, unless the bishop has already made proper provisions for one.[18] An auditor may likewise be designated from the group of auditors already appointed by the bishop.

The duties which may be entrusted to the auditor have been enumerated in detail in the *Instructio,* to the point where the entire probatory stage of the process, exclusive of the actual passing of the sentence, may be performed by the auditor.[19] Nevertheless, the statement of canon 1577, § 1, to the effect that the tribunal should act as a body, expresses the mind of the legislator that the tribunal should proceed collegiately whenever possible, even in those acts which precede the sentence. Accordingly, whenever possible, all of the judges should be present at each session of the trial.[20]

B. Must an Auditor be Appointed?

Since canon 1580 and article 23 use the word *"potest,"* it is obvious that the appointment of an auditor is not absolutely necessary.

C. Should an Auditor be Appointed?

Roberti strongly urges that the judges themselves should act as auditors in order to obtain that intimate knowledge of the persons and acquaintance with the details of the causes which only a personal understanding can bestow.[21] On the other hand, some authors contend that the frequent contact of the judge with the parties during the preparation of the judicial acts would render it difficult for him to be absolutely impartial in the passing of the final sentence; accordingly, they deem this consideration the fundamental reason for the appointment of an auditor distinct from

[18] Art. 23, § 1; cf. can. 1580, § 2.

[19] Cf. especially Tit. IX, *De Probationibus*, Cap. I to VI, and art. 96, § 1, and art. 68, § 3.

[20] Cf. Cappello, *Summa Iuris Canonici* (Romae: Apud Aedes Universitatis Gregorianae, 3 vols., 1928-1936), III, n. 32.

[21] Roberti, *De Processibus*, I, n. 111, p. 182.

the judge.[22] It is probably more correct to assume that through the direct and personal contact with the parties and witnesses the judge who acts as auditor derives a greater knowledge of the true facts and circumstances of the cause brought to trial.[23]

Here, so it seems to this writer, it is necessary to distinguish between the ideal—namely, that the tribunal or at least one of the judges acting as auditor have personal contact with the deponent—and practical necessity as determined by circumstances. The chief reason for providing an auditor seems to lie in the necessity of providing assistance to the judge—presiding or collegiate—in his multitudinous tasks, and to expedite the conclusion of the trial. The assumption that only the one who personally interviews a party, witness, or expert, could utilize properly all the circumstances accompanying the answers is false. Even the judge who has acted as auditor must reach his decision *ex actis et probatis*[24] and not from personal or private knowledge; thus, if he should perceive any important indications which will help explain the words themselves of the answer, he should see that they are placed in the acts. A competent auditor, though he be not a member of the collegiate tribunal, can describe fully in the judicial acts the significant facts, together with his own impressions of the person examined, for the benefit of the subsequent evaluation by the panel.

Two things may be noted concerning the relationship of the presiding judge to the auditor: a) neither the Code

[22] Cf. Matthaeus Conte a Coronata, *Institutiones Iuris Canonici* (5 vols., Vol. III, *De Processibus*, 3. ed., 1948 Taurini: Marietti), n. 1121; Wernz-Vidal, *Ius Canonicum*, VI, n. 98.

[23] Roberti, *De Processibus*, I, n. 113; Noval, *De Iudiciis*, nn. 126, 135, 443; Wernz-Vidal, *op. cit.*, VI, pars I, n. 98; Lyons, *The Collegiate Tribunal of First Instance*, The Catholic University of America Canon Law Studies, n. 78 (Washington, D.C.: The Catholic University of America, 1932), p. 60; Cocchi, *Commentarium in Codicem Iuris Canonici ad Usum Scholarum* (8 vols., Taurinorum Augustae: Marietti, 1920-1930), VII, n. 32, A.

[24] Can. 1869, § 2.

nor any subsequent instruction of the Holy See has limited the right of the judge to use the auditor *when* and *if* he considers it necessary and opportune,[25] and b) even though the auditor may be commissioned to conduct the interrogations, the judge does not thereby lose his right to interrogate whenever he considers it necessary and opportune.[26]

D. *Who May be Appointed Auditor?*

Insofar as possible, the auditor should be chosen from among the synodal (or pro-synodal) judges.[27] It would probably be preferable to have one of the judges of the college act as auditor.[28] The presiding judge himself may undertake the duties of the auditor, should he deem it necessary or expedient.[29] If it is necessary to appoint an auditor who is not one of the synodal judges, he should possess similar qualifications of learning, forensic experience, good judgment, and prudence.[30] A lay person may not be appointed as auditor in marriage causes.[31]

E. *When Should the Auditor be Appointed?*

Since the law does not specify the necessity of or the time for the appointing of an auditor, and in view of the fact that the principal purpose of an auditor is to assist the judge, it seems that such an appointment can be made at any time during the trial.

F. *How Many Auditors may be Appointed?*

Ordinarily, only one auditor need be appointed. However, the law clearly permits more than one auditor.[32] It

[25] Cf. Cans. 1580, 1582, 1715 § 2, 1773; art. 23, 24, 96.

[26] Wernz-Vidal, *op. cit.*, VI, n. 422.

[27] Can. 1581; art. 23, § 2.

[28] Roberti, *op. cit.*, I, 297.

[29] Art. 68, § 3.

[30] Doheny, *op. cit.*, I, 84.

[31] Cf. can. 118; Noval, *De Iudiciis*, n. 131; Lega (ed. Bart.), *Commentarius*, I, 142.

[32] Cf. art. 23: "... unum aut plures auditores ... pro certa causa, constituere potest."

seems, therefore, that as many auditors as are deemed necessary, or even simply useful, can be appointed. It is obvious, however, that one auditor should at least complete the examination of the party, witness, or expert with whom he has started.

G. Removal from Office

The auditor can be removed from office at any time during the trial by the one who selected him in a given case, provided there be a just reason and that no harm result thereby to the parties.[33]

Art. III. The Recording Judge

A. Appointing the Recording Judge

Only the presiding judge is qualified to appoint the recording judge of the collegiate tribunal.[34] Since canon 1584 uses the word *"debet,"* it is plain that the presiding judge may not omit the appointment of the recording judge,[35] unless he elects to take these duties upon himself with the consent of the tribunal.[36] However, in view of canon 11, the validity of the process does not depend upon the necessity of this appointment.[37]

[33] Can. 1583. Lega (ed. Bart.), *op. cit.*, I, 144, mentions as just reasons: "1) imperitia auditoris, 2) aut studium partium, scilicet animus praeoccupatus in unam vel alteram litigantium partem; 3) mala valetudo; 4) vel in genere aliqua superveniens causa unde auditoris status et conditio mutetur; ut ecce si auditor uni vel alteri parti fiat suspectus, aut si status eius mutetur ob novum officium aut novam dignitatem adeptam, et ita porro."

[34] Referred to as *ponens* or *relator*—cf. can. 1584. The duties of the recording judge are outlined above, p. 46.

[35] Coronata, *op. cit.*, III, n. 1132; Cappello, *op. cit.*, III, p. 33, n. 35; Noval, *op. cit.*, n. 137; Metz, *The Recording Judge in the Collegiate Tribunal*, The Catholic University of America Canon Law Studies, n. 287 (Washington, D.C.: The Catholic University of America Press, 1949), p. 51; Lyons, *The Collegiate Tribunal of First Instance*, p. 58.

[36] Art. 22, § 2; Cocchi, *Commentarium*, VII, p. 52, n. 23.

[37] Cappello, *loc. cit.*

B. Who may be Appointed?

Canon 1584 simply states that the presiding judge should appoint one of the collegiate judges. The presiding judge may therefore appoint either one of the other judges as recording judge. With the assent of the other members of the panel, the presiding judge himself may serve as recording judge.[38] If, however, the other two judges do not give their assent, it will be necessary for the presiding judge to appoint one of his associate judges to serve in this capacity. If the presiding judge were to appoint himself in spite of the others' disapproval, this fact would not invalidate such a self-appointment, nor would it affect the validity of the sentence later on passed by the collegiate panel.[39] Such a disregard of the majority opinion would certainly render illicit the self-appointment of the presiding judge.

Whether or not the presiding judge should appoint himself seems to depend upon circumstances—the number and ability of judges available, the number of causes pending, etc.;—in any case, a proper distribution of the duties among the members of the tribunal seems to indicate that whenever possible the presiding judge should appoint one of the other judges of the panel to act as recording judge.[40]

The recording judge could also be the auditor.[41] In smaller dioceses, where the abilities and the knowledge of the three judges may be quite disparate, it would be advisable for the best qualified judge to assume both duties. Since the presiding judge may be either the auditor or the recording judge, it follows, in view of the lack of explicit law to the contrary, that the presiding judge could be the audi-

[38] Art. 22, § 2.

[39] Metz, *op. cit.*, p. 63. It may be noted that can. 1584 does not exclude self-appointment by the presiding judge, nor does it require the assent of the panel.

[40] Metz, *loc. cit.*

[41] Cf. Roberti, *De Processibus*, I, 296-7; Noval, *op. cit.*, n. 132; Muñiz, *Procedimientos Eclesiásticos* (2. ed., 3 vols., Sevilla, Imp. y. Lib. de Sobrino de Izquierdo, 1925), I, 132-133; Lega (ed. Bart.), *op. cit.*, I, 145.

tor *and* the recording judge. It seems, however, that such a concentration of judicial functions in one judge to the exclusion of the other two would rarely if ever be advisable.

C. Manner of Appointment

Usually the appointment of the recording judge is made in writing.[42] The presiding judge has the discretionary authority to make the appointment orally,[43] in which case he should write a memorandum for insertion into the acts.[44]

D. Time of Appointment

Neither the Code nor the *Instructio* determines the time for the appointment of the recording judge. It is obvious from the nature of the duties of the recording judge, that his appointment should take place as soon as possible in the trial. Roberti suggests that the appointment be made soon after the joinder of issue.[45] Noval (1861-1938) stated that it is highly important that the recording judge be appointed very early in every cause, so that there may be at least one of the panel thoroughly conversant with the case.[46] Metz concludes that the recording judge should be designated at the very beginning of the trial, since without this appointment the special attention of the recording judge to the progress of the cause would be made more difficult.[47] It would be practical for the presiding judge to incorporate into the decree designating the *turnus* a specific designation to one of the judges as recording judge.[48]

[42] Roberti, *op. cit.*, I, 287; Metz, *op. cit.*, p. 50.

[43] Noval, *op. cit.*, n. 139.

[44] Cf. can. 1642, § 1.

[45] *De Processibus*, I, p. 387, n. 109.

[46] *De Iudiciis*, n. 137.

[47] *Op. cit.*, p. 60, c.

[48] Vaughan, *Constitutions for Diocesan Courts*, The Catholic University of America Canon Law Studies, n. 210 (Washington, D.C.: The Catholic University of America Press, 1944), p. 143; Noval, *op. cit.*, n. 137; Lega (ed. Bart.), *op. cit.*, I, p. 146, n. 9; Metz, *op. cit.*, p. 61.

E. Substitution of Another Recording Judge

The presiding judge may at his discretion, for a just reason, transfer the duties of the recording judge from the one first appointed to another of the collegiate panel.[49] Doheny suggests that a just reason for such a transfer could be the "fact that the original *ponens* did not agree with the majority opinion, and consequently would find it difficult to formulate reasons for an opinion from which he personally differed."[50] Other just reasons could be occasioned by sickness, by the pressure of other duties, and the like.[51] This substitution, of course, affects only such duties as pertain to the office of the recording judge; the judge himself will remain a member of the collegiate tribunal.[52]

ART. IV. ADVOCATES AND PROCURATORS

The judicial procurator or proxy represents one of the principals, or parties, before the tribunal; his civil counterpart is the attorney. The role of advocate has its civil counterpart in the lawyer or counsellor at law.[53]

A. Appointing an Advocate

The party may select his own advocate.[54] Should a negligent or incapable advocate be chosen, the presiding judge, after consulting with the collegiate tribunal, may select another lawyer, so that the client's cause is properly presented before the court.[55] Moreover, the judge himself can and should see that proofs are supplied when these are not furnished by the advocate.[56]

[49] Can. 1584; art. 22, § 1.

[50] *Canonical Procedure in Matrimonial Caes,* I, 483.

[51] Metz, *op. cit.,* p. 70.

[52] Doheny, *Practical Manual for Marriage Cases* (Milwaukee, Bruce Pub. Co., 1938), p. 135, IX, n. 2.

[53] Cf. Hogan, *Judicial Advocates and Procurators,* The Catholic University of America Canon Law Studies, no. 133 (Washington, D.C.: The Catholic University of America Press, 1941), pp. 3-4.

[54] Art. 43, § 1.

[55] Art. 43, § 2; cf. can. 1655, § 2.

[56] Can. 1619, § 2.

Ordinarily, in matrimonial causes there is no need for both parties having an advocate; however, both may have their respective advocates if they should so desire, or if the presiding judge should consider it opportune. In view of the office of the defender of the bond, whose duty it is to defend the marriage bond with every legitimate means, it would be rare that another advocate for the defendant would be necessary. Nevertheless, the defendant may choose an advocate to whom arguments and proofs may be furnished by the party in furtherance of the cause; sometimes it may even be advisable for the judge himself to appoint another advocate, not because the judicial process requires it, but for the prudent assurance to the defendant that his rights will be safeguarded.[57]

B. Appointing a Procurator

Ordinarily the same person is designated to fulfill the twofold rôle of advocate and procurator; however, should the party so desire, he may appoint a procurator distinct from, and in addition to, the advocate.[58] Even though the parties have appointed an advocate and a procurator, they themselves are nevertheless bound to appear in court in person whenever the law or the judge demands their presence;[59] the judge therefore would not have the discretionary authority to permit the procurator or the advocate to perform all the duties of the parties, such as serving in place of the party at his interrogation.

Doheny is of the opinion that in the event no procurator has been commissioned, the parties may be considered to have entrusted his prerogatives to the advocate, unless the presiding judge has decreed the designation of a procurator.[60] Hogan questions this,[61] and points out that the strict requirement of law with reference to the express, written

[57] Cf. art. 43, §§ 3-4.
[58] Art. 44.
[59] Can. 1647; art. 45.
[60] Doheny, *Canonical Procedure in Matrimonial Cases,* I, 163.
[61] Hogan, *op. cit.,* p. 82.

mandate would preclude such implicit designation of the procurator.[62] Authors are generally agreed that the Code has rendered impossible the assumption of a presumed judicial mandate.[63]

C. *Numbers of Advocates and Procurators*

Each party to the trial may appoint only one procurator, who, in turn, may not substitute another procurator, unless he has the express authorization to do so.[64] The judicial reason for this restriction is obvious. The procurator or proxy stands before the court in a very definite capacity, representing the legal person who has commissioned him to do so. Since the principal has but one juridical personality, it is evident that he should be represented by but one agent at a time. Furthermore, in view of the inevitable confusion that would follow an attempt to act through several procurators simultaneously, practical reasons as well have dictated this regulation.[65]

Sometimes for a just reason a party may designate several tentative proxies with the proper authorization of the presiding judge.[66] The just reason to be determined according to the discretion of the judge,[67] could consist, for example, in the amount of litigation in which the party is involved, or perhaps in the mass of judicial work with which a particular agent is engaged.[68]

Nevertheless, the general rule holds that only a single agent is to function at a time. When the commissioning of a plurality is permitted, the individual procurators must be authorized *in solidum,* which arrangement makes the principle of exclusive precedence, or the rule of prior claim,

[62] Can. 1659, § 1; art. 49.

[63] Cf. Noval, *De Iudiciis,* n. 280; Roberti, *De Processibus,* I, 332; Cappello, *Summa Iuris Canonici,* III, 145.

[64] Can. 1656, § 1; art. 47, § 1.

[65] Cf. Doheny, *op. cit.,* I, 166.

[66] Art. 47, § 2; cf. can. 1656, § 2.

[67] Cf. Noval, *op. cit.,* n. 274.

[68] Hogan, *op. cit.,* p. 78.

operative.[69] A plurality of procurators can be appointed only in such a way that the one who precedes the others by actually assuming the representation of his principal excludes the others from so doing. Such actual precedence and the resulting exclusion of all others is effected by the delivery of a legitimate citation, or by the spontaneous entry of the parties into court.[70] Prior to the Code, upon the joinder of issue the procurator gained control in a trial to such an extent that he became empowered to substitute another in his place. This is no longer possible, without an express permission from the party, as was mentioned above.

With regard to the number of advocates who may be called upon for legal aid by a party in one and the same trial, the law makes no restriction.[71] A plurality of advocates for the same process may be designated simultaneously or at intervals as the occasion demands.[72]

D. *Residence of Advocate and Procurator*

No restriction is placed upon the residence of the advocate; for the procurator, the general rule is that he should reside in the same city where the tribunal is situated or in a near-by place, unless the presiding judge permits otherwise on account of special circumstances.[73] Since the purpose of this regulation is to have the procurator near at hand whenever his presence is required by the court, the judge may well be lenient in granting exceptions to this general rule, in view of modern means of rapid communication and travel.[74]

[69] Blat, *De Processibus* (Vol. V of a six volume work, *Commentarium Textus Codicis Iuris Canonici,* Romae: Institutum Pontificum Internationale "Angelicum," 1927), p. 162, points out that this should be made clear to the several procurators commissioned in this fashion.

[70] Can. 1725, n. 5. Cf. can. 1568; Cf. Noval, *op. cit.*, n. 274; Coronata, *Institutiones*, III, 89.

[71] Cf. can. 1656, § 3; art. 47, § 3.

[72] Blat, *op. cit.*, p. 162.

[73] Art. 47, § 4. Since the law places no limitation, it seems that the presiding judge has full discretionary authority to evaluate the special circumstances permitting this.

[74] Doheny, *op. cit.*, I, p. 167.

E. Qualifications

In view of the stringent requirements in respect to the personal qualifications for procurators and advocates, particularly for the latter,[75] there could arise in many dioceses a great difficulty, if not an impossibility, of fulfilling these requirements. It seems that the presiding judge may admit, by way of exception, to the office of advocate or procurator one who lacks the full legal training demanded by the *Instructio*, provided that the appointed one otherwise meets the requirements of canon 1657.[76]

F. Legitimate Mandate

It is the duty of the presiding judge to see to it that the procurator has a legitimate mandate from the party;[77] likewise, in order to undertake the pleading of a cause, the advocate must have proper authorization from the party, or from the judge when the court appoints the advocate, similar to the mandate of the procurator; mention of this authorization should be incorporated in the acts.[78]

G. Rejection and Resignation

The collegiate tribunal is expressly empowered to reject advocates and procurators from practice in ecclesiastical courts.[79] This rejection may take place at the very outset of the process, or it may prove to be a necessary measure during the course of the trial.[80] This discretionary power of the tribunal cannot be exercised arbitrarily; for the rejection or expulsion of these officials, there must be a just and

[75] Cf. Art. 48, which in addition to the general requisites urges three years training for advocates and one year for procurators, preferably in the S. R. Rota.

[76] Hogan, *op cit.*, p. 91; Canon 1657, § 1: Procurator et advocatus esse debent catholici, aetate maiore, bonae famae; acatholicus non admittitur, nisi per exceptionem et ex necessitate. § 2. Advocatus debet praetera esse doctor vel alioqui vere peritus, saltem in iure canonico.

[77] Art. 49, §§ 1-3; cf. cans. 1659, 1660.

[78] Art. 49, § 4; can. 1661.

[79] Can. 1663; art. 51.

[80] Cf. Blat, *De Processibus*, p. 169.

grave reason, proportionate to the rejection, in the prudent opinion of the court.[81] For example, should an advocate or a procurator prove incapable from a technical point of view,[82] by lacking in proper respect and obedience to the court,[83] by being unworthy because of improper legal practice,[84] or by being unfitted because of a deficient moral standing,[85] the court would be well within its discretionary authority in banishing that person from the tribunal.[86] Advocates and procurators may be removed by the person who appointed them; nevertheless, the obligation of paying the fees due them remains.[87] Neither advocate nor procurator, during the trial, may resign his office, without a just reason approved by the presiding judge.[88]

H. Gratuitous Advocacy

Advocates whom the bishop has listed in the legal register[89] are bound, upon receipt of a mandate from the presiding judge of the tribunal, to give gratuitous assistance to those to whom this privilege has been granted by the tribunal.[90] The advocate thus designated may not withdraw from his task, unless for some reason approved by the presiding judge,[91] such as illness, incompatible assignments, special obligations, and the like.[92] Should the advocate resign without the judge's approval, he can be punished by the presiding judge—which punishment may be increased by the collegiate tribunal even to suspension from

[81] Art. 51; can. 1663; cf. cans. 1657; 1658; 1659.
[82] Cf. cans. 1657; 1619.
[83] Can. 1640, § 2.
[84] Cans. 1665, 1666.
[85] Cans. 2263; 2294.
[86] Wernz-Vidal, *Ius Canonicum,* VI, 204; Coronata, *Institutiones,* III, 93.
[87] Can. 1664, § 1; art. 52, § 1.
[88] Art. 54, n. 3.
[89] Cf. art. 53, § 1.
[90] Art. 53, § 2; cf. can. 1916; arts. 237-240.
[91] Art. 240, § 1.
[92] Doheny, *op. cit.,* I, 571.

office.[93] If the advocate thus appointed does not fulfill his duty with proper diligence he may be reprimanded by the judge.[94] If the advocates fail seriously in their duty, a fine may be imposed upon them or they may be removed from office.[95]

Neither the Code nor the *instructio* makes any mention of any fees granted by the court in the event of gratuitous legal assistance. Doheny remarks that the custom of the Rota in this matter might well be followed by diocesan tribunals —the advocate is presented a few hundred *lire* at the trial's end.[96]

[93] Art. 240, § 1; cf. cans. 1916, § 1; 1663; 1666.

[94] Art. 240, § 2; this the judge may do either *ex officio*, or upon the demand of the defender of the bond or the promoter of justice.

[95] Cans. 1625, § 3; 1666.

[96] Doheny, *op. cit.*, I, 572. In the U.S. a relatively greater amount would be indicated.

CHAPTER III

PRELIMINARIES IN THE TRIAL

ART. I. THE *Libellus* OR BILL OF COMPLAINT

The *libellus* or bill of complaint is the formal request addressed to the tribunal, by a legally authorized party, apprising the court of the object of the controversy and invoking the service of the judge to declare the nullity of the marriage in question.[1] The importance of a properly drawn up *libellus* is evident from the fact that the tribunal is restricted in its judicial examination to the claims set forth in the *libellus*, and according to it judgment is to be given.[2]

A. *Form of the Libellus*

The purpose of the law seems to call for the introduction of every cause by way of a written *libellus*, regardless of the means by which the *libellus* comes before the judge. Thus, while it is desirable that the plaintiff or his proxy submit the *libellus* in person, there is nothing in the law that forbids the submitting of it to the tribunal or to the ordinary by means of private messenger or public postal service.[3] Some discretion is allowed to the judge in regard to the requirement of a *libellus*, but only in matters of minor importance and of easier investigation and, hence, of expeditious definition.[4] To be enumerated among such matters are causes incidental to the principal cause at issue and

[1] Doheny, *op. cit.*, I, 186. The minute details that must be incorporated in the *libellus* are outlined in canon 1708 and article 57.

[2] Canon 1873, § 1, n. 1; art. 196; cf. Kealy, *The Introductory Libellus in Church Court Procedure*, The Catholic University of America Canon Law Studies, no. 108 (Washington, D. C.: The Catholic University of America, 1937), p. 21.

[3] Coronata, *Institutiones*, III, n. 1237; Roberti, *De Processibus*, I, n. 279, 1; Kealy, *op. cit.*, p. 25.

[4] Canon 1707, § 2.

frequently necessitating determination before the principal question,[5] e.g., exceptions of incompetence, of suspicion of a member of the tribunal, questions of suspension of the exercise of a right involved in the principal question.[6] These and similar questions may, at the discretion of the judge, be presented orally.

B. Omission of the Libellus

The omission of the *libellus* would not, in every instance, nullify the judicial proceedings, for the claim of the plaintiff may be sufficiently determined in the summons or in the joinder of issue, so that the trial will not be lacking any essential element.[7] In fact, it is difficult to conceive a case in which a trial is invalid with reference to the requirement of the bill of complaint.[8] Of course, this would not give the judge any discretionary authority to proceed apart from the *libellus* simply because its absence would not invalidate the process; however, this knowledge can relieve the judge of unnecessary scruples concerning the format of the *libellus*, particularly if he knows the petition of the plaintiff from other sources.[9]

C. Exceptional Presentation of the Libellus

The law itself makes an exception in favor of those who do not know how to write or are unable to do so because of some impediment, such as an incapacitating injury or paralysis.[10] Persons so poor as to be unable to procure suitable materials might be included among the "legitimately hindered."[11] When the judge thus admits oral petitions in

[5] Cans. 1837-1839.

[6] Cans. 1672-1674; cf. Kealy, *op. cit.*, p. 27.

[7] Cans. 1708; 1715, § 1; 1726-1728; cf. Wernz-Vidal, *Ius Canonicum*, VI, nn. 370, 400; Roberti, *op. cit.*, I, nn. 297, 301.

[8] Noone, *Nullity in Judicial Acts*, The Catholic University of America Canon Law Studies, n. 297 (Washington, D.C.: The Catholic University of America Press, 1950), p. 80.

[9] Cf. Noone, *op. cit.*, p. 81.

[10] Art. 56; canon 1707, § 1.

[11] Roberti, *op. cit.*, I, 427; Kealy, *op. cit.*, p. 27.

accordance with the discretion allowed him, he is to order the notary to put the oral petition into writing; the written statement is then read to the petitioner for approval, and if approved, is signed by the petitioner by tracing a sign of the cross on the document, in view of his inability to write. The notary should append a note attesting to the significance of the mark.[12] Article 58 of the *Instructio* emphasizes the necessity of properly identifying the petitioner, which duty belongs to the *officialis*.[13]

D. Admission or Rejection of Libellus

The first duty of the collegiate tribunal after receiving the *libellus* is to ascertain: a) its own competency, and b) the legal capacity of the petitioner.[14] Little if any discretionary authority of the tribunal is discernible in the deciding of these two questions, since the limits set by the law are quite definite; a further discussion, therefore, either of the competency of the court or of the legal capacity of the plaintiff is beyond the scope of the present work. In passing, one may note that the generally accepted opinion in reference to the debarment of non-Catholics from acting as plaintiffs in matrimonial causes is that this disqualification is restricted to causes which are introduced before the collegiate tribunal for formal trial, and that non-Catholics are not estopped from acting as petitioners or plaintiffs in summary cases.[15]

The *libellus* should be admitted or rejected by the collegiate tribunal.[16] Since art. 61 omits the word *iudex* of canon 1709, § 1, retaining only the word *tribunal,* it evidently is the mind of the Church that in matrimonial trials the

[12] Art. 56; cf. can. 1707, §§ 1-3.

[13] Identification is to be effected according to the norms issued by the Sacred Congregation of the Sacraments on March 27, 1929—*AAS,* XXI (1920), 490. The same precautions are to be taken as regards the identity of the witnesses, experts, etc.—Art. 97; cf. *infra,* p. 93.

[14] Cf. canon 1709, § 1; art. 61.

[15] Gasparri, *Tractatus Canonicus de Matrimonio,* II, n. 1260, p. 293; Noone, *op. cit.,* p. 50.

[16] Cf. art. 61; can. 1709, § 1.

collegiate tribunal should decide the acceptance or rejection of the *libellus*. Thus, Doheny concludes that the opinion advanced by some authors permitting the *officialis* to accept or reject a *libellus* in matrimonial causes is no longer tenable.[17] However, there seems to obtain a partial exception from this general rule: in 1938, the Cardinal Archbishop of Milan asked the Sacred Congregation of the Sacraments, relative to the *Instructio* of 1936, whether for the rejection of a petition impugning a marriage, a decree of a collegiate tribunal is always required, or whether a decree of the *officialis* is sufficient when the impugnment has no juridical foundation and the incapacity of the plaintiff to impugn the marriage is evident, or the tribunal lacks jurisdiction. The Sacred Congregation replied that the *officialis* can reject the petition by a well-founded decree, if it is *evident* either that the impugnment has no juridical foundation, or that the plaintiff is incapable of impugning the marriage, or that the tribunal is without jurisdiction. There remains the option of a recourse against such a decree of the *officialis*, but it lies exclusively to the college of judges, which shall proceed according to law. On his part, the *officialis*, when he alone rejects the petition with his decree, must expressly mention in the decree the plaintiff's right to interpose a recourse to the college. If the college rejects the recourse made to itself, or confirms the decree of the *officialis*, the plaintiff has a right to seek redress with the higher tribunal according to canon 1709, § 3.[18]

Moreover, private action by the judge or the tribunal is not beyond possibility. The rules of judicial action on the *libellus* do not prevent the judge or the tribunal from suggesting privately to the prospective plaintiff the corrections needed to make his bill acceptable. Thus, embarrassment for the future may be avoided for the one who drew up the incorrect *libellus;* however, neither the erroneous bill

[17] Doheny, *op. cit.*, I, 203.

[18] Private reply, S. C. de Sacramentis, 18 ian., 1938; cf. Bouscaren, *Canon Law Digest*, II, 544-546.

nor the suggested corrections are mentioned in the acts.[19]

The admission or rejection of the *libellus* should be decided as soon as possible *(quantocius)* after the *libellus* reaches the tribunal.[20] It seems to be the purpose of this regulation to preclude needless procrastination rather than to effect immediate action by the court. Each cause may present its own difficulties; consequently, the law does not specify an absolute time for the taking of action by the tribunal, until the lapse of a month without action establishes the presumption of neglect of duty or at least of undue postponement.[21] It seems therefore that the word "*quantocius*" should have a relative rather than an absolute connotation.[22]

ART. II. THE CITATION

A. The Necessity of the Citation

After the *libellus* or the oral petition has been accepted, the summons or the citation is in order, namely the calling or the citing of the other party and of the defender of the bond into court to contest the alleged claim; these steps may be taken upon the instance of the plaintiff or even *ex officio*.[23] Of course, if both parties appear in court of their own initiative to press their cause, there is no need of a summons; however, the notary should indicate in the record that the parties appeared formally in court of their own accord for the purpose of initiating litigation.[24] There is no need to formally cite the plaintiff;[25] however, the citation of the defendant should be intimated to the plaintiff, so that he likewise may appear on the given day and hour.[26]

[19] Cf. Coronata, *op. cit.*, III, 145; Kealy, *op. cit.*, pp. 54-55.

[20] Art. 61; can. 1709, § 1.

[21] Canon 1710; art. 67.

[22] Kealy, *op. cit.*, p. 51. As to undue delays, see can. 1710 and art. 67.

[23] Art. 74, § 1; cf. can. 1711, § 1.

[24] Art. 74, § 2; can. 1711, § 2. cf. Whalen, *The Value of Testimonial Evidence in Matrimonial Procedure*, p. 154.

[25] Except when the cause is initiated by the promoter of justice.—art. 75.

[26] Art. 74, § 3; cf. can. 1712, § 3.

The summons of the defendant is so necessary that, if it is omitted, or if it lacks the elements required by law, or if it is not lawfully served, the subsequent acts of the process and the ensuing sentence are remediably null.[27] Even when the summons seems superfluous or when it is impossible to consign it to the defendant personally, a summons at least by way of an edict is required for the validity of the juridical process.[28]

B. Means of Presenting Citation

If possible, the summons should be carried by the court messenger, and should be presented personally to the party summoned.[29] If the presiding judge or the auditor deem it advisable, he may order the court messenger even to enter the territory of another diocese.[30] When, because of the distance, or for some other reason[31] it is difficult to serve the summons by court messenger, the judge can order it to be transmitted through the public mails, provided that the letter is registered and a return receipt is demanded, or by any other means that is most secure according to the local laws and conditions.[32] In practice, the serving of the summons by means of registered mail will most frequently obtain in the United States; however, before it can be validly adopted, an order of the judge is required.[33] An implicit order of the judge may suffice, for instance, one that is implied in the customary practice of the tribunal.[34]

Whenever, after careful investigation, the whereabouts of the party to be summoned remains unknown, the sum-

[27] Art. 84; cans. 1723; 1894, n. 1; cf. Noone, op. cit., p. 81; cf. *infra*, p. 72 footnote n. 51, regarding summoning of the defender of the bond.

[28] Art. 83; can. 1720.

[29] Art. 79, § 1.

[30] Art. 79, § 2.

[31] E.g., inclement weather, poor roads, danger inherent in the journey—cf. Lega (ed. Bart.) *op. cit.*, II, 533.

[32] Can. 1719; art. 80.

[33] Noone, *Nullity in Judicial Acts*, p. 90; can. 1719 and can. 1723.

[34] Noone, *loc. cit.*

mons may then be made by way of an edict, i.e., the summons may be affixed to the Curia door for a time to be determined by the prudent judgment of the presiding judge, and the notice is also inserted in some public newspaper; if not both of these can be done, then either manner of publication suffices.[35] For all practical purposes, the affixing of the summons to the door of the Curia in the United States would be absolutely useless for obvious reasons; consequently, this means of publishing the summons need not be considered, at least in this country.[36] While the diocesan newspaper—if there is one—would seem preferable to a secular paper, the choice of the paper should be controlled by the consideration of the best means of intimating the summons to the defendant.[37] Thus, in citing a non-Catholic, the secular press would be more likely to reach him. The law does not determine how often the edict should be inserted in the newspaper; hence, it can be argued that even if it were published only once, the subsequent acts of procedure in the cause would not be invalid on the grounds of an illegitimate summons.[38] However, the judge should try to make the publishing of the summons more than a mere gesture, and probably should insert it in such papers as are likely to reach the defendant, at least two or three times.

C. The Response to the Citation

The determination of the length of time between the issuance of the edictal citation and the time when the defendant must appear in court is discretionary with the judge. It should be of sufficient duration to allow the summons to reach him[39] and to permit the necessary preparation. If it is too brief, the summons is not invalid, but the

[35] Art. 83; can. 1720.

[36] Cf. Lega (ed. Bart.) *op. cit.*, II, 535.

[37] Lega, *loc. cit.;* Wernz-Vidal, *Ius Canonicum,* VI, n. 389, p. 335; Roberti, *op. cit.*, I, n. 294, p. 445.

[38] Noone, *Nullity in Judicial Acts,* p. 90.

[39] Cf. art. 68; *Normae S. R. Rotae Tribunalis—AAS,* XXVI (1934), 449-490.

defendant has just cause for not appearing, or, if he does appear, he may seek more time in which to deliberate. If such a brief period expires, and the judge issues a decree of contempt of court, the defendant without any prejudice is to be admitted in the trial if he appears in court within a reasonable time.[40] If the defendant fails to comply with the summons, and he does not offer an explanation for not appearing, or at least not a valid one, the judge should not proceed to pronounce him guilty of contempt of court, unless it is sufficiently evident that the summons was legitimately issued and brought to the notice of the defendant within due time, or at least should have come to his notice.[41]

D. Repeating the Citation

Although every summons is by its nature peremptory, it is left to the discretion of the presiding judge to repeat it, especially if there is a reasonable cause to doubt whether the summons actually reached the person cited.[42] The citing of non-Catholics, particularly, must be effected with considerable prudence if it is not to offer offense.[43]

E. Citation of Witnesses and Experts

Witnesses and experts must also be legitimately cited. If the adverse party does not interpose an objection, the judge commands each witness to be cited for examination at determined hearings of the trial.[44] If, on the other hand, the adverse party does interpose an objection against a witness, an incidental question arises,[45] which must be de-

[40] Wernz-Vidal, *op. cit.*, VI, n. 386; Noone, *op. cit.*, p. 87.

[41] Can. 1843, § 1, nn. 1-2; cf. Noone, *op. cit.*, p. 92.

[42] Art. 86.

[43] Cf. art. 115. Reg. 38, *Regulae Servandae*, states: "Si citatus praecepto comparendi obtemperarae renuerit, videat iudex an renovanda sit citatio, vel aliis modis magis opportunis et efficacibus uti expediat, ut foret interventus personae amicae vel auctoritate gravis. A remediis coercitivis, ut flectatur contumacia, abstinere ut plurimum prudens erit."

[44] Cf. cans. 1715-1724; 1765; and 1981.

[45] Cf. Roberti, *op. cit.*, II, n. 339, pp. 51-52.

cided according to the norms.[46] The citation of witnesses is made by the presiding judge or the auditor after the names of the witnesses are presented to and accepted by the court.[47]

F. Contumacy

Canon 1842 clearly states that a defendant who has been summoned and who fails to appear in court, either personally or through attorney, without a just reason, may be declared contumacious or guilty of contempt of court. A person cannot be declared contumacious if he appears in court in answer to a summons, but nevertheless refuses to answer questions. Hence a mere appearance in court sufficiently fulfills the strict requirements of law, to let one escape the condemnation of contumacy.[48]

Art. III. The Joinder of Issue

The joinder of issue *(contestatio litis)*, in which the object or matter of the trial is definitely established, consists in the formal denial of the plaintiff's claim by the defendant, made with the intention of contesting the claim judicially.[49] The joinder of issue is effected by the formulation of the mutually acknowledged points in dispute *(concordatio dubiorum)* in the presence of the presiding judge, according to the formula, "*an constet de matrimonii nullitate in casu.*"[50]

A. The Procedure in Effecting the Joinder of Issue

The procedure to be followed at the session of the joinder of issue is not complicated; no special formalities are required. The presence of the presiding judge and the notary would suffice to insure the validity of the joinder of issue; for a valid procedure at least the summoning of the defender

[46] Cf. *infra*, p. 151.
[47] Cf. can. 1582; art. 24. See also can. 1761; 1764 §§ 1-3.
[48] Doheny, *op. cit.*, I, 364.
[49] Canon 1726; art. 87.
[50] Art. 88; cf. art. 68, § 2.

of the bond or his actual presence is explicitly required.[51] The parties appear before the judge, the complaint of the plaintiff and the denial of the defendant are clearly determined, and records of this procedure are inserted in the acts of the cause at trial.[52]

B. The Necessity of the Joinder of Issue

Although required for lawful procedure, and therefore not within the discretionary authority of the judge deliberately to omit, a formal joinder of issue is not required for the validity of the trial itself.[53] As long as the object of the controversy is determined, the judicial process will not be lacking any essential constituent,[54] and nowhere in the present legislation is the formal joinder of issue required under positive sanction of nullity. The claim of the plaintiff will be known both from the bill of complaint and from the judicial summons. Any denial of this claim by the defendant, made with the intention of contesting it judicially, will serve to determine the object of the legal dispute. The Sacred Roman Rota has sustained the validity of trials in which the joinder of issue was omitted, inasmuch as despite the omission the litigants were fully aware of the object of the trial.[55]

That a formal joinder of issue is not absolutely necessary for the validity of the trial appears also from the procedure that is permitted when the defendant is contumacious. In

[51] Art. 74, § 1; art. 15; cans. 1586-1587. If the defender of the bond happens to be present even though not duly summoned, the acts of the session of the court are valid; if he has been duly summoned, but does not appear, the acts of the session are likewise valid. In this latter case, however, the acts of the session should afterward be submitted to his scrutiny, so that he may have the opportunity of submitting objections or suggestions.—Doheny, *op. cit.* I, 247. If the defender of the bond is neither cited nor present, the joinder of issue is invalid as a formal procedure; however, the trial itself would not be invalid. Cf. can. 1680; see also following paragraph.

[52] Can. 1727.

[53] Noone, *Nullity in Judicial Acts*, p. 94.

[54] Cf. can. 1680, § 1.

[55] Cf. Noone, *op. cit.*, p. 94.

such an instance the trial can be conducted and the definitive sentence pronounced even though there has not been any joinder of issue.[56]

There is greater necessity for the formal joinder of issue when the cause is a difficult and involved one, namely when the petition of the plaintiff is neither clear nor simple, and the denial of the defendant is beset with difficulties. If in such circumstances the formal joinder of issue is neglected, it may happen that the object of the dispute will remain undetermined, so that the trial will be lacking in an essential constitutive element.[57] In causes relating to marriage the point at issue will rarely be in doubt; moreover, it will frequently happen that the defendant will affirm the claim of the petition, rather than deny it.

[56] Can. 1844, § 2.
[57] Can. 1728; cf. Wernz-Vidal, *op. cit.*, VI, nn. 399, 400.

CHAPTER IV

JUDICIAL EVIDENCE

Art I. Meaning of Judicial "Probatio"

Some four hundred years ago Mascardus (d. 1588) gave this classical definition: "Probatio est ostensio rei dubiae per legitimos modos iudici facienda in causis apud ipsum iudicem controversis."[1] This same definition is given with little change by the majority of later commentators.[2] This definition presents an objective and broad view of *probatio,* and allows one to distinguish two aspects in it: a) the *ostensio* or *demonstratio* itself—i.e., the actual presentation of the proofs before the judge for the purpose of convincing him;[3] and b) the contents of the *ostensio*—the legal arguments themselves.[4]

A more specific definition, injecting the subjective element of the conviction of the judge, was given by Schmalzgrueber (1663-1735), who described *probatio* as "actus judicialis, quo per instrumenta, aut testes, aut idonea argumenta judici de re, aut facto dubio, et controverso fit fides."[5] This definition is substantially retained by Wernz (1842-1914)-Vidal (1867-1938)[6] and by Noval (1861-1938).[7]

[1] *De Probationibus: Conclusiones Omnium Probationum,* (Frankfurt, 1684) I, q. II, n. 17.

[2] Cf. Reiffenstuel, *Jus Canonicum Universum,* lib. II, tit. XIX, n. 5; Lega (ed. Bart.), *Commentarius in Iudicia Ecclesiastica,* II, 628; Coronata, *Institutiones,* III, n. 1272; Roberti, *op. cit.,* II, n. 324; Vermeersch-Creusen, *Epitome Iuris Canonici* (3 vols., Vol. I-II, 5. ed. 1933-34; Vol. III, 4. ed., 1931, Romae-Mechliniae: H. Dessain), III, n. 163.

[3] Cf. Noval, *op. cit.,* p. 305, n. 439.

[4] Cf. Lega (ed. Bart.), *op. cit.,* II, p. 629, n. 2.

[5] *Op. cit.,* lib. II, tit. XIX, n. 1.

[6] Probatio est rei dubiae seu controversae per legitima argumenta iudici facta ostensio, sive actus iudicialis, quo per argumenta idonea in forma legitima proposita de re dubia et controversa iudici fit fides. —*Ius Canonicum,* VI, 375.

[7] Actus iudicialis quo partes per argumenta idonea et a lege ad-

From these two general types of definitions, judicial proof *(probatio)* can be considered objectively and subjectively in relation to the judge: first, in the objective or broad sense, either as the presentation of proofs for the purpose of convincing the judge—or as the proofs themselves available for presentation; and secondly, in the subjective or restricted sense, as the effect of that presentation when it brings about moral certainty in the mind of the judge. Taken in the objective or wide meaning, proof *(probatio)* seems to agree with what is called "judicial evidence" in the Anglo-American systems of law,[8] which term will be employed in this work to signify *probatio* in the broad sense.

With these distinctions in mind, one can readily solve the question of whether or not the confession of the parties *(confessio partium)* is to be classified under *probatio*. Obviously, in the objective or broad sense of judicial evidence, the *confessio partium* is indeed *probatio;* it is likewise evident that the *confessio*[9] alone cannot be considered *probatio* in the subjective or restricted sense, particularly in matrimonial causes.[10]

missa fidem iudici faciunt de re inter ipsas controversa.—*De Iudiciis*, p. 305, n. 439.

[8] In Anglo-American common law, judicial evidence is defined as "any knowable fact or group of facts, not a legal or a logical principle, considered with a view to its being offered before a legal tribunal for the purpose of producing the effect of persuasion, positive or negative, not of law or of logic, on which the determination of the tribunal is to be asked." Cf. Wigmore, *The Principles of Judicial Proof as given by Logic, Psychology and General Experience and Illustrated in Judicial Trials* (Boston: Little, Brown & Co., 1913), p. 5, § 1.

[9] Sane probatio in sua generica notione est *ostensio rei controversae;* confessio autem ex can. 1750 est "asseveratio de aliquo facto in scriptis aut oretenus ab una parte contra se et pro adversario coram iudice sive spote sive iudice interrogante facta." Qua ex notione patet confessionem consistere in *asseveratione facta de eo quod ab adversario intenditur;* et hinc convenire in genere probationis, quatenus est *ostensio rei controversae.*—Lega (ed. Bart.), *op. cit.*, II, p. 643, n. 2.

[10] Ratio ob quam fides detrahitur simplici asseverationi sive *ac-*

ART. II. KINDS OF "PROBATIO"

Authors over the years have devised many different categories of judicial evidence.[11] For the purposes here to be considered, only the types of judicial evidence that are listed in the Code, Lib. IV, Tit. X, *de probationibus*, are of practical value. The Code in Tit. X repeats in substance the species of proof enumerated by Mascardus in the verse:

Aspectus, sculptum, testis, notoria, scriptum,
Iurans, confessus, praesumptio, fama probavit.[12]

1. *Aspectus* is found in Tit. X, *De probationibus*, Cap. IV, *De accessu et recognitione iudiciali*, canons 1806-1811. It seems that the code anticipates a use for this proof chiefly in causes wherein property or fixed objects that cannot be brought to court are to be inspected.[13] Thus, this chapter is entirely omitted in the *Instructio*. However, there may be judicial notice of objects, such as documents, that are brought to the court,[14] or of persons.[15] Thus in cases of

toris sive *rei* in iudicio illa praecipua est, quia *nemo* in proprium damnum praesumtur testar velle.—Lega (ed. Bart.), *op cit.*, II, p. 657, n. 2. Cf. Art. 117: "Depositio iudicialis coniugum non est apta ad probationem contra valorem matrimonii constituendam." Cf. also cans. 1747, n. 3 and 1751; Lega (ed. Bart.), *op. cit.*, II, p. 644, n. 3.

[11] E.g., according to Noval, *op. cit.*, n. 439, p. 306: "Probationes, *ratione medii seu argumenti* adhibendi vel adhibiti, dividuntur in plures species, utputa probationes *per confessionem, per testes*, etc. *Ratione modi* quo obtinentur, aliae sunt *directae*, quae, scilicet ex partium destinatione constitutae sunt ad probationem faciendam, v.g, *instrumenta, depositiones testium*, etc.; aliae sunt *indirectae*, quae, uti *praesumptio*, deducuntur ex facto non destinato a partibus ad probationem faciendam. *Ex tempore constitutionis*, quaedam dicuntur *praeconstitutae*, quia ante iudicium constitutae, ut sunt depositiones testium receptae ante litis contestationem ad perpetuam rei memoriam, instrumenta confecta ad fidem faciendam de aliquo actu; aliae dicuntur *constituendae*, quae in ipso iudicio constituuntur, ut probatio *per confessionem, per testes, per peritos*, etc. *Ex parte formae*, dividuntur in *iudiciales* et *extraiudiciales*. Considerato *effectu* seu vi persuadendi, possunt esse *plenae* et *semiplenae*."

[12] *Op. cit.*, I, q. IV, nn. 1-2.

[13] Wanenmacher, *Canonical Evidence in Marriage Cases*, n. 329.

[14] Cf. can. 1808, § 1.

[15] Wanenmacher, *loc. cit.*

insanity nothing prevents the judge from confirming with his own senses the reports of experts as to the present mental condition of a party.[16] For reasons which are at once obvious it is not becoming that ecclesiastical judges should undertake judicial inspection in the causes of non-consummation or impotence, even when the person to be inspected is the husband.[17] It would be possible, in a trial involving, for instance, the impediment of abduction or detention, that the judge would find it necessary to inspect the place where the woman was held.

2. *Sculptum* and *scriptum* are summed up in Cap. V, *De probatione per instrumenta,* canons 1812-1824.

3. *Testis* is contained in Cap. II, *De testibus et attestationibus,* canons 1754-1791, and in Cap. III, *De peritis,* canons 1792-1805.

4. *Notoria* is briefly summarized in canon 1747, n. 1, and Art. 93, n. 1: "Non indigent probatione... facta notoria, ad normam can. 2197, nn. 2-3." Thus all notorious facts, whether they be notorious as the result of notoriety of law or of fact, no longer call for proof. How much probative effect is inherent in the notorious fact will have to be judged from the circumstances of the trial.

5. *Iurans* is contained in Cap. VII, *De iureiurando partium,* canons 1829-1836. This chapter refers, not to the oaths to tell the truth *(de veritate dicenda)*, etc., taken by the parties, witnesses, or experts during the judicial examination, but to the various kinds of probatory oaths: suppetory *(suppletorium)*, appreciatory *(aestimatorium)*, or decisory *(decisorium)*. These oaths are either not admissible or not relevant as judicial evidence in marriage causes regarding the matrimonial bond,[18] and hence this chapter

[16] Wernz-Vidal, *Ius Canonicum,* VI, n. 501.

[17] Wanenmacher, *loc. cit.*

[18] Cf. cans. 1834-1835, n. 1, for the decisory oath; cans. 1832-1833, for the appreciatory oath; can. 1830, § 2, for the suppletory oath. But as regards the merely civil effects of matrimony, this category of proof is admissible.—Cf. Torre, *Processus Matrimonialis* (Neapoli: M. D'Auria, 1947), p. 7, at § 3.

is omitted by the *Instructio.*[19] In a broad sense, the oaths to tell the truth and of having told the truth are probatory, inasmuch as a deposition which is sworn to has more probatory value than an unsworn deposition. The suppletory oath used in prenuptial investigations[20] can come into question, when the issue of freedom of status for marriage is submitted to judicial trial under can. 1552 *(factum iuridicum)*, or can. 1035 (claimed right) together with can. 1667 (the right of action).

6. *Confessus* is contained in Cap. I, *De confessione partium*, canons 1750-1753. A confession is properly an *"assertio de aliquo facto contra se et pro adversario."*[21] Since this particular conflict or juxtaposition of parties is frequently missing in marriage trials, the *Instructio* speaks rather *"De partium depositione."*

7. *Fama* is implicitly contained in the chapter on presumptions, canons 1825-1828, according to Noval.[22]

The *Instructio*, in title IX, *de probationibus*, lists five types of judicial evidence used in marriage trials: 1) the deposition of the parties; 2) the testimony of witnesses; 3) the opinion of experts; 4) documents; 5) presumptions. By far the major portion of the probatory stage of a marriage trial is taken up in the judicial examinations of the parties, witnesses, and experts.

Art. III. Discretionary Authority of the Judge in Rejecting Evidence

The presiding judge should not allow the presentation of

[19] But see can. 1830, § 3: the suppletory oath can at times serve as a means for determining in accord with can. 1764, §§ 4-5, the rejection of a witness.

[20] Cf. Fulton, *The Prenuptial Investigation*, The Catholic University of America Canon Law Studies, n. 274 (Washington, D.C.: The Catholic University of America Press, 1948), pp. 101-102.

[21] Cf. can. 1750.

[22] *De Iudiciis*, p. 310, n. 443: "... fama, id est, communis, constans et concors populi vel hominum alicuius loci assertio de aliqua re... per se nihil probat licet praesumptionem inducat, quapropter accensenda est praesumptionibus."

evidence when its purpose appears to be the delay of the trial.[23] If proofs are requested which would unduly delay the progress of the trial—such as the examination of a witness who lives at a great distance or whose domicile is unknown, or the verification of a document that cannot be readily secured—the presiding judge has the right, after consultation with the parties and the defender of the bond, to decide whether the requested proofs should be admitted. He should admit such proofs if they seem necessary or if other proofs are lacking or are insufficient.[24] The examples given in canon 1749 and article 95 of proofs which delay the trial are not meant to reflect a complete list of the ways in which a party may seek to evade a decision unfavorable to himself.[25] It is a well-known fact in all courts that parties who fear the outcome of the trial will seek to delay the progress of the proceedings by means of subterfuge and divers other means.[26]

The judge, therefore, is given the right in law to refuse to admit proofs that are invoked simply with a view to delaying the trial. However, he should weigh the matter carefully before deciding to reject any possible source of proof.[27]

One can easily conceive possible sources of delay, such as the temporary illness of a witness, or the presentation of a document in a foreign language whose translation is delayed in consequence of the difficulty of finding a translator, in which there is no intention to impede the progress of the trial. The judge, therefore, before rejecting any proof, should carefully examine the circumstances to determine whether the intent to delay the trial is actually present. He should admit such evidence if it seems necessary or if

[23] Art. 95, § 1; cf. can. 1749.

[24] Art. 95, § 2; cf. can. 1749.

[25] Cf. Lega, (ed. Bart.), *Commentarius*, II, p. 642, n. 3.

[26] Doheny, *Canonical Procedure in Matrimonial Cases*, I, 306.

[27] "...quotidiana experientia...docet...minimam varietatem in circumstantiis facti magnam solere inducere iuris diversitatem"—Lega (ed. Bart.), *Commentarius*, II p. 641. n. 1.

other proofs are lacking or insufficient—even if the obtaining of such evidence considerably delays the trial.[28]

[28] Cf. art. 95, § 2. Cardinal Lega defined the situation well: "... si probationes exhibeantur cum intentione longius differendi causae solutionem, vel expetitas probationes sit nimis difficile dare executioni, quacumque demum de causa quia exempla in canone [1749] adducta sunt *demonstrative* non *taxative* posita, eademque non videantur iudici necessariae pro rei controversae demonstratione, ista non admittendas esse decernit et decretum, ad normam can. 1840, § 3, *rationes quibus innititur in iure et in facto breviter exponat necesse est....* Iudex autem probe sciat, decretum quo expetita probatio non admittitur esse gravis ponderis et graves consequentias secumferre posse nedum in damnum partium pro veritate et iustitia litigantium, sed etiam quia inde moveri potest quaestio incidentalis maius temporis dispendium et expensarum importans."—Lega (ed. Bart.), *op. cit.*, II, p. 642, nn. 3-4.

CHAPTER V

THE TIME AND PLACE OF JUDICIAL EXAMINATIONS

ART. I. THE TIME OF JUDICIAL EXAMINATIONS

A marriage trial officially begins with the joinder of issue[1] and should ordinarily be completed within two years.[2] The presiding judge should designate an appropriate time within which the parties are to present their proofs, and he can according to his discretion lengthen this time.[3] The particular time during the trial at which the judicial examinations will be held is left to the judgment of the presiding judge or auditor,[4] except that the examination of the plaintiff is to take place first, unless some grave reason suggest a different sequence.[5] There are times, however, when the plaintiff cannot be called first to testify. For instance, if the plaintiff should become suddenly ill, then, with a view to not delaying the trial, the defendant could be heard; or if the defendant should not be available, a witness could be heard. The reason for hearing the parties first is founded in canon 1742 and article 113, and orderly procedure likewise demands such a sequence.

The presiding judge should set the precise day and hour for the examination, in his citation.[6] He should try to set a time which is acceptable to the party or the witness.

The presiding judge may admit proofs even before the

[1] Can. 1732.
[2] Can. 1736.
[3] Can. 1731, 2°; cf. art. 68, § 2.
[4] Cf. can. 1577, § 2; can. 1582.
[5] Art. 110.
[6] Can. 1715, § 1. While the law prohibits judicial procedure on holy days, it does not, as it did in the pre-Code legislation, invalidate judicial acts executed on these days (can. 1639).

joinder of issue, according to the principles of canon 1730.[7] The phrase in canon 1730, *"vel ob aliam iustam causam,"* indicates that the judge may permit this means of securing evidence *whenever,* in his judgment, there is danger that this source of proof be lost, in order to preserve such proof for future remembrance *(ad futuram rei memoriam).*[8]

The judge can apply canon 1730 in the situation wherein the defendant is absent without malice and cannot be located; the defendant's part can otherwise be supplied in such cases by the promoter of justice.[9] Such evidence should be accepted in a judicial manner. It will then have the same probative value as judicial evidence that is gathered after the joinder of issue.[10] Another just cause for applying canon 1730 would be present when there is danger that the witness might forget the facts.[11] The prohibition in canon 1730 applies only to the principal cause, for incidental questions should be settled immediately;[12] likewise, various documents

[7] Art. 68; can. 1730 states: "Antequam litis contestatio locum habuerit, iudex ad testium aliarumve probationum receptionem ne procedat, nisi in casu contumaciae, aut nisi testium depositionem recipere oporteat, ne ipsa ob probabilem testis mortem, ob discessum eiusdem vel ob aliam iustam causam recipi postea nequeat, aut difficulter possit."

[8] Cf. Coronata, *Institutiones*, III, n. 1255, p. 162; According to Pope Innocent III (1198-1216): "Quoniam frequenter in dubium revocatur a multis an, *lite non contestata,* testes recipi valeant, auctoritate praesentium duximus declarandum, regulariter verum esse quod lite non contestata non est ad receptionem testium procedendum, ***nisi forte de morte testium timeatur*** vel ***absentia diuturna.*** In quibus casibus ... ne veritas occultetur et probationis copia fortuitis casibus subtrahatur, *senes et valetudinarii et alii testes* de quibus ex aliqua rationabili causa timetur, etiam lite non contestata, sunt procul dubio admittendi, sive pars conventa sit contumax, sive sit absens absque malitia ut conveniri non possit."—5, X, *ut lite non contestata non procedatur ad testium receptionem vel ad sententiam definitionam,* II, 6 (Italics inserted).

[9] Lega (ed. Bart.), *op. cit.*, II, p. 557, n. 4.

[10] *Ibid.*, p. 559, n. 5.

[11] Coronata, *loc. cit.*

[12] Wernz-Vidal, *Ius Canonicum*, VI, p. 404, note 17.

pertaining to the cause can be deposited in the chancery at any time.[13]

ART. II. PLACE OF JUDICIAL EXAMINATIONS

As a rule, the parties, witnesses, and experts must be examined in the diocesan tribunal.[14] However, certain prelates and civic leaders may choose the place where they will testify.[15] In special cases, the judge may interrogate the cited person at the latter's residence. The Code enumerates the following: All those who are prevented by illness or some other bodily or mental ailment, or by their state of life (e.g., nuns) from appearing in court.[16] It seems that the presiding judge or the auditor could likewise interview non-Catholic witnesses at a place of their choice, if they refuse to come to the tribunal, and if the securing of their testimony is considered necessary or useful; the judge can interrogate witnesses anywhere in his jurisdiction.[17]

Those who live in distant sections of the diocese, so that neither they can go to the court nor the judge to them without great expense, can be interviewed by a local priest appointed by the judge; the priest should be assisted by another person acting as notary, and he is held to interrogate the witnesses according to the questionnaire and instructions sent by the judge.[18] In many of our more thinly populated sections, it could well happen that the only priest in the area would not be able to find even a competent lay person to act as notary. In such cases, the delegated priest alone may secure the testimony, acting both as auditor and notary, to which offices he should expressly and officially be appointed.[19] In every case an authentic copy of such appoint-

[13] Muñiz, *Procedimientos Eclesiasticos,* III, 244.

[14] Can. 1770, § 1.

[15] Cf. can. 1770, § 2, 1°.

[16] Can. 1770, § 2, 2°.

[17] Cf. can. 1636.

[18] Can. 1770, § 2, 4°. It is to be noted that in such a case the presence of the defender of the bond or of a substitute is not necessary.

[19] Cf. Reg. 24, § 4, *Regulae Servandae*—AAS, XV (1923), 397.

ments should be placed in the acts. It could also happen that a non-Catholic in the situation wherein his testimony is secured at his residence or under similar conditions would refuse to be interviewed by more than one person; or the auditor might reasonably judge beforehand that the non-Catholic would resent the presence of a third party; in such cases, the delegated auditor alone could secure the testimony.

The rogatory commission should be utilized to secure the testimony of those who dwell outside the diocese and cannot without grave inconvenience return to appear in the court.[20] However, the parties have the right to request that persons living in another diocese come to the tribunal of the court trying the case, provided these persons agree to do so.[21]

[20] Can. 1770, § 2, 3°.

[21] Art. 98, § 2. Concerning fees and expenses, see below, p. 157.

CHAPTER VI

JUDICIAL EXAMINATIONS IN GENERAL

Art. I. The Oaths

It is a general rule that all judicially conducted examinations concerning marriage causes should begin with the deponent taking the oath to tell the truth *(de veritate dicenda)*,[1] and should terminate with the taking of the oath that the truth has been told and that secrecy will be observed *(de veritate dictorum et de secreto servando)*.[2] It is not within the scope of the work here to enter into an explanation of oaths or of the obligations arising from the taking of oaths.

A. The Form of the Oath

Oaths are to be administered with the invocation of the Divine Name, while the person touches the book of the Gospels;[3] for a priest, it suffices that he touch his breast.[4] The examining judge may, at his discretion, administer the oath in either the declaratory or the interrogatory form.[5] The wording of the oaths is not precisely determined by the law. Ordinarily, written formularies will be found in their proper place in the interrogatories.

In the declaratory oath, the oath-taker repeats word for word, after the judge, the oath; for example: "I swear to tell the truth, the whole truth, and nothing but the truth, regarding those things about which I shall be questioned, so

[1] Art. 96, § 1; cans. 1744, 1767, § 1; Reg. 39, *Regulae Servandae—AAS*, XV (1923), 400. Cf. however, can. 1758: unfit and suspect are exempted from this rule.

[2] Art. 104, § 2; canons 1769, 1780; Reg. 46, *Regulae Servandae—AAS*, XV (1923), 402.

[3] Cf. art. 96, § 1.

[4] Can. 1622, § 1.

[5] Cf. Moriarity, *Oaths in Ecclesiastical Courts*, p. 44.

help me God." In the interrogatory form, the judge asks, for example: "Do you swear to tell the truth, the whole truth, and nothing but the truth concerning all about which you will be questioned, so help you God?" And the oath-taker replies, "I do."

While actually it matters little which form is used, the declaratory form seems better calculated, by its word for word repetition, to impress the oath-taker.

B. The Admission of Unsworn Depositions

If the summoned person refuses to testify under oath, and if the presiding judge or the auditor nevertheless considers that the testimony will be of value to ascertain the truth, he may receive the testimony; but mention should be made in the acts of the fact of the refusal to take the oath and the reason for it.[6] The judge would be the more inclined to admit such depositions, the less direct be the connection which the person about to be questioned has with the parties. Thus it would be practically inconceivable that the plaintiff himself would be interrogated unsworn, since he would either be a Catholic and thus have no reason not to swear, or, if a non-Catholic, he would presumably be willing to co-operate with canonical procedure, else he would never have presented a petition to the court. However, it would be possible for a plaintiff to be admitted, even when he sincerely believes that he should not take an oath, since the law does not advert to any exceptions. On the other hand, the defendant would more likely have some legitimate reason for refusing to swear; in view of this and of the importance of the defendant's deposition, the judge will be more ready to receive his unsworn deposition.

Witnesses, especially those who are not connected with the parties through some bond of intimacy, could more readily be admitted to testify unsworn, since there would be less likelihood of their trying to conceal some pertinent fact. Obviously, if sufficient evidence is already on hand, or

[6] Art. 96, § 1.

if the witness has little to add in the way of evidence, the judge would have no reason to accept his unsworn statements. Entering into the judge's consideration of the matter of admitting such testimony would also be the witness's reputation and standing in the community coupled with the sufficiency of his reason for refusing to swear.

In short, in arriving at a decision whether to admit the unsworn deposition of a person in court, the judge should consider: a) the person himself, whether he is the plaintiff, the defendant, or simply a witness; b) his reasons for refusing to swear; c) the availability of other proofs; and d) the amount of evidence obtainable from him. No set rule can be given, except that when in doubt as to the advisability of admitting unsworn testimony the judge should proceed with the interrogation, indicating fully his reasons for the doubt. Thus, when the collegiate tribunal examines the evidence, the proper importance of such evidence can be more fully gauged in the over-all comparison and sifting of the judicial evidence.

C. The Oath of Secrecy

This oath may be administered to bind the person until the publication of the process, or even for life if the judge deems it necessary.[7] If the nature of the cause or if the evidence itself be such that from the divulging of the proceedings and proofs or any part thereof the good reputation of others might be endangered, or discord, scandal, or other unpleasant consequences might result, the presiding judge or the auditor may bind the consorts, witnesses, or experts to the oath of secrecy for life.[8] Probably it would be sufficient to bind the deponent to life-long secrecy only concerning certain more important points in the trial; such a procedure would surely be within the discretionary power of the judge, and would relieve the person of the possible

[7] Art. 104, § 2; cf. can. 1623, § 3.

[8] Doheny, *Canonical Procedure in Matrimonial Cases*, I, 321; cf. Lega (ed. Bart.), *Commentarius*, II, p. 698, n. 6.

worry of violating the oath over rather inconsequential matters.[9]

D. Penalties for Falsehoods and Perjury

A party, witness, or expert who either refuses to answer when legitimately questioned, or who gives false testimony in an ecclesiastical trial, may be punished[10] by means of a temporary exclusion from the rightful performance of authorized ecclesiastical acts; if the falsifier does either of these things while under oath, he is guilty of perjury and may be punished more severely: with a personal interdict if he is a layman, with suspension if he is a cleric.[11] These penalties are of a *ferendae sententiae* character and may be inflicted at the discretion of the presiding judge or of the auditor.[12] Recourse against the acts of the presiding judge or of the auditor may be lodged with the collegiate tribunal, whose function it is to issue a decree or an interlocutory sentence after consultation with the defender of the bond, and with the promoter of justice, if he is present.[13] Since the law does not expressly provide otherwise, the appeal or the recourse from these penalties operates to suspend their effect *(datur in suspensivo)*.[14] With the exception of the penalties of degradation, deposition, and the deprivation of office or benefice and of the case in which there is urgent demand that the given scandal shall be repaired, it is left to the discretion of the judge to suspend the execution of an ordinary penalty inflicted by way of condemnatory sen-

[9] Cf. Lega (ed. Bart.), *op. cit.*, II, p. 707, n. 5.

[10] Can. 1743, § 3, uses the word "*puniatur.*" It seems, in the light of cans. 2219, § 1, and 2223, that "*puniatur*" should be translated as "may be punished" rather than more positively as "is to be," "must be," or "shall be punished." Thus, the more benign opinion would leave the judgment of whether or not to inflict the punishment to the judge's discretion.

[11] Cans. 1743, § 3; 1755, § 3; 1794.

[12] Cf. Coronata, *Institutiones*, III, n. 1270, p. 176; Moriarty, *op. cit.*, p. 46.

[13] Art. 69.

[14] Can. 2287.

tence, if the offense punished is the first one of a delinquent who prior to its commission had lived a blameless life; with the condition, however, that if, within three years, the delinquent commits the same crime or a different one, he will be subject to the penalties owing for both.[15] Vindictive penalties are terminated by way of expiation (on the part of the delinquent) or by way of dispensation granted by the one enjoying the power to do so, in accordance with canon 2236.[16]

Canon 2323 states that those who are found guilty of perjury in extra-judicial matters—i.e., outside of court cases —are to be punished, especially if they are clerics, at the discretion of the ordinary. Some have concluded from this that the judge should never punish a perjurer without first consulting the ordinary and obtaining his permission;[17] however, it seems that canon 2323 cannot be applied to judicial trials, and that the judge could exercise his discretion without the knowledge or permission of the ordinary.[18]

In canon 1743, § 3, can be distinguished four different ways in which the deponent can violate his obligations when legitimately interrogated:

1) by simply refusing to respond;

2) by responding untruthfully;

3) by refusing to respond after taking the oath to tell the truth;

4) by responding untruthfully after taking the same oath.

Fundamentally, the negative aspect is not as serious

[15] Can. 2288.

[16] Can. 2289.

[17] E.g., Moriarity, *op. cit.*, p. 46.

[18] Cf. Doheny, *op. cit.*, I, 308. Lega (ed. Bart.) *op. cit.*, II, 610: "Canon § 3, loquitur de iudice ad exclusionem Ordinarii, qui nempe in causa non sit iudex, arg. can. 2323, quippe tantum iudex est competens sive ordinarius sive delegatus ad hance poenam applicandam quousque tamen perdurat iudicium; quo absoluto, si iudex suo munere legitime non sit functus, Ordinarius, alias competens, poenae applicationi devenire posset, maxime in vim can. 2222, ne grave crimen remaneat impunitum."

as the positive, i.e., it is ordinarily more serious to tell an actual falsehood than it is simply to say nothing; doing either while under oath adds a more serious aspect. The oath to tell the truth is a promissory oath, in which the deponent not only promises to tell the *truth,* but first of all to *tell* the truth.[19]

The penalty which may be inflicted in the first two instances forbids the guilty person, whether layman or cleric, to administer ecclesiastical goods and property; to act as a presiding judge, as an examining judge *(auditor),* as a recording judge *(relator),* as defender of the bond, as promoter of justice and of the faith, as a notary, a chancellor, a messenger, a bailiff, an advocate and a procurator in ecclesiastical causes; to act as sponsor in the sacraments of baptism and confirmation; to vote in ecclesiastical elections; and to exercise the right of patronage.[20] However, this penalty need not be inflicted indiscriminately.[21]

In the case of perjury, the interdict which may be inflicted upon a layman is the one which bars him from entering a church *(interdictum ab ingressu ecclesiae);* the suspension incurred by clerics could be made to comprise a suspension

[19] Cf. Ayrinhac-Lydon, *Penal Legislation,* p. 176, n. 227.

[20] Canon 2256, 2°; cf. Moriarity, *op. cit.,* p. 45.

[21] Iudex obtemperans generalibus normis pro poenarum applicatione statutis et in primis can. 2223, perpensa delicti seu culpae (can. 2195) gravitate, debet determinare attentis rerum et personarum adiunctis *actum legitimum* (et non omnes actus, indiscriminatim, habent eamdem gravitatem a quo delinquens removeatur nec non *tempus* remotionis.

Iudici vero cavendum est ne partem ab eo actu removeat qui iudiciali contentioni praeiudicet utpote obiectum controversiae, veluti remotio ab administratione rei controversae ecclesiasticae; unde deveniendum esset ad sequestrationem.

Quod si, et casus forsan non est infrequens, non subsit actus legitimus cuius decernatur suspensio aut iudex decernendo remotionem ab actu legitimo non posset efficaciter compescere culpam delinquentis, utputa ab eiusmodi actibus exercendis alieni, unde remotio ei foret iucunda, ad normam can. 2223, n. 3 valeret, loco remotionis, adhibere remedium poenale (c. 2306) aut poenitentiam (c. 2312)—Lega (ed. Bart.), *op. cit.,* II, 610.

of all power of orders as well as of jurisdiction.[22] Here, likewise, the penalty should not be imposed indiscriminately, but in whole or in part as the case warrants in the discretion of the judge. The *interdictum ab ingressu ecclesiae* in its fullest application forbids attendance at divine services and prohibits ecclesiastical burial. Nevertheless, if the interdicted person attends divine service in a church he need not be expelled; if he is accorded ecclesiastical burial, there is no obligation to exhume and remove the corpse.[23] Such an interdict does not prohibit assistance at divine services in oratories—public, semi-public, or private—nor does it forbid the reception of the sacraments.[24]

After determining the penalty, the presiding judge or the auditor has the discretionary authority to determine the length of time within which the perjured layman or cleric must remain under the ban of ecclesiastical penalties.[25] In determining this time, as well as the penalty itself, the first consideration is the person who commits the perjury; the judge should take into account whether the person is the plaintiff, the defendant, a witness, or an expert. The responsibility and consequent guilt seem to be greater in the plaintiff than in the defendant, for the plaintiff has voluntarily presented his petition, and accordingly he could be expected to give all co-operation possible. In dealing with witnesses, the judge should examine the situation carefully to determine whether the deponent might not be excused from answering some particular question in view of the rulings contained in canon 1755, § 2.[26] This would seem to

[22] Can. 2279, § 1; cf. Moriarity, *op. cit.*, p. 47.

[23] Can. 2277.

[24] Conran, *The Interdict*, The Catholic University of America Canon Law Studies, n. 56 (Washington, D.C.: The Catholic University of America, 1930), pp. 140-142.

[25] Cf. can. 2223.

[26] Concerning the obligation of the witnesses, Lega remarks: "At iudex advertat oportet ut plurimum, maiorem dolum habere testem scientier mendacem quam partem quae falsum proferendo aut verum occultando suo commodo seu defensioni suae magis quam veritati indulget." Lega (ed. Bart.), *op. cit.*, II, p. 665, n. 8.

apply even more aptly to experts, who are engaged in the trial at their own volition.

Finally, all those who presume to induce either witnesses or experts by gifts, promises, etc., to falsify their testimony or to hide the truth, are subject to the same penalties.[27]

In inflicting the penalties enumerated above, the judge should bear in mind particularly the principles of canons 2199 and 2218:

1. The imputability of a crime depends on the malice of the delinquent or on his culpability as arising from his ignorance of the law violated or from his omission of due care; therefore all causes increasing, diminishing, or excluding malice or culpability automatically increase, diminish, or exclude the imputability of a crime.[28]

2. In imposing penalties there must be maintained a just proportion with the crime in view of its imputability, the scandal caused, and the resulting injury. Therefore consideration must be given not only to the object and the seriousness of the law which is violated, but also to all the circumstances under which the crime was committed, such as the age, the knowledge, the training, the sex, the status, and the sanity of the delinquent; the rank of both the delinquent and the person injured; the purpose for which, the place in which, and the time at which the crime was committed; the existence of passion or serious intimidation as influences in the commission of the crime; repentance on the part of the delinquent and his attempts to forestall the consequences of his crime; as well as other similar circumstances.[29]

[27] Can. 1755, § 3. Lega (ed. Bart.), *op. cit.*, II, 666; "Attendendum vero est verbum *praesumpserit* quod ad mentem c. 2229, § 2, exigit plenam cognitionem et deliberationem. Nihilominus, quamvis corruptionis conatus non obtinuerit effectum, vel ex quadam levitate magis quam ex plena voluntate delinquendi positus fuerit, si ex adiunctis rei vel personae scandalum enatum sit (utputa si clericus corrumpere ausus sit), potest esse locus poenae ad normam c. 2222." But it must be noted that the *conatus* is here punished; cf. cans. 2212, § 4; 2223, § 1.

[28] Can. 2199.

[29] Can. 2218, § 1.

3. Not only those circumstances which relieve one of all, but likewise those which excuse one of grave culpability, serve to excuse one from all penalties, even in the external forum, provided the excusing circumstances can be proved in the external forum.[30]

Art. II. The Judicial Interrogations in General

In the judicial interrogations, every question, no matter from what source, is to be proposed by the examining judge —presiding judge or auditor, as the case may be—and by no one else, not even by the defender of the bond.[31] The parties, witnesses, and experts are obliged to reply truthfully to the judge lawfully questioning them.[32]

A. Identification of the Deponent

The examining judge should admit no one to testify until he has satisfied himself as to the deponent's proper identification, either by means of a lawful document or through personal recognition by one of the members of the court.[33] The identity of the parties, witnesses, and experts should be established in accordance with the *Normae* of the Sacred Congregation of the Sacraments of March 27, 1929,[34] which stated, in part:

1) ... they [the *officiales*] must require an appropriate document duly drawn up by the ecclesiastical or civil authority, which is to be kept in the records of the case, either in the original or in a certified copy.

2) In case the certified copy cannot report all the marks of personal identification which are usually reported in such

[30] Can. 2218, § 2.

[31] Art. 101; cf. cans. 1742, § 1; 1773.

[32] Cans. 1743, § 1; 1755, § 1; arts. 111; 121, § 1.

[33] Articles 58 and 97. The sufficiency of the identification of the consort *qua* party lies with the *officialis* (art. 58); the sufficiency of the identification of the parties, witnesses, and experts presenting themselves for judicial interrogation seems to rest with the examining judge (cf. art. 97).

[34] *AAS*, XXI (1929), 490.

documents, as, for example, a photograph of the person, it must, nevertheless, carefully report such marks of identification as will certainly distinguish one person from another.

3) In case such a document cannot be obtained, the identity of persons must be placed beyond doubt by other equivalent documents, or by the testimony of witnesses; and such documents or testimony must likewise be preserved in the records.

4) If the judge who draws up the case, or the *Defensor Vinculi,* or the notary, is well acquainted with the petitioner or the defendant, they shall, without requiring a document of identity, certify in the record to their certain personal knowledge of the party or parties.

5) In the course of the judicial inquiry the same precautions are to be taken as regards the identity of the witnesses and of the experts.

The insistence of the *Instructio* is so emphatic and repeated, that it is clear that every tribunal must observe this ruling meticulously.[35]

B. Ex officio Proposed Questions

As often as the judge deems it necessary or useful to ascertain the truth or to define it more accurately, he may *ex officio* add other questions to those already presented, or to those which the defender of the bond, the synodal judges if present, or the parties when present by special permission of the judge,[36] have requested to be proposed during the course of the examination.[37] No hard and fast rule can be formulated for the questioning which is to be undertaken *ex officio* by the examining judge, since only the actual interrogation will bring to light circumstances demanding additional questions—circumstances which could not have been foreseen by the defender of the bond when he drew up

[35] Doheny, *Canonical Procedure in Matrimonial Cases,* I, 192-194; 309.

[36] Arts. 114 and 128.

[37] Art. 101; can. 1742, § 1.

the questionnaire. Moreover, the prepared questionnaire can hardly be expected to elicit complete and exhaustive information about all the phases of a case, in view of the fact that the defender of the bond is chiefly interested in safeguarding the validity of the marriage. Consequently, the examining judge should be prepared to ask questions designed to supplement the defender's submitted questionnaire, particularly in seeking out all the arguments to establish the objective fact of validity *or* invalidity.[38]

It is therefore left to the prudent discretion of the examining judge to carry on the interrogations in such a manner as to leave nothing obscure or incomplete as the interrogation proceeds—adding a question here and there, or demanding a fuller explanation to an ambiguous answer. The examining judge should be particularly careful to include further questions, when necessary, as to the source of the knowledge: how, whence, and when the fact referred to was ascertained; specifically, whether this knowledge was secured as an eyewitness or from personal experience, or directly from an eyewitness, or only indirectly from hearsay, rumors and the like; particularly, the definite time when such knowledge was gained—whether under suspect circumstances in point of time *(tempore suspecto)*, or not, etc.[39]

C. Qualifications of the Interrogatory

The Code clearly states the qualities of the questions: they should be brief, not complex, not captious, not crafty, not leading, not offensive in any way, and relevant to the matter under consideration.[40] The *Instructio* adds that they should be adapted to the intelligence of the persons being examined and expressed in the ordinary language of the people.[41] The responsibility of seeing that these recommendations are put into practice will naturally belong to the examining judge. It will be his duty not only so to

[38] Cf. Doheny, *op. cit.*, I, 312.
[39] Cf. art. 100.
[40] Can. 1775.
[41] Art. 102.

phrase his own questions, but to see to it that all of the questions proposed to the deponent be worded in the manner demanded by canon 1775 and article 102. If the judge discovers that the deponent does not understand the questions properly, he should explain and simplify them, excluding irrelevant questions wherever that is indicated.

In general, the examining judge has no discretionary authority to omit or materially change the questions proposed by the defender of the bond.[42] If, however, the defender of the bond has formulated long and involved conditional questions, the examining judge should simplify them; he may likewise alter the question if the defender of the bond asks for opinions, such as, "What would be your impression," "What do you think he might have done," etc., instead of asking for facts.[43]

D. Apprising the Deponent

In formulating his questions, and in proposing questions from other sources, the judge should particularly avoid framing any question so as to indicate the answer desired —a leading question, as it is called.[44] Moreover, he should never acquaint the parties, witnesses, or experts beforehand with the questions that are going to be asked them,[45] but should only indicate in a general way the object of the examination.[46] If, however, the matters concerning which they are to testify belong to a period so remote that the witness could not answer with certainty unless he had time to reflect, the judge has the discretionary authority before the examination to tell a witness to reflect on certain facts, if he believes that the witness can do so without prejudicing

[42] Cf. can. 1968, 1°: "... interrogatoria ... a iudice ... proponenda."

[43] Cf. Doheny, *op. cit.*, I, 318; Lega (ed. Bart.), *op. cit.*, II, p. 715, n. 10.

[44] *Sacrae Romanae Rotae Decisiones seu Sententiae Quae Prodierunt Anno 1909*—(Romae: Typis Vaticanis, 1912—), IV (1912), p. 39, n. 10 (hereafter cited: S.R.R., *Dec.*)

[45] Art. 103, § 1, a; can. 1776, § 1.

[46] Cf. cans. 1715; 1724; 1765; *Regulae Servandae apud S.R.R.*, § 114, n. 8.

his testimony.[47] Very likely this intimation should not occur in the citation, since ample time would then be afforded to consult with the parties or other witness, which could possibly result in collusion. Rather, if the judge deems some forewarning concerning certain specific items to be necessary, he can intimate this shortly before the examination while the person is waiting to face the court.[48]

E. Use of Interpreter

If a person who is ignorant of the local language appears before the court, and if the judge or auditor does not understand the language spoken by the person, an interpreter under oath, appointed by the presiding judge or auditor, should be utilized, after consultation with the parties and the defender of the bond, so that they may be enabled to lodge an exception against the interpreter if they wish.[49] According to Doheny,[50] it is only necessary that the examining judge understand the language of the person in question; thus it would be permissible to have a substitute auditor who understands the language and can interview the person in question, instead of resorting to the expedient of appointing an interpreter. While the law nowhere states that the defender of the bond must be able to understand the language of the witness, it seems, from the very nature of the defender's obligations and the law's insistence upon his presence at every session,[51] to be implied that he also understand the replies of the deponent. Moreover, it would be impossible for the notary to function if he did not understand the replies. Accordingly it appears to this writer that when a party or a witness is to be examined who

[47] Canon 1776, § 2.

[48] Such limited forewarning should occur only "si agatur de factis antiquis aut alias remotae cognitionis, et de testibus omni exceptione maioribus aut certe probis, quibus si rei cognitio non desit, nunquam deerit voluntas dicendi veritatem." Lega (ed. Bart.), *op. cit.*, II, p. 714, n. 9.

[49] Art. 108. [50] *Op. cit.*, I, 327.

[51] Cf. art. 15, §§ 1-2; can. 1587.

does not speak the local language, it would simply be a question either of using an interpreter, or of not interviewing the person at all, or of hearing him in the presence only of the substitute auditor. And in a cause wherein this person is one of the parties, or a witness whose testimony is of the utmost importance to the arriving at the truth, the judge should make every effort to secure the services of a reliable interpreter. Of course, wherever possible, the judge could always resort to the examination by means of a duly appointed court, whose personnel—examining judge, defender and notary—is sufficiently qualified through the fact that it understands the deponent's language.[52]

F. Answers Not Given Orally

Answers to the questions should as a general rule be made orally.[53] However, the dumb are not excluded as witnesses.[54] Certainly, the fact that they cannot speak effects little or no impairment of their powers of perception. In the situation wherein a party, a witness, or what is even less likely, an expert is mute, or for some reason temporarily unable to use his voice—which could occur, for instance, from an attack of laryngitis, etc.—it would be possible to receive his replies in writing.[55] When the speechlessness is temporary, it would probably be better to postpone the examination until the person can again speak. Meanwhile the court could proceed with the trial through the interrogation of others, etc. However, if such a postponement would unduly delay the trial, or even be moderately inconvenient, it seems that the judge would be justified in permitting the deponent to write down answers to the questions proposed in the examination. Another possibility, in his dealing with

[52] The court must of course be appointed by the bishop. Cf. can. 1572, § 1.

[53] Art. 103, § 1, b; cf. can. 1777.

[54] Cf. Whalen, *The Value of Testimonial Evidence in Matrimonial Procedure*, p. 112.

[55] Reason to be stated in acts, and the written answers are to be filed (cans. 1819-1820; 1814-1818).

the dumb, would be the employment of an intermediary (after the manner of an interpreter), who understands the sign language.

G. Reading of the Answers

The answers to the questions proposed in the examination should never be read from a prepared paper, unless in the opinion of the judge this becomes necessary in answering questions involving numbers, dates, or calculations of a mathematical nature.[56] The exceptions mentioned in Canon 1777 need not be understood as the only possible reasons allowing an answer to be read.[57]

H. Recording of the Depositions

There is some conflict between the Code and the *Instructio*: Both canon 1778 and article 103, § 2, state that the reply of the deponent is to be immediately committed to writing by the notary not only in substance but in the identical words. Then each continues in a silghtly different vein: canon 1778: "... nisi iudex, attenta causae exiguitate, satis habeat unam depositionis substantiam referri"; but article

[56] Can. 1777; cf. *Regulae Servandae apud S.R.R.*, 4 aug. 1910, § 114, n. 8—*AAS* II (1910), 821.

[57] "Sane hac in materia est abs re prohibere documenti lecturam secus attestatio reddi non potest. Ergo, reapse, magis quam exceptio habetur complementum regulae. Unde regula ita enunciata, non secus ac quaecumque regula admittere dicenda est exceptiones quas ipsa subicta materia infert. Ut ecce agitur de causa matrimonii quod nullum ex gravi metu esse accusat mulier ad coniugium coacta, ipsa asserit, ob violentam patris voluntatem. Pater, ut testis et in actu examinis, petit a iudice ut sibi fas sit legere litteras ad se datas a filia: si hoc ei permittat iudex quoad unam vel alteram epistolam quis dicet, attestationem non esse *oretenus* redditam, contra praescriptum nostri canonis? Praxis quoque nostri fori ita hactenus interpretata est legem de attestatione orali; nec littera canonis iubet ut ab hac praxi recedamus, iuxta dicta."—Lega (ed. Bart.) *Commentarius*, I, p. 715, n. 11. The reason for such procedure should be stated by judge for the record. Cf. art. 163-164. Likewise, the matter read should be filed as a document in the record (cans. 1819-1820; 1814-1818), either in the original or as a copy, authenticated in each case.

103, § 2: "... si id instructori videbitur necessarium vel opportunum, aut partes, testes, periti id postulent..." The two conditional clauses radically differ in adding significance to the body of the regulation: according to the sense of the words, art. 103, § 2, indicates that the replies are to be written down verbatim only if the judge thinks it necessary or opportune, or the deponent demands it, whereas canon 1778 indicates that the replies should always be written down verbatim, unless in matters of slight importance the judge deems a substantial recording to suffice. The explicit mention of the parties, witnesses, and experts as made in article 103, § 2, adds little new, since they could add, suppress, correct, or change anything in their testimony at the conclusion of their deposition.[59] One might be inclined at first to conclude that the *Instructio* is less exacting than the Code.[60] However, in view of the principle that the *Instructio* is not new legislation, but simply interpretative of the Code,[61] and in view also of the constant practice of the previous legislation in demanding verbatim reports wherever possible,[62] one must understand article 103, § 2, in the light of canon 1778. It could be put this way: the replies of the deponents are *always* to be recorded verbatim whenever possible; wordy responses which contribute little to the solution of the case may at the discretion of the judge be recorded in substance, unless the deponent demands otherwise.[63] In such a case the judge would dictate the response, and with the approval of the deponent have it placed in the record.[64]

I. Conclusion of the Interrogation

Upon the completion of the questioning, the replies which

[59] Cf. can. 1780.

[60] Doheny, *Canonical Procedure in Matrimonial Cases*, I, 319.

[61] Cf. Schmidt, "The Juridic Value of the *Instructio* provided by the *Motu Proprio "Cum Iuris Canonici"—The Jurist*, I (1941), 289-316.

[62] Cf. Noval *De Iudiciis*, p. 344, n. 497; Lega (ed. Bart.), *op. cit.*, II, 716-717.

[63] Cf. Roberti, *De Processibus*, II, n. 349, p. 65.

[64] Cf. can. 1707, § 3; Analogously, can. 20. See also art. 129.

the notary has committed to writing must be read to the party, the witness, or the expert, and permission granted them to add, suppress, correct, or change whatever they wish, in accordance with the oath *de veritate dicenda* which they earlier uttered.[65] After the final oath, the deponent affixes his signature to the deposition along with that of the judge, the defender of the bond, and the notary.[66] If the deponent is unable or refuses to sign his name, a note to that effect should be made in the record indicating the reason for the non-signing, along with a statement that the deposition was read verbatim to the deponent.[67] It seems that the deponent should be asked to indicate his approval of his deposition as recorded and read, and an annotation to this effect should be made in the record.[68] The judge may prudently seek by means of ecclesiastical penalties to compel the party, the witness, or the expert to affix his signature in the face of an unreasonable refusal to do so;[69] however, this measure should be resorted to but rarely in the case of Catholics, and never in the case of non-Catholics. In the latter case the applying of penalties would accomplish nothing but the antagonizing of an individual who cannot be expected to appreciate the Church's rights in this matter. The person who simply does not know how to write should mark a cross on the record, and the notary should indicate the significance of the mark.[70] Unsigned testimony should be placed in the acts with an explanation for the deponent's refusal to sign; its evaluation will then be made in due course by the tribunal.

[65] Art. 104, § 1.

[66] Art. 104, § 2; can. 1780, § 2.

[67] Can. 1643, § 3.

[68] Cf. can. 1707, § 3, can. 20, and reason of non-signature, art. 96, § 1, analogously.

[69] Cf. cans. 1640, § 2; 1766, § 2.

[70] Cf. art. 56; Roberti, *op. cit.*, I, n. 188; II, n. 349.

CHAPTER VII

THE JUDICIAL DEPOSITION OF THE PARTIES[1]

ART. I. HOW PARTIES ARE CONSTITUTED

The parties in a marriage cause are the husband and wife in the marriage whose nullity is disputed; they become parties, informally, when the bill of complaint *(libellus)* is drawn up and presented to the court; they are formally parties when the trial officially starts with the joinder of issue *(litis contestatio)*. The one who presents the petition is called the plaintiff *(actor)*, the other party the defendant *(reus)* or summoned party *(pars conventa)*.[2] The latter party could also be called the respondent, in view of the fact that the defendant in marriage causes not only rarely objects to the petition, but often is in accord with it.[3] It is for this reason, too, that the defender of the bond plays such an important part in a marriage trial, for it is his duty to safeguard the marriage bond, regardless of whether the defendant agrees with the plaintiff's action or opposes it.[4]

ART. II. OBLIGATION TO INTERROGATE THE PARTIES

Roman law provided that the judge should question the parties at his discretion.[5] Canonical procedure customarily followed the civil law in this matter, but the custom was not brought into written law until 1840, in an Instruction of the Sacred Congregation of the Council.[6] While in causes of a civil nature it was always left to the discretion of the

[1] This Chapter treats only the interrogation of the parties made during the trial; cf. *infra*, p. 169, for a discussion and evaluation of evidence from the consorts.

[2] Cf. Roberti, *op. cit.*, I, 534.

[3] Cf. Reg. 5, § 2, *Regulae Servandae—AAS* XV (1923), 393.

[4] Art. 15; cf. can. 1587. Cf. Roberti, *op. cit.*, I, p. 316, n. 2.

[5] D.(11, 1) 21.

[6] S.C.C., instr., *Cum moneat Glossa*, 22 aug. 1840—*Fontes*, n. 4069.

judge whether or not to interrogate the parties, in 1883 the Sacred Congregation for the Propagation of the Faith commanded that the parties be interrogated in marriage trials.[7]

The Code specifically commands the judge to judicially interrogate the parties;[8] this interrogation can be omitted only in the case of impossibility of hearing the party.[9]

Art. III. Obligation of the Parties to Reply

The parties, when lawfully questioned by the judge, are obliged to answer and to tell the truth, except that they are exempted from the necessity of confessing their personal delicts.[10] In the latter situation, the law does not forbid the party to volunteer this information, but rather states that he cannot be obliged to incriminate himself with his own words. The judge has the right and the duty to question the party, in order to learn the truth;[11] since laws which contain an exception from the law are to be interpreted in a strict sense,[12] it follows from a correlation of can. 1743, § 1, and 1742, § 1, that, though the party is not obliged to incriminate himself by answering, interrogations on the part of the judge which are concerned with a party's personal crime are legitimate and lawful.[13] If the party refuses to respond, no obligation to do so can be imposed upon him, nor can his refusal be in any way construed as a confession of his guilt, since his refusal is legally justified.

[7] S. C. de Prop. Fide, instr., *Causae matrimoniales*, a. 1883, n. 18—*Fontes*, n. 4901; cf. Wanenmacher, *Canonical Evidence in Marriage Cases*, p. 50, n.93.

[8] Can. 1742, § 1.

[9] In the case of contumacy of the plaintiff, see cans. 1849-1851, and art. 91; in the case of contumacy of the defendant, see cans. 1844, 1848 and art. 115, and the entire chapter on contumacy in general.

[10] Can. 1743, § 1.

[11] Can. 1742, § 1.

[12] Can. 19.

[13] Cf. Roberti, *op. cit.*, II, n. 321; Coronata, *Institutiones*, III, n. 1270.

It is the well-founded opinion of Clune[14] that if such interrogations concerning a personal crime are to be proposed to the party, then the party should be advised beforehand that his refusal to answer will not be considered as tantamount to a confession of guilt. For if the party is not aware of this fact of non-obligation, the purpose of, or the reason for, this exception from the law is defeated, and the contention of Cappello, that to interrogate directly concerning one's personal crimes is unlawful, while seemingly lacking a foundation in law, would at least appear to have a basis in equity.[15] Reiffenstuel, in commenting upon the obligation of the party to respond, gave it as his opinion that, if the penalty attached to the commission of a crime was very grave, in such an instance the party was justified in denying his guilt.[16]

Sometimes, in matrimonial causes, the decision hinges upon the wrong doing of one of the parties which may amount to a delict, e.g., on the fact that the party was guilty of abduction, which fact furnished the basis for the invalidity of the marriage. In such an instance, some authors[17] contended that the party would be obliged to answer truthfully when questioned about his crime, since the delict was considered as being merely incidental to the main question, the validity of the marriage. In such a case, the party's silence would redound to the continuance of an invalid union. This opinion seems untenable, after the *Instructio* of 1936. Article 111 applies canon 1743 verbatim to marriage trials, thus clearly indicating that, while the parties are bound to reply truthfully to the lawful interrogations of the judge, they are not so bound in the matter of a delinquency committed by themselves. Consequently, in mar-

[14] *The Judicial Interrogation of the Parties*, The Catholic University of America Canon Law Studies, n. 269 (Washington, D.C.: The Catholic University of America Press, 1948) p. 115.

[15] Cappello, *Summa Iuris Canonici*, III, n. 166.

[16] Reiffenstuel, *Jus Canonicum Universum*, lib. II, tit. XVIII, n. 166.

[17] E.g., Wanenmacher, *Canonical Evidence in Marriage Cases*, p. 57, n. 100.

riage causes the furnishing of information regarding personal delicts must rest on a voluntary basis on the side of the deponent.[18] In every event the judge should examine whether or not a party's refusal to answer is justified.[19]

Art. IV. Collusion

If both parties have impugned the marriage, or if the defendant replies that he has no objections, the examining judge should carefully investigate the reasons why the parties agree—or at least why they do not disagree.[20] When both parties impugn the validity of their marriage, there is danger of collusion. When the suspicion of collusion arises from the replies of the parties, the judge should strive to determine the truth of the matter, even calling in witnesses if necessary.[21] However, the suspicion of collusion must be such that it is well-founded, and not presumed simply because the parties do not disagree. The defender of the bond is to be informed of this suspicion of collusion, so that he may take due cognizance of it in formulating the questions of his interrogatory.[22]

Sometimes the parties' depositions are made according to a pre-arranged and fraudulent understanding between them. Rota decisions offer these examples of collusion: 1) when two parties who have been enemies for a long time, suddenly renew friendly relations at the prospect of a decision favorable to nullity;[23] 2) when the parties attempt to keep members of their families from testifying in the case;[24] 3) when one party has recently received a large sum of money from the other or the other's relatives, although the parties had long been separated;[25] 4) when the depositions of the parties are in such perfect accord that the slight-

[18] Doheny, *op. cit.*, I, 330; Clune, *op. cit.*, p. 116.

[19] Can. 1743, § 2; art. 112.

[20] Art. 113, § 2.

[21] Art. 113, § 3.

[22] Doheny, *op. cit.*, I, 332.

[23] S.R.R. *Dec.*, VI (1914), 60.

[24] S.R.R. *Dec.*, IV (1912), 259-260.

[25] S.R.R. *Dec.*, VI (1914), 342-344.

est details are the same, or the identical language is used by both parties.[26]

Art. V. Questioning of the Woman in Impotence or Non-Consummation Causes

An exception to the general rule that only the presiding judge or auditor is to propose the questions is found in marriage trials based on impotence or non-consummation. According to a decree of the Holy Office in 1942, the interrogation of the woman who is a party in the cause should always be done before the tribunal *by a physician,* who must be of a solidly religious and moral character, of some years of experience, and proof against imputable exceptions *(omni exceptione maior);* he is to be appointed by the ordinary himself.[27] It is to be noted that the physician does only the questioning; the judge still directs the procedure.[28] Moreover, the judge is not specifically excluded from proposing questions of his own directly to the woman party. That is to say, the intent of the Holy Office seems to be that the physician propose all those questions that pertain to the medical and physical aspects of impotence or non-consummation. However, it would surely be within the discretionary authority of the judge to tender the opening oath, to ask the general questions,[29] and to tender the concluding oath. The physician should be made acquainted with the cause sufficiently in order that he may intelligently present the questions prepared by the defender of the bond;[30] should he propose spontaneous questions of his own as the need arises from the responses of the woman, the notary should affix a notation that these questions were proposed *ex officio* by the physician.[31] It would be appropriate to ask the

[26] S.R.R. *Dec.,* VII (1915), 351.

[27] S. C. S. Off., decr. 12 iun. 1942—*AAS,* XXXIV (1942), 200-202.

[28] Cf. can. 1577, § 2.

[29] Cf. art. 99.

[30] Cf. art. 147, § 2.

[31] Cf. Torre, *Processus Matrimonialis,* p. 91: The physician's questions should have judicial approval after a hearing from the defender of the bond *(audito defensore vinculi.)*

physician his opinion of the deponent; however, the judge need not follow this opinion.[32] The decree of the Holy Office also enacts more precise regulations concerning the physical inspection of the woman.[33]

ART. VI. DIVERGENT TESTIMONY OF THE CONSORTS

After the examination, the party may be invited to propose any questions that he or she may wish, upon which the other consort is to be interrogated.[34] If the replies of the party questioned second in order[35] differ notably from those of the other consort, the judge (either *ex officio* or upon the instance of the defender of the bond) should propose questions intended to dispel the difficulties and doubts. The judge may use his own discretion on whether or not he should mention the contradictory statements of the other consort. Furthermore, the judge may recall the other party for reexamination, if he deems it necessary, and propose the discrepancy in their depositions, or even arrange a confrontation of the two parties.[36]

ART. VII. FAILURE OF THE CONSORTS TO APPEAR IN COURT

If the plaintiff fails to appear to testify after he has been duly summoned, he should be cited anew, upon the instance of the defendant, with the threat of the charge of contempt of court. If he still persists in his failure to heed the summons, the cause should be declared abandoned by the presiding judge, unless the defendant urges the nullity of the marriage.[37]

If the defendant does not appear in court to testify after

[32] Cf. art. 154, § 1.

[33] Cf. *infra.* p. 134.

[34] Art. 114, § 1; these questions should be submitted to the defender of the bond (art. 70, § 1, n. 2, and art. 71, § 2).

[35] Cf. arts. 110; 113, § 1: the plaintiff is usually questiond first, and the defendant second.

[36] Art. 114, § 2. Cf. *infra*, p. 139, for a discussion of the *confrontatio.*

[37] Art. 115; cans. 1849, 1850 § 1; cf. art. 91.

being duly summoned, the presiding judge or the auditor has the right, after consultation with the defender of the bond, to determine whether the summons should be repeated or whether other opportune measures should be resorted to in an effort to induce the party to appear, such as employing the intervention of a friend, or invoking influential authority.[38] However, should the defendant still persist in refusing to appear in court, the collegiate tribunal (and not the presiding judge or auditor) should decide whether he is to be declared contumacious or whether canonical penalties are to be applied in an effort to overcome his refusal.[39]

[38] Can. 1848, art. 115; cf. Reg. 38, § 2, *Regulae Servandae*: "A remediis coërcitivis, ut flectatur contumacia, abstinere ut plurimum prudens erit."—*AAS*, XV (1923), 400.

[39] Art. 115; cf. cans. 1844, 1845.

CHAPTER VIII

WITNESSES[1]

ART. I. INTRODUCTION OF WITNESSES

In marriage causes as in all others, proof by witnesses is admissible, under the direction and moderation of the presiding judge or the auditor.[2] Witnesses may be introduced by the plaintiff, by the defendant, by the defender of the bond, or by the promoter of justice if he takes part in the trial.[3] The introduction of witnesses consists in presenting the names and addresses of the desired witnesses to the judge, along with an indication of the facts to which these witnesses can attest, in order that he may summon them to court.[4] If this presentation of names is not made within the time designated by the judge, the party is presumed to renounce his demand to have the witness heard.[5] However, the judge or the collegiate tribunal itself is to cite witnesses *ex officio* if this is considered expedient in any manner for the completing of the proofs.[6] Volunteer witnesses may present themselves to the court; the judge may admit or reject them according to his discretion.[7]

When an important witness cannot be induced to testify, the judge may seek to supply the information from extrajudicial evidence through witnesses *de auditu* (hearsay) and private documents.[8]

[1] Cf. *supra*, p. 85, for those parts of the interrogation which are common to parties, witnesses, and experts.

[2] Canon 1754.

[3] Art. 123, § 1; cf. can. 1759, §§ 1, 2.

[4] Cans. 1761, § 1; 1765.

[5] Can. 1761, § 2.

[6] Art. 123, § 1; cf. can. 1619, § 2.

[7] Art. 124; cf. *infra*, p. 122.

[8] Cf. *infra*, pp. 185, 211.

ART. II. PERSONS EXEMPTED OR EXCLUDED AS WITNESSES

Canon law follows the law of nature in disqualifying some persons, but it also goes beyond this in expressly repelling some who would be fit to testify, if the natural qualifications alone were considered. In the Decretals are found many disqualifying circumstances: women, slaves, stage players, soldiers, the blind, the deaf and dumb were generally not received as witnesses,[9] although exception was made to admit even such persons as witnesses in marriage causes.[10] Most of these disqualifications have no place in modern law, and the Code makes no specific mention of them. Even the blind, deaf and dumb may be admitted as witnesses of those things which they were able to perceive.[11]

In general, all persons may act as witnesses,[12] and when lawfully questioned by the judge are obliged to answer and tell the truth.[13] Certain persons, although in general competent to act as witnesses, are exempted from the obligation of replying to the judge concerning certain things; other persons are partially or relatively excluded from giving testimony as unfit or suspect; still others are absolutely disqualified from testifying.

A. The Exempt

Canon 1755 lists the following as being exempt from the obligation of testifying; priests concerning whatever has been manifested to them by reason of their sacred ministry, outside of sacramental confession; civil magistrates, medical doctors, obstetricians, advocates, and notaries and all others who are bound to professional secrecy, even by reason of advice pertaining to matters falling under this secre-

[9] Cf. c. 17, C. XXXIII, q. 5; c. 10, X, *de verborum significatione*, V, 40.

[10] C. 33, X, *de testibus et attestationibus*, II, 20; c. 3, X, *qui matrimonium accusare possunt, vel contra illud testari*, IV, 18; c. 2, *de iudiciis*, II, 1, in VI°.

[11] Cf. Lega (ed. Bart.), *Commentarius*, II, 669.

[12] Can. 1756; art. 118.

[13] Can. 1755, § 1; art. 121, § 1.

cy.[14] Article 121 adds this exception: unless they have been released from the obligation of secrecy by the persons concerned, and feel that they may prudently testify. Also exempted are persons who fear that infamy, dangerous vexations, or any other serious harm may result from their testimony, either for themselves, their blood relations, or their relatives by affinity in any degree of the direct line or in the first degree in the collateral line.[15]

The judge should advert to the fact that the listing of those who may be bound by a professional secret is not an exhaustive one. Hence, besides the ones enumerated, procurators, pharmacists, nurses and everybody to whom a secret was committed for the purpose of obtaining advice are exempt also.[16] The existence of a professional secret is a fact as also is the claim to exemption because of it; therefore, a claim to exemption and its reason must be noted in the acts.[17] In doubt as to whether the matter comes under professional secrecy, it seems that the law of secrecy obtains, because the common good is involved; probability cannot, it seems, be used.[18]

The judge nevertheless may summon the exempt, and during the examination determine whether there are any details about which they could in justice testify.[19] When the

[14] Cf. Wanenmacher, *Canonical Evidence in Marriage Cases*, n. 210.

[15] Can. 1755, § 2, 1° and 2°; art. 121, §2, 1° and 2°.

[16] Whalen, *op. cit.*, p. 99. Regarding the professional secret which exempts from testifying, Lega remarks [(ed. Bart.), *op. cit.*, II, 663]: "Haec autem pertinent ad *secretum commissum;* nam secretum *naturale* et *promissum* vel iuratum non eximit ab onere respondendi iudici legitime interroganti. Expedit enim rei publicae haec secreta pandi ut iudicia expedire possint. Quare exemptio ab obligation respondendi tantum habetur in secreto *commisso,* quod si est *sacramentale* nullam admittit exceptionem; neque illam quam extra sacramentale admittere explicavimus; et planum est ob inviolabilem sanctitatem secreti sacramentalis."

[17] Cf. can. 1755, § 3.

[18] Cf. Noldin-Schmitt, *Summa Theologiae Moralis* (23. ed., 3 vols., Oeniponte: Rauch, 1935), I, 236.

[19] Noval *De Iudiciis*, p. 326, n. 462.

person pleads exemption from answering on the basis of fear of harm to himself or to his relatives, the judge must discreetly ascertain the existence and sufficiency of the reasons for the alleged fear and the consequent exemption. According to some authors the judge can scarcely inquire into and evaluate the sufficiency of the reasons for exemption without forcing the witness to reveal precisely the information which by law the latter is excused from revealing, and thus the purpose of the exemption would be frustrated.[20] In such an event, however, it seems that the judge could persuade the witness to testify with a promise of not revealing the name of the witness;[21] or the judge could inquire into the reasons for the fear, in order to ascertain whether they are justified or not, and if they are justified, the inquiry made to ascertain them need not be recorded.[22] Otherwise a witness who did not wish to testify could plead fear, and there would be no way to ascertain the truth of the matter. Decretal law granted to witnesses the same exemption, but made the validity of its claim subject to the approval of the judge, who could notwithstanding compel the witness to testify, especially if the desired information was not otherwise available.[23] It seems that the examining judge has this same discretionary authority,[24] in view of canon 1823, § 2, which permits the judge to decide to what extent documents containing deleterious information should be exhibited.

B. The Unfit and the Suspect

The presiding judge or the auditor may at his discretion hear the unfit and the suspect in court; in such an event he is to issue a decree declaring that their hearing is expedi-

[20] Wernz-Vidal, *Ius Canonicum*, VI, n. 463, p. 401; cf. Coronata, *Institutiones*, II, n. 1282, p. 191; Muñiz, *Procedimientos Eclesiasticos*, III, n. 319.

[21] Cr. art. 130, § 2.

[22] Because *testificatio* is strictly to be interpreted (cf. can. 19: *exceptio a lege*).

[23] C. 3, X, *de testibus cogendis vel non*, II, 21. Cf. Reiffenstuel, *Ius Canonicum Universum*, lib. II, tit. XXI, nn. 9, 20, 24.

ent.[25] They are generally not put under oath, in order to avoid the danger of perjury.[26] However, the judge may receive their statements under oath, if he deems the individual to have a sufficient awareness of and reverence for the nature of an oath.[27] Such evidence, even when given under oath, does not have the probatory value of other sworn depositions, but is merely indicative of the truth.[28] However, it may reveal or disclose sources of proof or evidence of which the court was hitherto unaware; at other times, it may support depositions of the parties or other witnesses in important details. For instance, in a case of coercion and fear, younger children in the family might well furnish indications of proof to the court or lend support to the testimony of others in details of importance.[29]

The fact that the witness is unfit or suspect, or that the oath was not administered to him, must be mentioned in the acts, to be properly evaluated by the judges later on. The hearing of the unfit and the suspect can be proposed by the parties, by the defender of the bond, by the promoter of justice or by the judge himself.[30] In his decree of admission, the judge should express his reasons for admitting such persons.[31]

1. *The unfit.* Those who have not attained the age of puberty[32] and persons who are feeble-minded[33] are rejected

[24] Cf. art. 68, § 2: "...exhibitionem documentorum imponere..."

[25] Can. 1758.

[26] Noval, *op. cit.*, p. 332, n. 470.

[27] Lega (ed. Bart.), *op. cit.*, II, p. 677, n. 20.

[28] Canon 1758.

[29] Doheny, *Canonical Procedure in Matrimonial Cases*, I, 355.

[30] In the latter case, the judge would inform beforehand the defender of the bond (also the promoter of justice if present) and the party concerned, of the name of the witness (cf. can. 1763 and art. 126).

[31] Lega (ed. Bart.) *op. cit.*, II, p. 677, n. 21.

[32] A young man is considered to reach the age of puberty after completing the fourteenth year, and a girl after completing the twelfth. —can. 88, § 2.

[33] The Code, in using the words "*mente debiles*," seems to refer to *any* mental aberration or defect which may impair a person's ability

as unfit to give testimony in ecclesiastical trials.[34] The determination of who is unfit will ordinarily pose no great problem, since lack of age and insanity are usually indicated by external signs. When a serious doubt arises as to the fitness of a witness, the judge may ask for documentary proof of age, or consult an expert concerning the mental condition of the witness.[35] Whether to admit such testimony is another question. The judge should be guided by the availability of other proofs and the amount of valuable information likely to be secured from this particular person.

It is to be noted that persons are not excluded from testifying to facts witnessed in childhood—they are merely considered unfit to testify in court until they have attained the age of puberty. However, when an adult thus testifies to something that happened in childhood, the age of the person at the time of the event should be noted so that the judges later on may properly evaluate the testimony.[36] In marriage causes, the testimony of adults to what they witnessed after reaching the age of reason but before reaching the age of puberty may even at times constitute full proof, if the judge is satisfied with the testimony, and especially if the facts were witnessed at an age approaching puberty.[37]

to perceive correctly, or to recount correctly what has been perceived. This concept differs considerably from that of psychopathology, in which the term "feeble-minded" is used generically to include all degrees of mental defect due to arrested or imperfect mental development; grave mental disorders acquired after birth are called "psychoses"—usually referred to in law simply as insanity. Cf. Cavanagh-McGoldrick, *Fundamental Psychiatry* (Milwaukee: Bruce Pub. Co., 1953), pp. 287-296; 492-507.

[34] Can. 1757, § 1; art. 119, § 1.

[35] The judge here is not concerned with the specific type of mental deficiency or sickness, but rather with the juridical capacity or incapacity of the witness to testify.—Pickett, *Mental Affliction and Church Law* (Ottawa: U. of Ottawa Press, 1952), pp. 2-3.

[36] Doheny, *op. cit.*, I, 347.

[37] S.R.R., *Dec.*, VII (1915), 392-393: "Unus e praecipuis testibus qui nullitati matrimonii favent, est procul dubio Iustina, quae de vexationibus matris, eiusque minis testatur; atque haec, tempore dicti matrimonii, erat adhuc adolescentula, et proinde inidonea testis.

Not only are the insane and feeble-minded excluded as unfit, but also any person who was in such a condition at the time when the alleged fact occurred that he could not have correctly witnessed it; thus a person who attempts to testify to a fact witnessed while he was drunk is unfit to be a witness.[38]

2. *The suspect.* The suspect are persons who, although they have the right use of reason, are nevertheless open to the suspicion that they cannot be depended upon to speak the truth. Determining just who may be suspect can at times be very difficult. According to canon 1757, the following are suspect: excommuniated persons, perjurers, and infamous persons, after a declaratory or condemnatory sentence; those who are of such a debased moral character as to be considered unworthy of credence; public and implacable enemies of the party.[39] When no judicial declaration or condemnation has been made, the excommunicated are not *ipso facto* suspected, but the judge may hold their testimony in suspicion if the facts warrant it.

Determining the suspect when a sentence has been passed causes no difficulty; while the judge may use his discretion

Verum, ut recte animadvertit iudex primae instantiae, agitur de auditis et visis uti sunt minae et arreptio cultri, ad quod memorandum non requiritur aetatis prudentia, sed satis est audiendi et videndi facultas et rerum praeteritarum memoria, quae in pueris et puellis est valde tenax." S.R.R., *Dec.*, XVI (1924), 23, n. 6: "Et revera etiamsi illo tempore Iulius non fuerit iure pubes, tamen factus pubes potest legitime testificari de his quae impubes vidit, quaeque tunc poterat percipere... In casu tamen agitur de pubere qui deponit se, cum adhuc esset impubes [quattuordecim annos natus], factum vidisse ex quo grave indicium desumitur de copula inter matrem et Stephanum habita."

[38] Cf. Noval, *op. cit.*, n. 464. Lega makes an interesting observation about women as witnesses: "De foeminis nihil cavetur expresse iure nostro, sed quia, naturâ sua, mentem habent debiliorem, prae viris et mutabile ingenium, iudicis est aestimare in singulis casibus quanti earum attestatio habenda sit, et in nonnullis causis ex subiecta materia veluti in causis matrimonialibus testimonium mulieris esse locupletissimum canones admittunt ut facile percipitur."—Lega (ed. Bart.), *Commentarius*, II, p. 669, n. 5.

[39] Can. 1757, § 2, nn. 1, 2, 3; art. 119, § 2, nn. 1, 2, 3.

with respect to the testimony of such persons, he should be very cautious in admitting them to testify. Determining the suspect in other cases will considerably exert the judge's prudent discretion, especially with regard to persons of low moral character. Obviously, in this regard no sharp dividing line can be drawn; if the person is simply of a weak character and easily enticed to crime, he should be considered less suspect than the vicious, habitual criminal.

Paupers are no longer considered suspect for the reason simply that they are poor; they may well be suspect, however, not because they are paupers, but because in fact they may be low moral characters.[41]

Enmity towards one or both of the parties gives rise to suspicion against a witness however high his character or veracity; for when occupied with enmity toward a person, the mind cannot engage itself with objective truth, but seeks to avenge the injury.[42] If the enmity is not public but comes to light in the course of the trial, the judge will use his discretion as to how far the testimony is suspect. Witnesses are not rendered suspect because of an enmity that formerly existed but later was eradicated. Nor need the testimony of an enemy be suspected if he testify in favor of his enemy.[43]

Although the *Decree* of Gratian excluded apostates from the Faith as witnesses,[44] the Code does not mention them in this matter, and so they are not *ipso facto* excluded. Nor

[40] Lega (ed. Bart.) *op. cit.*, II, p. 670, n. 8: "Iudicis est aestimare in singulis casibus quinam, considerata etiam causae gravitate, sit moribus abiectus seu vilis conditionis in publica aestimatione, ut testis fidem non mereatur et hinc sit repellendus. Talis est qui lenocinio meretricio favet, qui furibus ut res furtivas occultent et distrahant, adiuvat, qui se exhibet ad reddendum testimonium pecunia conductum; ii omnes uno verbo qui facile suam conscientiam produnt ut lucrum vel tenue et vile faciant." Cf. also can. 2293, § 3, *re*: *infamia facti.*

[41] Lega (ed. Bart.), *op. cit.*, II, p. 670, n. 9.

[42] S.R.R., *Dec.*, XIII (1921), 10

[43] Wanenmacher, *Canonical Evidence in Marriage Cases*, n. 202, p. 125.

[44] C. 24, C. II, q. 7.

are Protestants and other non-Catholics *ipso facto* excluded; canon 2027, § 1, for instance, allows them as witnesses in beatification causes; they are all the more admissible in marriage causes.[45] Protestants and other non-Catholics have been declared acceptable witnesses both in nullity causes and in causes wherein they testify to the freedom of a party to marry.[46] But the judge may hold their testimony suspected when there is sufficient reason.[47]

C. The Disqualified

In principle the disqualified are not even to be summoned to appear in court; however, the disqualification can be doubtful, in which event it may be subjected to judicial examination upon the citing of the person.[48] After enumerating the unfit and the suspect, canon 1757 describes the disqualified: 1) Those persons who are the parties in the cause or who take the place of the parties, such as a guardian in the cause of his ward, the judge or his assistants, the advocate, and others who are assisting or who have assisted the parties in the same cause; 2) Priests, in whatever concerns any knowledge they may have received through sacramental confession, even though they may have been released from the obligation of the seal; even more, anything whatsoever heard by anyone or in any way on the occasion of confession may not be accepted as even an indication of the truth; 3) One consort in the cause of the other consort.[49]

At the outset one should remark that, while the parties cannot be witnesses strictly so called in their own marriage trials, nevertheless they must be heard, and their depositions

[45] Wanenmacher, *op. cit.*, n. 200, p. 123.

[46] Wanenmacher, *loc. cit.*

[47] S.R.R., *Dec.*, IX (1917), 166.

[48] Lega (ed. Bart.), *op. cit.*, II, p. 672, n. 11.

[49] Can. 1757, § 3, 1°, 2°, and 3°; art. 119, § 3, 1°, 2°, and 3°. Can. 1757, § 3, n. 3, also excludes relatives of the parties, except when the public good demands that they be admitted, or the knowledge of the truth cannot be secured from any other source. Can. 1974 and art. 122 specifically allow relatives as witnesses in marriage causes.

have great influence upon the ultimate outcome of the trial.[50]

The exclusion of all matter which may have been learned from a sacramental confession is so absolute, that no passing of time, nor death even of the penitent, nor release from the seal of confession on the part of the penitent, can remove the incapacity. However, confessors of the parties are not disqualified from testifying to events they know from other sources than the confessional, even when they have similar knowledge that derives from the confession.[51] Nevertheless, their testimony may be suspected because of the very restraint under which the confessor must testify in such cases.[52]

Those persons who are debarred because of having acted for the parties or participated in the trial are enumerated demonstratively, not all-inclusively. It would be possible to admit as a witness an advocate or an expert, especially after a severance of his professional relation to the client, who wishes to testify about some fact whose knowledge he did not acquire from the party, if this is deemed necessary in order to complete the proofs.[53] The Rota has admitted the testimony of those who furthered the cause in the capacity of advocates and other similar positions.[54]

Moreover, in view of the fact that judges, advocates, ex-

[50] Cf. *infra*, p. 169; can. 1742, § 2.

[51] Wanenmacher, *op. cit.*, n. 205, p. 127.

[52] Wanenmacher, *loc. cit.;* S.R.R., *Dec.*, II (1910), 341: "At ommisso quod hic testis non est omni exceptione maior utpote quia ratione sigilli sacramentalis non omnia revelare potest . . ."; cf. Noval, *De Iudiciis*, n. 468, p. 331.

[53] Lega (ed. Bart.), *op. cit.*, II, p. 673, n. 14.

[54] S.R.R., *Dec.*, X (1918), 76: "Fides tamen deneganda non est . . . sac. Bartolo excusso in processu suppletorio. Hic quidem ad concubinatus scandala avertenda auctor fuit, ut causa introduceretur, verum iste zelus non debet ipsum a priori suspectum reddere . . ."; S.R.R., *Dec.*, XIII (1921), 218: "Neque hic testes tenore can 1767, § 3, n. 1 [*sic*], repellendus est, quia ab eo tamquam advocato, ante causae introductionem actrix consilium petiit; nam nec in hoc iudicio neque in alio partibus assistit vel adstitit, sed refert quae a partibus tempore non suspecto accepit." The citation obviously is a printing error, and refers to can. 1757, § 3, n. 1.

perts, etc., are debarred only by positive law, and not as severely as are the parties and their procurators, it can be asked whether it would be possible, either at the instance of the parties or *ex officio,* to hear one who has acted as a judge, advocate, or expert, merely to secure an indication or support of the truth, as allowed in canon 1758 for the unfit and the suspect. Lega gives a qualified affirmative to this question, thus explaining it:[55]

> "Excluso iudice dum ius dicit, seu quousque pro tribunali sedet, alii et in his iudex qui in causa iudex fuit, possunt si res postulet, audiri saltem ut habeatur indicium... quando aliae non suppetant probationes et maxime intersit cognoscere veritatem... earum attestationem aestimare saltem uti *indicium et praesumptionem veritatis,* pro rerum personarumque adiunctis, iudicis est, uti in ceteris probationibus aut probationum adminiculis. Certe graviores requiruntur rationes seu absoluta necessitas ut iudex qui sententiam protulit, audiatur in alia instantia sed absolute incapax non est ad indicium saltem faciendum vi c. 1758."

However, this opinion seems not justified in the canons themselves, since can. 1758 makes no mention of the disqualified. Lega himself answers this difficulty:[56]

> "1) personas, in hoc munere, renunciatas *incapaces,* non *taxative* sed *demonstrative* indigitari; unde mens legis est, in iis determinandis non parum deferre legitimae iudicis aestimationi; 2) in numero insequenti n. 2° ubi absolute excluduntur confessarii, cavet lex, hos ne *ad indicium quidem recipi posse;* quae prohibitio quum praetermissa sit in n. 1°, inferre licet, hanc non contineri in legis intentione, et hinc implicite admitti *incapaces* ex n. 1 *ad indicium* posse audiri; eo magis quod de *incapacibus* ex n. 3°, in causis boni publici quando rei notitia aliunde haberi non possit statuitur, recipi posse in testes, quamvis heic incapacitas determinata sit taxative quoad *certas personas.* Quare in n. 1° statuitur regula generalis, quam nemo

[55] Lega (ed. Bart.), *op. cit.,* II, p. 674, n. 15.

[56] *Loc. cit.*

non approbat; sed non excluditur casus partialis exceptionis, ad normam c. 1758."

Art. III. Communicating the Names of the Witnesses to the Parties

The presiding judge or the auditor[57] should see to it that the names of the witnesses are made known in due time to the party concerned, so that he will be enabled, if he wishes, to lodge an exception of disapproval of the witness.[58] The judge could inform the parties to notify each other;[59] however, the practical reason for article 126 in specifying that the obligation of seeing that this notification takes place belongs to the court lies in the fact that the parties were often remiss in this duty, and even when they did notify the other party, they frequently had no means of proving the fact of this notification.[60] The actual notification of the parties is, as a rule, done by the notary at the instance of the court;[61] he may employ the court messenger or the mails for this purpose. Records should be kept in the files of the exact date of this notification, as the other party is ordinarily allowed only three days in which to lodge an exception of disapproval.[62]

If for some grave reason, in the prudent judgment of the presiding judge or auditor, or upon the instance of the defender of the bond, this notification is not viewed as expedient before the examination of the witness, it should at least be made known to the party before the publication of the testimony.[63] Ordinarily, there would be no reason for delay

[57] Art. 126, § 1, uses the word "*tribunal*"; however, from the fact that the word "*instructor*" is used in § 2, and that can. 1763 states, "Partes debent sibi invicem nota facere . . . ," it can be deduced that this is not reserved to the collegiate tribunal.

[58] Art. 126, § 1.

[59] Can. 1763.

[60] Cf. Doheny, *Canonical Procedure in Matrimonial Cases*, I, 362.

[61] Art. 73.

[62] Can. 1764, § 4.

[63] Art. 126, § 2; cf. c. 1763.

in announcing the names of the witnesses to the opposing party.[64]

If a witness will testify only on the condition that his name be not revealed to one or both of the parties, the presiding judge or the auditor has the discretionary authority to admit his testimony; in such a case, the judge should select two or three persons to whom the name of the witness can be given, so that they may investigate the credibility and the honesty of the witness.[65] The testimony of such a witness is published, in order that the party may take exception, if he desires, to the testimony; but the identity of the person remains a secret. If the auditor has good reasons for believing that the testimony of a certain witness would be of great importance, he may induce that witness to testify with the promise that his identity will be kept secret.[66]

ART. IV. THE IMPEACHMENT AND THE EXCLUSION OF WITNESSES

The presiding judge and the auditor have the right to restrict the number of witnesses lest they become too numerous.[67] An excessive number of witnesses should be particularly guarded against when witnesses are introduced in the following circumstances: a) for a matter that does not

[64] Lega (ed. Bart.) *op. cit.*, II, p. 684, n. 9: "... per accidens, posset haberi hisce in causis gravis, difficultas in denunciatione nominum testium ante examen, utputa, si pars adversa, cognito testis nomine, forsan ob timorem attestationis sibi valde contrariae, saevire posset in testem ut eum a veritate pandenda deterreret. Item si adesset periculum ne testes corrumpantur aut alii inducantur corrupti ad dstruendam aliorum attestationem. Hoc in casu legitime iudex decerneret, testis aut testium nomina pandenda esse tantum una cum attestationum publicatione." Ordinarily, the delay allowed by art. 126, § 2, would be sufficient. The course here prescribed in the last sentence could be justified, it seems, in line with the norms of art. 130, § 2.

[65] Art. 130, § 2. The persons thus selected are not to be interested in the cause and must be above all suspicion as regards the party or parties, in so far as this can be determined.

[66] Doheny *op. cit.*, I, 370.

[67] Can. 1762.

directly pertain to proof or hardly has a necessary relationship with it; b) in order to delay the case or harm the other party; c) when a cause can be sufficiently established with fewer witnesses.[68] No pre-determined number of witnesses can be established in any given case. The judge should strive for sufficient evidence in the trial to establish full proof. The Code does not indicate any limitation regarding the number of times the parties may present the names of witnesses; the judge will have to follow canon 1762 and article 123, § 2, according to his prudent judgment.[69]

When the presiding judge or the auditor realizes that too many witnesses have been listed, he should ascertain the names of the witnesses considered most important for the plaintiff and the ones viewed as most important for the defendant; by careful inquiry he can discover those who are most likely to furnish valuable and trustworthy information to the court.[70]

Witnesses who appear of their own initiative to testify may be admitted or refused according to the discretion of the judge; they are by all means to be rejected if it appears that their purpose is to delay the trial or to obstruct justice and truth in any way.[71] Ordinarily, persons do not volunteer to testify in a marriage trial, and as witnesses would usually be suspect.[72] The judge should be reluctant to admit volunteer witnesses, because both parties and their advocates usually submit the names of the best witnesses available; if other witnesses are discovered during the course of the trial, their names are likewise presented to the court. Hence, if witnesses come of their own accord, it is possible that they intend to harm one party or to distort truth to aid the other, or at times may even be suborned.[73] The judge,

[68] Art. 123, § 2.

[69] Cf. Lega (ed. Bart.) *op. cit.*, II, 682-683.

[70] Doheny, *op. cit.*, I, 360. Cf. also can. 1761, § 1.

[71] Art. 124; cf. can. 1760.

[72] Roberti, *De Processibus*, II, n. 338, p. 49.

[73] Cf. Reiffenstuel, *Ius Canonicum Universum*, lib. II, tit. XX, n. 415; Muñiz, *Procedimientos Eclesiasticos*, III, n. 301, pp. 238-239.

therefore, before admitting such witnesses should cautiously investigate their reasons for volunteering, their character, etc., in view of the personal presumption *(praesumptio hominis)* against them.[74]

Ordinarily, a witness should be excluded by means of a judicial decree, which gives the reasons for the exclusion (cf. can. 1785). When a witness is obviously incompetent by reason of canon 1757, the judge should exclude him immediately.[75]

> "Raro contigit rationes exclusionis esse notorias; quare ut plurimum a iudice investigationes sunt instituendae, uti in aperto ponantur. Huiusmodi investigationes non sunt propriae iudiciales, quia non spectant ad rem controversam iudicialiter dirimendam; attamen de iisdem ex actis processus constare debet . . . ; fas enim est parti cuius interest impetere decretum exclusionis a iudice editum . . . Quod si iudex huiusmodi exclusionis documenta pandere non valeat, quin grave contingat accedere scandalum vel aliud malum, tunc vel aliis argumentis reprobare contendat huiusmodi testes eorumque attestationes; vel alias compareṫ probationes quibus veritas et iustitia in tuto collocetur. Non excluditur quod rationes reprobationis sub arctissimo secreto pandantur promotori aut defensori, ut hi non excipiant adversus testium ex officio reprobationem."[76]

The exclusion of a witness for want of the proper qualifications takes place either *ex officio* or at the instance of an interested person. Usually the parties are in a better position than the judge to know the circumstances that stand against admitting a witness, and so they too are allowed to offer objection against the witness who, they should be able to show, should be excluded.[77] Yet it rarely happens in marriage causes that the parties seek to exclude witnesses,

[74] Doheny, *op. cit.*, I, 361.

[75] Can. 1764, § 1.

[76] Lega (ed. Bart.), *op. cit.*, III, 686-687. It may well be noted, however, that a right of a party is involved here; a judicial right, in cans. 1754; 1756; 1759, §§ 1-2.

[77] Can. 1764, § 2.

partly because they are not aware of their right in this matter, and partly because in many causes both parties jointly petition the declaration of nullity, or at least the respondent does not actively oppose the suit. The defender of the bond is more likely to take advantage of his right to take exception to a witness.[78]

A party may renounce the right to have his witness testify, even though suggested by him; however, in such a case the other party and the defender of the bond have a right to have the witness summoned to testify before the court.[79] A party may even raise an objection to a witness whom he has presented, for some reason that has subsequently occurred.[80] It is not difficult to imagine that during the long period required for a matrimonial trial a party might change his opinion about the worth of the testimony of a certain witness. In all such cases the presiding judge or the auditor has the discretionary authority to admit or reject the exception as he deems it appropriate.[81]

The parties should place their objections to witnesses within three days after they have received notification of the names, unless in the opinion of the judge the distance of the places demands a longer period of time.[82] A protest entered at a later date is not to be admitted unless the party proves or at least confirms under oath that he did not previously know of the objectionable quality of the witness.[83] The reason for this prescription is the presumption that the person who thus takes exception to a witness is acting maliciously and repudiates a witness after he knows from the published attestation that the witness testified against him.[84]

[78] Wanenmacher, *Canonical Evidence in Marriage Cases*, n. 214. It seems, therefore, that the judge should forewarn the parties of their rights in this matter.

[79] Art. 132, § 1; cf. can. 1759, § 4.

[80] Art. 132, § 2; cf. can. 1764, § 3.

[81] Cf. can. 1759, §§ 2-4.

[82] Art. 131, § 1.

[83] Can. 1764, § 4.

[84] Coronata, *Institutiones*, III, n. 1293, p. 205; cf. Reiffenstuel, *op. cit.*, lib. II, tit. XX, n. 537.

Unless the reason for the objection is determined in law (i.e., the witness is unfit, suspect, or disqualified), the presiding judge or the auditor should set a brief period of time within which the objecting party is to furnish proof, after which he will proceed to settle the question as an incidental issue.[85] If the objection cannot be immediately and easily proved, its discussion should be postponed until the end of the trial;[86] in the meantime the witness is to be examined.[87] The presiding judge or the auditor should immediately with a decree rule out all futile and dilatory requests for the rejection of a witness.[88]

There is an important difference between taking exception against the person of a witness and taking exception against his testimony. For a party may still object to the testimony when he cannot repudiate the witness. Thus, nothing prevents a party from taking exception to the testimony of witnesses produced by himself,[89] or from taking exception against testimony even after the acts have been published.[90] Testimony may be objected to on two grounds:[91] a) that the manner of taking the testimony was faulty; b) that the testimony itself is faulty—i.e., the statements made were doubful, wavering, obscure, contradictory, improbable, irrelevant, or evidently false.[92]

[85] Art. 131, § 2; for incidental issues, cf. *infra*, p. 151.

[86] What does "*in finem litis*" mean? According to Doheny (*op. cit.*, I, 372), Roberti (*op. cit.*, II, n. 341, p. 53), Coronata (*op. cit.*, III, n. 1293, p. 205), and Vermeersch-Creusen (*Epitome*, III, n. 176, p. 68), "*in finem litis*" means *after* the publication of the testimony; Noval (*De Iudiciis*, n. 479, p. 335), Lega (ed. Bart.) (*op. cit.*, II, p. 691, n. 11), and Claeys-Bouuaert-Simenon (*Manuale*, III, n. 1104) hold that "*in finem litis*" means *before* the publication of the testimony. The latter opinion seems more in conformity with cans. 1783, n. 1, and 1763.

[87] Art. 131, § 3; cf. can. 1764, § 5.

[88] Art. 131, § 4.

[89] Can. 1764, § 3.

[90] Can. 1783, n. 2.

[91] Cf. Wanenmacher, *op. cit.*, n. 218; Whalen, *The Value of Testimonial Evidence in Matrimonial Procedure*, p. 195.

[92] Cf. can. 1783, n. 2.

Art. V. Character Witnesses

The judge is to demand, *ex officio,* testimony regarding the religious character, the probity and credibility of all witnesses, for the stronger the evidence of the requisite qualities of good character, the greater the credence to be given to the witness.[93] Ordinarily, the testimonials for the witnesses will be received from the pastor. If this means is not sufficient or satisfactory, they may be obtained from any source that the judge thinks reliable and well informed.[94] All such testimonials are to be published unless, in view of the content of the depositions, the collegiate tribunal decides otherwise in order to avert great harm.[95] The general rule that all the acts are to be published is so important that only the collegiate tribunal, not the presiding judge or the auditor, can make the decision not to publish the testimony of character witnesses. It is to be noted that article 138 refers only to the character witnesses for witnesses, not for the parties.[96] This silence does not mean that the character and credibility of the parties is not to be ascertained,[97] but merely that character witnesses as such are not as a general rule demanded for the parties. Witnesses in a marriage case should also be interrogated concerning the credibility of the parties. Character witnesses called specifically to vouch for the parties are given the technical name of *septimae manus* witnesses. In cases involving impotence or non-consummation of the marriage, *both* consorts must present to the court

[93] Art. 138, § 1. Cf. can. 1789, n. 1.

[94] Doheny, *op. cit.*, I, 382; Benedetti, *Ordo Iudicialis Processus Canonici Super Nullitate Matrimonii Instruendi* (Taurini: Marietti, 1937), p. 85: "Iudex testimonium de testis credibilitate quaerere qumodocumque potest, sed praesertim opera parochorum, qui inquirere tenentur et, gravata eorum conscientia, quae sciunt tradere debent; possunt tamen etiam *partes* et advocati documenta de probitate et bona fide ab ipsis collecta Iudici praesentare, quibus Iudex utitur, post diligentem inquisitionem, ad veritatem cognoscendam." Cf. also Torre, *Processus Matrimoniales*, p. 107.

[95] Art. 138, § 2.

[96] Cf. Benedetti, *loc. cit;* Torre, *loc. cit.*

[97] Cf. Reg. 25, *Regulae Servandae—AAS*, XV (1923), 397.

the names of at least seven witnesses, who should be chosen from among the blood relations or the relatives by marriage, or at least from among neighbors of good reputation, or persons acquainted with the circumstances attending the cause under investigation.[98]

[98] Art. 137; can. 1975, § 1.

CHAPTER IX

EXPERTS

Expert inspection and testimony were recognized in the Mosaic and in the Roman law,[1] although no systematic legal method of procedure was adhered to.[2] Until the reestablishment of the Rota in 1909, experts were not viewed as a means of proof distinct from that acquired by witnesses.[3] Experts may be appointed or designated according to the following norms.[4]

ART. I. NECESSITY OR UTILITY OF EXPERTS

The judge may call upon the services of experts at any period of the trial when he deems these necessary for the completing of the evidence.[5] Most of the marriage causes do not require the use of experts to implement the available evidence. However, in causes involving impotence, non-consummation, and insanity, the opinion of experts is strictly demanded.[6] Certain reasons excusing the court from making an examination in impotence and non-consummation causes will be discussed subsequently. In all causes other than the three just enumerated, the presiding judge or the auditor may decide whether or not an expert

[1] Noval, *De Iudiciis*, n. 514.

[2] Wernz-Vidal, *Ius Canonicum*, VI, n. 491.

[3] Wanenmacher, *Canonical Evidence in Marriage Cases*, p. 172, n. 275.

[4] Analogously to the appointment or designation of a notary, experts may be said to be *appointed*, if they have never been previously presented to the court; *designated*, if selected from among those who have been previously presented to the court as qualified experts. Cf. Lega (ed. Bart.), *op. cit.*, II, pp. 748-749, n. 2. There is no strict legal distinction, however, as in the appointment or designation of the notary (cf. *supra*, p. 47).

[5] Cf. can. 1792.

[6] Art. 139; cans. 1976, 1982.

opinion is needed, either *ex officio* or upon the instance of the parties.[7] This will most frequently happen where the authenticity of the handwriting is questioned.[8] In each situation of this kind the defender of the bond should be heard.

The judge may have occasion to call for medical experts and require an examination with a view to determining the existence or nature of some fact, disease, or disorder other than impotence and insanity.[9] In a cause tried in four instances, the expert testimony of physicians was called upon for the purpose of ascertaining whether the woman in question was afflicted with a certain disease. The husband having suspected the presence of this ailment had given his marital consent under the express proviso that the woman did not have such a disease. The first, third and fourth instances of trial gave sentence for nullity based on expert testimony.[10]

ART. II. THE APPOINTMENT OF EXPERTS

Only the presiding judge may appoint the experts,[11] even in causes wherein the auditor may have decided that it is necessary that experts be employed.[12] However, the decree of the Holy Office in 1942 specified that if men physicians are to conduct the examination of the woman consort in causes involving impotence and non-consummation, they should be appointed by the ordinary, with the consent of the woman.[13] In each cause the defender of the bond should be heard.[14] In view of the fact that the auditor can determine that an expert is required, it seems that he could also desig-

[7] Art. 140, § 2, which concludes: "Partibus dissentientibus, instructor rem collegio deferat."

[8] Cf. art. 140, § 1.

[9] Wanenmacher, *op. cit.*, p. 177, n. 285.

[10] S.R.R., *Dec.*, I (1909), 68; S.R.R., *Dec.*, II (1910), 299; S.R.R., *Dec.*, III (1911), 292.

[11] Art. 141.

[12] Cf. Doheny, *Canonical Procedure in Matrimonial Cases*, I, 384-385.

[13] S.C.S. Off., decr. 12 iun. 1942, n. 3; cf. *infra*, p. 134.

[14] Cf. art. 141; can. 1793, § 2.

nate an expert who has been previously recognized by the court as a qualified expert, or is permanently employed as such by the court, without reference to the presiding judge. The requisite qualities demanded in experts are listed in articles 142 and 143 of the *Instructio*.

If the experts become suspect before they have undertaken the examination ordered by the court, or if they have been found unqualified for the task, other experts must be substituted in their places by the presiding judge after consultation with the defender of the bond.[15] It is not always easy, however, to determine the qualifications of all experts. Since article 144 does not specify whose judgment is to be relied upon in the appraising of the qualifications of experts, it seems that the auditor could determine the necessity of securing another expert, even though the actual appointment is usually reserved to the presiding judge.

Art. III. Objections to Experts

Experts, if they are suspected of partiality, can be objected to by either or both of the parties.[16]. The parties can also object to the experts on other grounds, if they have reason to suspect that the experts are not qualified, etc. In every such event the presiding judge must by means of a decree determine whether or not the objection is to be sustained.[17] The judge would be wise to accede as far as possible to the wishes of the interested party.[18]

Art. IV. The Number of Experts

The determining of the number of experts is left to the prudent discretion of the auditor or the presiding judge, according to the nature and difficulty of the cause,[19] except in causes of impotence and non-consummation, when at

[15] Art. 144.
[16] Can. 1796, § 1.
[17] Art. 145; cf. can. 1796, § 2.
[18] Wanenmacher, *op. cit.*, p. 183, n. 297.
[19] Cf. can. 1793, § 3.

least two experts are to be appointed.[20] In the past, the Sacred Congregations have allowed that, when under the circumstances prevailing in missionary countries two experts cannot conveniently be had, one is sufficient for the bodily examination of either the man or the woman; but the findings of this one are to be referred to two other experts, even though they live in a distant place, who shall under oath examine the findings and declare their agreement or disagreement with the conclusions reported.[21] The Rota has upheld this practice and declared the marriage null even though the defender of the bond took exception to the impotent woman's having been examined by only one expert.[22]

The judge would be wise to appoint as few experts as necessary—preferably only one. Securing the opinion of experts is time-consuming, and usually adds to the expenses; moreover, if several experts disagree, matters are complicated rather than simplified.[23] The one criterion for the judge in this matter is the effort to reduce all the judicial evidence to proof in the strict sense; if he feels that the matter is too involved or serious to rely on one expert's opinion, he may appoint two, or even more, experts.[24]

ART. V. THE TIME FOR THE EXAMINATION BY EXPERTS

After determining in his decree the points about which the study of the experts should concern itself,[25] the presiding judge or the auditor may specify the time within which the examination should take place, and the opinion submitted to the court.[26] The judge should bear in mind the attendant

[20] Cans. 1976, 1979, §§ 1-2. Art. 151 states, "In causis amentiae unus vel, pro casus gravitate, duo medici deputentur..."

[21] S.C.S. Off., instruction, 20 iun. 1883,—*Fontes*, n. 1076; S. C. de Prop. Fide, instructio, *Causae matrimoniales*, a. 1883,—*Fontes*, n. 4901; cf. Reg. 89, § 2, *Regulae Servandae*—*AAS*, XV (1923), 409-410.

[22] S.R.R., *Dec.*, X (1918), 1.

[23] Cf. Lega (ed. Bart.), *Commentarius*, II, p. 749, n. 3, a).

[24] Cf. art. 151; Lega (ed. Bart.), *op. cit.*, II, p. 750, b)-c).

[25] Art. 147, § 1.

[26] Art. 147, § 4; cf. can. 1799, § 2.

circumstances and the nature of the expert's profession. It could not be reasonably expected, for instance, that a busy psychiatrist would cancel his appointments on short order for the convenience of the court. If the judge has reason to believe that the expert chosen will conduct his examination and render an opinion in a reasonably brief time without urging, the judge should simply omit setting a definite time.[27] At least, if a time is set, it should be conveyed to the expert in such a way so as to show him that the court has no reason to doubt that he will expeditiously fulfill the appointment. When a definite time is set, it may be extended by the judge for such reasons as the sickness of the expert, unforeseen obstacles of a business nature for the expert, etc. The parties should be consulted concerning this extension. It may here be noted that, whereas witnesses are *summoned*, experts are *invited.*[28]

Ordinarily, the experts should conduct their examinations individually and apart from one another. However, for a special reason,[29] the presiding judge or the auditor may decide that the examination be conducted by the experts together in a group. In such an event the divergent opinions, if any, should be noted in the report together with the reasons for the divergency.[30]

Cardinal Lega discusses[31] whether, in a joint report, the names of the experts are to be set down, and whether the joint report should be signed before a notary:

> "Quaeritur an in relatione etiam nomina peritorum adnotari debeant, adeo ut iudex sciat peritorum vota et quodnam singuli periti protulerint votum. Ratio dubitandi est, quia canon iubet adnotari varias sententias, si periti non fuerint concordes, sed de peritorum nominibus nihil innuit; et ex alia

[27] Cf. can. 1799, § 2.

[28] Cf. Lega (ed. Bart.), *op. cit.*, II, p. 753, n. 9.

[29] E.g. "...si periti discordent sive quoad ea quae perlustrando reperirent, sive in conclusione finali."—Reg. 93, § 2, *Regulae Servandae—AAS*, XV (1923), 411.

[30] Art. 148, § 2; cf. cans. 1802; 1980; Reg. 93, § 2, *Regulae Servandae—loc. cit.*

[31] Lega (ed. Bart.), *op. cit.*, II, p. 766-767, nn. 7-8.

parte plures Codices vetant significari in relatione collegiali qualem opinionem habuerint singuli periti nominatim expressi. Prohibitionis ratio est quia iudex attendere debet non pondus auctoritatis, sed vim rationum; et nimis facile est, iudicem assentire voto periti magnae auctoritatis, rationibus suae sententiae minime libratis posthabito contrario voto alterius periti valde minoris famae et auctoritatis qui tamen forsan rem plenius et studiosius examinavit et in conclusionem devenit veriorem, uti eius probabilissimae rationes demonstrant. . . . Respondendum censeo rationem prohibitionis certe non esse spernendam imo gravem haberi, sed . . . in nostro foro hanc prohibitionem non vigere dicendum est; nisi in aliquo casu, ob peculiares rationes iudex peritos iubeat unam facere relationem, non significatis nominibus singulorum peritorum. Quod a iudice praescribi posse non est dubium, quia lex non vetat. Canon praescribit, relationi collegiali singulos peritos subscriptionem apponere, ast non praecipit istam coram notario seu actuario in sede tribunalis apponi. . . . Unde consequitur a iudice exigendum esse ut subscriptiones fiant coram notario si periculum sit quod dein exceptiones de authenticitate scripturae moveantur aut aliqua fraus timeatur."

ART VI. EXPERTS IN CERTAIN CAUSES

The ones most frequently employed by matrimonial tribunals are: first, handwriting experts, and secondly, doctors of medicine who are particularly proficient in questions of insanity, impotence, and non-consummation.

A. Handwriting Experts

Art. 149 of the *Instructio* states that, when the authenticity of someone's writing is to be investigated, the rules of canon 1800 are to be observed. In general, the judge has the discretionary authority to select, upon the proposal of the parties, what documents are to be compared by the experts, or to have the author of the writing in question come before him and write whatever the judge or the experts at the direction of the judge shall dictate.

B. Experts in Causes of Impotence and Non-Consummation

The decree of the Holy Office issued in 1942 must be borne in mind with reference to the matter of expert examination in causes of impotence and non-consummation.[32] Two physicians are to be appointed for the examination of the man; for the woman, these physicians should be women physicians.[33] According to art. 150, two men physicians may be appointed to examine the woman with her consent, *or* at the decision of the collegiate tribunal, which provision could lead one to believe that the tribunal could come to this decision without the woman's consent. The Decree of the Holy Office clarifies this point when it states that, in the event that women physicians are not available, the ordinary may, *with* the consent of the woman, appoint two men physicians; and if the woman objects to the examination itself or to the presence of men, the inspection is not to be urged.[34] The physical examination of the parties, especially that of the woman, may be omitted:

1) if a consummation was impossible inasmuch as neither time nor place offered opportunity for the consummating of the marriage;

2) if it is already certain that the woman has lost her physical virginity;

3) if in view of the moral excellence of the parties and the witnesses, and upon serious consideration of their attitude of mind and of other circumstances and arguments, there is already, in the judgment of the ordinary, abundant proof of impotence or non-consummation;

4) if it is fully proved from the inspection of the man that he was incapable of consummating the marriage, the inspection of the woman shall be omitted.[35]

If the examination of the woman consort is conducted by

[32] S.C.S. Off., decr. 12 iun. 1942—*AAS*, XXXIV (1942), 200; for English translation, cf. Bouscaren, *Canon Law Digest*, II, 549 ff.

[33] Art. 150, §§ 1, 2; S.C.S.Off., decr., n. 2.

[34] S.C.S.Off., decr., nn. 3-4.

[35] S.C.S.Off., decr., n. 1; cf. Reg. 86, *Regulae Servandae*—*AAS*, XV (1923), 409.

women experts, the judge should interrogate these experts in the presence of a physician, who may make remarks and put appropriate questions.[36] Apparently, in this event the physician puts the questions directly to the woman expert, rather than through the judge, although in each case he should receive the judge's permission; or the judge may request that the physician make his observations and present relevant questions. The judicial interrogation of the woman consort herself should be conducted by a physician, as has been explained.[37]

C. Experts in Insanity Causes

One expert may suffice, unless the seriousness of the situation would demand that the judge appoint two.[38] Care must be taken for the appointment of qualified psychiatrists, whose principles are in accord with Catholic teaching. These experts need not be Catholic, but they must exercise their office according to Catholic principles.

ART. VII. INTERROGATION OF THE EXPERTS

After the reports of the experts have been duly submitted ot the court, the auditor is to summon them so that they may individually identify their conclusions, confirm them by oath, and reply to the questions duly prepared by the defender of the bond.[39] Doheny advises that the experts be examined by the collegiate tribunal, and that the judges should beforehand read over the reports so that they will be prepared to ask pertinent questions to ascertain fuller information.[40]

ART. VIII. APPOINTMENT OF SPECIAL EXPERTS

If the experts disagree in their conclusions, the presiding judge or the auditor may appoint, after due consultation

[36] S.C.S.Off., decr., n. 5.
[37] Cf. *supra*, p. 106; S.C.S.Off., decr., n. 6.
[38] Art. 151.
[39] Art. 152.
[40] Doheny, *op. cit.*, I, 396.

with the parties and with the defender of the bond, another expert who is better qualified; this *peritior* is to conduct an examination in the same manner as the first experts, and he is not merely to examine the conclusions of these other experts.[41]

The selecting of a *peritior* presents a practical difficulty. The judge will have chosen the best available experts for the initial examination, and will usually be rather nonplused in his task of securing a more qualified expert. In such a case, the judge could select another expert at least as well qualified, since there is no limit to the number of experts whom the judge can appoint. Generally, the securing of an expert truly better qualified than those first chosen would involve great expense in bringing one from another section of the country. The *Instructio* does not determine the criterion according to which the *peritior* is to be selected; Doheny states that the authority of either the presiding judge or the tribunal seems sufficient to decide upon the qualification of different men, after proper and sufficient measures have been taken for the obtaining of reliable information.[42] It is to be noted that the judges in passing sentence are not under any definite obligation to follow the opinions of the experts.[43]

[41] Art. 153.
[42] Doheny, *op. cit.*, I, 397.
[43] Art. 154, § 1; cf. can. 1804, § 1; cf. *infra*, p. 205.

CHAPTER X

RE-EXAMINATION AND CONFRONTATION

ART. I. RE-EXAMINATION OF PARTIES, WITNESSES, AND EXPERTS

A. *Re-examination before the Publication of Testimonies*

The presiding judge or the auditor[1] has the discretionary authority to recall the parties, witnesses, or experts for further questioning, as often as he deems it expedient or necessary.[2] This he can do *ex officio,* or at the instance of the parties (in either case after consulting the defender of the bond), or at the instance of the defender of the bond himself.[3] If the presiding judge or the auditor does this at the instance of the parties, he should be particularly careful to guard against collusion and dishonesty.[4]

How many times can the same person be recalled for examination? As often as this seems necessary or useful according to the prudent discretion of the judge.[5] Obviously, an overly scrupulous approach to re-examining a witness should be avoided.

[1] Art. 107 speaks only of the tribunal; but in view of the fact that art. 135 allows the judge (who according to art 96, § 1, can be either the presiding judge or the auditor) to permit the re-examination even *after* the publication of the testimony for a grave reason, it follows that the presiding judge or auditor could also decree a re-examination *before* the publication, and that accordingly the word "tribunal" is used in a generic sense in art. 107.

[2] Art. 107, § 1; cf. can. 1781.

[3] *Loc. cit.*

[4] Art. 107, § 2; cf. can. 1781.

[5] Noval (*De Iudiciis*, n. 500, p. 346), in commenting on can. 1781, stated: "*denuo*: quoties? Iuxta prudens iudicis arbitrium; . . . *necessarium vel utile*: ad formandum *internum sui animi motum* in ordine ad ferendam sententiam."

A re-examination is conducted in the same manner as any judicial examination.[6] The general questions already ascertained in the prior examination need not again be asked,[7] but the identity of the deponent as having previously appeared should be determined, and mention of it included in the record.

B. Re-examination after the Publication of Testimonies

The judge may allow the re-examination of witnesses even after the publication of the testimonies,[8] but with all caution: three conditions must be verified: a) there must be grave reasons; b) all danger of fraud and subornation must be averted as far as possible, and c) the other party, the defender of the bond, and the promoter of justice, if he is engaged in the case, must be heard. If the judge deems it advisable to permit the introduction of new evidence even after the conclusion of the cause, then the time for the interrogation of the parties is likewise extended.[9]

The parties also have the right to request the summoning anew of a witness, if from the investigation or inquiry there have come to light any facts of which the parties may have been ignorant.[10] Ordinarily, however, after the publication of the testimony the parties will not be able to vindicate the right to produce other witnesses.[11]

Since the prohibition of recalling a witness after the publication of the testimony specifically states, "denuo super

[6] Art. 107, § 3.

[7] Cf. art. 99, § 2.

[8] Can. 1786; art. 135; cf. also art. 175, § 4.

[9] Clune, *Judicial Interrogation of the Parties*, p. 98.

[10] Art. 135, § 2.

[11] Lega (ed. Bart.), *Commentarius*, II, p. 728, n. 10: "Recolatur ante publicationem attestationum partes monendas esse ut explicavimus de effectibus publicationis, quod scilicet, testes iam auditi denuo super iisdem articulis non interrogabuntur nisi gravi et legitima de causa. Quare partes annuentes publicationi, iuri alios testes deducendi censentur renuntiasse." This, of course, must be understood in the light of art. 135, § 2.

iisdem articulis ne interrogentur,"[12] it appears that the witness more readily could be recalled for questioning concerning new aspects of the case, unless these new aspects are contrary to what is already in the records.[13]

ART. II. THE CONFRONTATION OF PARTIES, WITNESSES, AND EXPERTS

During the Middle Ages, witnesses could not be heard unless the parties were invited to be present at the hearing.[14] The introduction of a written procedure which could be afterwards reviewed by the parties, and the danger lest some human respect incline the witnesses to favor the parties caused a change in this policy; thus, later instructions have demanded that the parties be absent during the hearing of the witnesses.[15] The present legislation in this regard in marriage trials is clearly given in article 128 of the *Instructio,* which states that ordinarily neither the parties nor their attorneys or advocates may assist at the examination of the witnesses; however, by way of exception the examining judge may give such permission according to his discretion.[16] A confrontation, however, is more than the mere presence of one of the parties; it implies that the persons in question be brought together for the purpose of resolving contradictions in their depositions which cannot be resolved otherwise; it is therefore a *joint* examination.

A. The persons to be confronted

The judge may bring about the collective examination, or confrontation, among any persons or groups of persons in the trial, according to his prudent discretion. Thus, a

[12] Cf. art. 135, § 1.

[13] Cf. Lega (ed. Bart.), *op. cit.,* II, p. 732, n. 15. It is there stated: "Hanc esse autem iuris intentionem, nempe super iisdem articulis, vel aliis etsi *directe* aut *indirecte* contrariis non licere producere testes qui oppugnant adversarii intentionem."

[14] C. 2, 41, X, *De testibus et attestationibus,* II, 20; Wanenmacher, *Canonical Evidence in Marriage Cases,* p. 142, n. 231.

[15] Cf. Wanenmacher, *loc. cit.*

[16] Cf. can. 1771.

confrontation can take place between the two parties,[17] between any of the witnesses or experts, and between either or both of the parties and any or all of the witnesses or experts.[18] There is no limitation in the number of persons potentially subject to confrontation; however, the fewer the persons who are confronted the lesser also the likelihood or possibility of the emergence of difficulties.[19] Nothing is specifically stated in the Code or in the *Instructio* concerning the confrontation of the experts; since, however, they are primarily witness, albeit of a special kind,[20] it may be deduced that the rules which in article 133 are more applicable for witnesses are by that very token applicable also for experts.

B. Reason for Confrontation

The judge's discretionary authority is much wider in permitting a confrontation between the two parties, than among the witnesses themselves or between the witnesses and the parties. For the confrontation of the parties themselves, article 114 simply states, *"si casus ferat,"* with no further conditions implied. Indeed, the parties have already confronted each other at the joinder of issue. The judge should particularly advert, however, to whether or not the parties are on friendly terms, and to what extent they are unfriendly, for the tribunal is no place to give occasion to quarrels.[21]

On the other hand, the Code enacts stringent rules for allowing the confrontation of the witnesses among themselves and between the witnesses and the parties. According to canon 1772, § 3, such a confrontation can take place *only* when all three of the following conditions are verified simultaneously:

1) if the witnesses disagree among themselves or with

[17] Art. 114.
[18] Art. 133; can. 1772, § 2.
[19] Cf. Lega (ed. Bart.) *op. cit.*, p. 708, n. 6.
[20] Noval, *op. cit.*, p. 356, n. 513.
[21] Cf. Lega (ed. Bart.), *op. cit.*, II, p. 708, n. 7.

the party in a serious matter pertaining to the very substance of the cause;

2) if there is no other easier way to discover the truth;
3) if there is no danger that scandal or dissensions will emerge from the confrontation.

These conditions so limit the discretion of the judge that in actual practice it would rarely be licit to allow such a confrontation, for the concomitant existence of all three conditions would seldom occur.[22] The judge should always consult the defender of the bond before proceeding with a confrontation.[23]

When considering the possibility of a confrontation, the judge would be wise to keep in mind the difference in qualifications and knowledge on the part of the witnesses, especially if these vary greatly.[24] Easier ways than confrontation are usually available for the ascertainment of the truth. For instance, the parties and the witnesses who are in disagreement may be summoned anew to testify as a

[22] Coronata, *Institutiones*, III, p. 214, n. 1301; cf. Doheny, *Canonical Procedure in Matrimonial Cases*, I, 374.

[23] Art. 133.

[24] Lega (ed. Bart.), *op. cit.*, II, pp. 707-708, n. 6: "Siquidem testium collatio habenda est uti medium extraordinarium. Nedum quia regula communis est, testes *seorsim* esse examinandos, sed maxime quippe facile non est unum testem cum alio vel cum parte conferre in punctis facti discordibus, eosdemque cohibere ne vagentur, et ne unus alteri imponat suam opinandi aut cognoscendi rationem, et ita magis implexa reddatur attestationum discordia; tum quia sive testis sive pars victor discedens a collatione, refutato adversario, magnum sibi acquirit pondus probationis, quae nisi obtineatur adhibitis omnibus cautelis, patet, magis praeiudicium quam subsidum praebere vertati. Sane si conferatur testis magnae auctoritatis cum altero teste minoris auctoritatis, nemo non videt quam grave sit periculum ut maior unius auctoritas alterum facile pertrahat in suam assertionem, non tantum evidentia veritatis quantum ex maiori praestantes [praestantia?] ex uberiori notitia et copiosore arte loquendi, unde plura refert facta vel factorum adiuncta quae alterum confundunt. Quocirca iudex caveat ne facile inter se conferat testes diversae auctoritatis. Item dicatur de testis collatione cum parte, quae testem non plene de re instructum a sua attestatione facile removebit."

means of clarifying difficulties;[25] this may be done without any danger of scandal or dissensions. A confrontation might develop into severe quarreling if animosity exists among the witnesses and the parties; family feuds could even break out anew during the course of a confrontation.[26]

A confrontation between experts and either the parties or the witnesses would ordinarily occasion a lesser danger of scandal or dissension, since the expert would usually be a disinterested party; however, there seems also to be less occasion for such a confrontation, since the expert does not testify to what he has actually perceived in favor of or against the parties, but rather gives an expert opinion. There could easily arise the utility of bringing the experts themselves together for the purpose of discussing their differences of opinion; in such an event the three conditions which when jointly present permit a confrontation would more readily be fulfilled. Indeed, the judge could request that the examination which is to be made by the experts be conducted *collegialiter*, and that their findings be issued as a joint report.[27]

C. *Time of Confrontation*

A confrontation between the parties can take place at any time during the trial when the judge deems it necessary, since article 114, § 2, indicates no limitations in this matter; ordinarily not, however, after the publication of the process.[28] The confrontation among witnesses and between witnesses and the parties can take place only after the interrogation of the witnesses and of the parties who are to be confronted has been completed.[29] The judge may decree that

[25] Cf. preceding article.

[26] Cf. Doheny, *op. cit.*, I, 374.

[27] Art. 148, § 2.

[28] Cf. Wernz-Vidal, *Ius Canonicum*, VI, n. 474; can. 1742, § 3.

[29] Can. 1772, § 2; "*edita testimonia*" does not mean after the publication of the testimony. See art. 175 with art. 134. The purpose here is to secure first the individual depositions of the persons concerned, in order to have on record their depositions freely given without out-

the evidence secured in judicial examinations be published immediately after the completion of the examination of all the witnesses,[30] or he may decide to postpone this until the publication of the whole process.[31]

D. *Manner of Executing the Confrontation*

Neither the Code nor the *Instructio* determines any specific rules as to the method of performing the confrontation. However, a confrontation is primarily a judicial re-examination—indeed, of two or more simultaneously rather than individually, but nevertheless a judicial examination. Therefore, a confrontation would be conducted as any other judicial examination,[32] i.e., the parties, witnesses, and defender of the bond should be cited and the oaths administered, the notary should record the acts,[33] the acts should be signed by each person present, etc. Doheny suggests that the individual parties or witnesses may be interviewed privately before the actual confrontation with a view to

side influence. Along this line, one way advert to Lega (ed. Bart.) *op. cit.*, II, 707, for the following: "Quod periculum suggestionis, in omnibus et cum primis diligenter evitandum, facile obreperet, si testis ab examine dimissus colloqueretur cum aliis adhuc examinandis. Hinc in Curia audientiae aula ita debet disponi, ut testis dimissus alios examen expectantes non alloquatur. Quare si testes audiendi sint plures vel omnes una sessione examini non valeant subiici, prudentis iudicis est, sessionem non claudere nisi ii auditi sint qui, pene super iisdem factis sunt excutiendi."

[30] Can. 1782, § 1.

[31] Can. 1782, § 2; cf. art. 175, § 2. Cardinal Lega advises: "Quocirca si iudex sperare potest ex aliis capitulis probationum, tantam lucem aut eam saltem effulgere ut veritas in tuto ponatur et attestationes pro veritate redditae solide confirmentur, multo melius est, testimonia non evulgare, nisi omnigenis probationibus absolutis. Ex adverso quando pene totum probationum pondus est in attestationibus et recurrendum est ad alia probationum media, si forte occurrant, quando desunt attestationes, tunc sane, absoluto omnium testium examine, est facienda evulgatio."—Lega (ed. Bart.), *op. cit.*, II, p. 725, n. 6.

[32] Cf. *supra*, p. 85 ff.

[33] The notary should indicate the source of each answer. Cf. Torre, *Processus Matrimonialis*, p. 97.

having the purpose of the session explained to them.[34] This procedure would certainly be permissible when the conditions mentioned in canon 1776, § 2,[35] are present, but only by way of exception. It does not seem necessary or even prudent that the citation indicate that the examination is to be a joint affair; however, the judge may decide that the wiser course is to inform those who are cited that it is to be a confrontation. In fact, when they have first assembled, the purpose of their joint presence could well be explained and the request made for their good will and co-operation.

[34] *Op. cit.*, I, 374.

[35] Canon 1776, § 2: "Attamen si ea quae testificanda sunt ita a memoria sint remota, ut nisi prius recolantur, certo affirmari nequeant, poterit iudex nonnulla testem praemonere, si id sine periculo fiera posse censeat"

CHAPTER XI

PUBLICATION OF THE PROCESS, CONCLUSION, AND DISCUSSION OF THE CAUSE

ART I. THE PUBLICATION OF THE PROCESS

After the judicial evidence thus far adduced by both sides has been duly examined by the defender of the bond, by the auditor if he functioned in the cause, and by the presiding judge, the communication of all of the acts to both parties must be implemented.[1] This is called the publication of the procedure (or process), and is authorized by means of the presiding judge's decree,[2] in virtue of which he grants to the parties and their advocates the authority to examine the testimony and all the other proofs which are contained in the acts and which have remained secret; they may also request a copy of the acts.[3]

Of the procedural factors and the furnished evidence much has already been made known to the parties at the time when the various proceedings took place. Thus, the introductory petition is made known to the respondent,[4] and all further petitions of either party are revealed to the other.[5] Both parties are summoned for the joinder and concordant specification of the issue.[6] Documents are at once opened to the inspection of the adversary.[7] Except in cases

[1] Art. 175, § 1.

[2] The Code was not clear as to whose authority was sufficient and necessary. Roberti (*De Processibus*, II, n. 435, p. 157) and Coronata, (*Institutiones*, III, n. 1387, p. 295) held that the authorization of the entire collegiate tribunal was necessary, whereas Muñiz (*Procedimientos Eclesiasticos*, III, n. 409) maintained that the authority of the auditor was sufficient for the issuing of this decree.

[3] Art. 175, § 2; cf. cans. 1858, 1859.

[4] Cans. 1712, § 1; 1715, § 1.

[5] Cf. can. 1724.

[6] Cans. 1712, § 3; 1727.

[7] Can. 1820.

of impotence and non-consummation, the parties may be present at the inspection or examination undertaken by the experts.[8] They may be present at the taking of judicial notice,[9] at the swearing in of witnesses,[10] and even at the hearing of testimonies, at the discretion of the judge;[11] or, if they are not present, the testimonies ordinarily should be published after the witnesses are all heard.[12]

In the Middle Ages when the parties in contentious causes were always permitted to be present at the hearing of the witnesses, there was no publication of the acts; the publication was introduced after the proceedings began to be held in secret, so that the necessity of the publication is simply a corollary of the secrecy of the trial.[13]

In the same decree, the presiding judge should determine an equitable period of time within which the parties and the defender of the bond may submit documents and adduce arguments by means of which the proofs and objections advanced by them may be corroborated, explained, and completed.[14] The parties still have the right to furnish new witnesses.[15] It is not easy to specify what should be the length of the equitable period of time to be provided by the presiding judge; it will vary according to the nature of the cause, and the circumstances surrounding it. Ordinarily, three weeks or a month should provide ample time; however, the period of time is to be determined according to the prudent judgment of the presiding judge.[16]

The court may publish the acts in one of three ways: a) by reading aloud the records to the parties; b) by granting permission to the parties and their advocates to inspect the acts, or c) by distributing copies of the originals,

[8] Can. 1797, § 2.
[9] Can. 1809.
[10] Can. 1767, § 2.
[11] Art. 128; cf. can. 1771.
[12] Art. 134; can. 1782, § 1.
[13] Wanenmacher, *Canonical Evidence in Marriage Cases*, n. 571.
[14] Art. 175, § 3.
[15] Art. 175, § 4; cf. *supra*, p. 109.
[16] Cf. Doheny, *Canonical Procedure in Matrimonial Cases*, I, 437.

either printed, typed, or handwritten.[17] In this latter event the parties should be prepared to bear the expense of securing authentic copies.[18]

Upon the expiration of time designated in the decree of the presiding judge or even sooner if the defender of the bond and the parties declare that they have nothing more to submit to the court, the conclusion of the cause takes place.[19]

Art. II. The Conclusion of the Cause

The conclusion of the cause is effected by means of the presiding judge's decree, in which it is stated that the provisions of the law have been duly fulfilled and that therefore the cause has been satisfactorily drawn up to the point of its termination.[20] The presiding judge should take care not to issue the decree of the conclusion of the cause if he thinks that anything necessary for the proper completion of the cause still remains to be investigated; in this event he may order to be supplied, after consultation with the defender of the bond, whatever is lacking.[21] Since matrimonial causes concern the public good and the salvation of souls, the judge has the added obligation of supplying proofs, or of lodging exceptions in the event that the parties, their attorneys, or their advocates have been remiss in so doing.[22]

New proofs may be admitted in matrimonial trials even after the conclusion of the cause, particularly if newly discovered documents are submitted or if there are presented any witnesses who could not, because of some lawful obstacle,[23] be brought before the court during the called for time. If the presiding judge thinks that this new evidence should be admitted, he authorizes this in a decree; if he should refuse to do this, recourse may be lodged with the

[17] Cf. can. 1859; Wanenmacher, *op. cit.*, n. 574.

[18] Wanenmacher, *loc. cit.*

[19] Art. 176.

[20] Art. 177, § 1.

[21] Art. 177, § 2.

[22] Can. 1619, § 2.

[23] Art. 178, § 1; cf. can. 1861, § 1; art. 135; cf. *supra*, p. 79.

collegiate tribunal.[24] It appears that the presiding judge has the obligation of informing the parties of their right of recourse in this case.[25]

After the new evidence has been admitted by the court, the parties and the defender of the bond should be informed of this fact by the auditor, and they should then be given sufficient time to study and impugn the new evidence; if this opportunity of viewing the new evidence is not given, the trial is null.[26] It is Doheny's opinion that the trial would not be invalid if the parties, although not canonically informed by the auditor, nevertheless had an opportunity to examine and even to impugn the new evidence, if they so wished.[27]

Art. III. The Discussion of the Cause

After issuance of the decree by means of which the conclusion of the trial is formally declared, the presiding judge designates the period of time within which the parties and their advocates are to present their briefs[28] and the defender of the bond is to submit his observations and comments *(animadversiones)*.[29] If certain difficult points are to be clarified, the presiding judge may decide to authorize an oral discussion;[30] but this is of rare occurrence in ordinary trials.

The length of time to be permitted by the presiding judge for the preparing of the briefs is not determined by the Code or the *Instructio*. The presiding judge should not be unduly lenient in determining this period of time. It should hardly ever exceed a month.[31] When the brief is prepared, it must be submitted to the presiding judge for his signature; he

[24] Art. 178, § 2.
[25] Doheny, *op. cit.*, I, 440.
[26] Art. 178, § 3; cf. can. 1861, § 2.
[27] Doheny, *op. cit.*, I, 440.
[28] Art. 179, § 1; cf. can. 1862, § 1.
[29] Art. 180, § 1.
[30] Art. 186, § 1.
[31] Doheny, *op. cit.*, I, 442.

then designates the number of copies that are to be prepared.[32] He may even order that copies be printed,[33] in which event the expenses are to be defrayed by the parties.[34] If copies are printed, the printers should be carefully selected and should usually be put under the oath of secrecy.[35]

After the brief of the parties has been received by the court, the defender of the bond should submit his observations within the period of time designated by the presiding judge.[36] The parties as well as the promoter of justice, if he is engaged in the cause, have the right to reply to these observations within a period of ten days.[37] After the rejoinder of the parties is accepted, the defender of the bond in turn may use the same right, if he wishes, of replying within another ten days.[38] The parties have the right to submit but one rejoinder, unless it appears to the judge that for some grave reason an opportunity for a second reply should be granted; if this permission is granted to one party, the same right is automatically conceded to the other party.[39]

The periods of time permitted for the observations of the defender of the bond, for the briefs of the advocates, and for the rejoinders and counter-rejoinders, may be extended by the presiding judge for a reasonable cause; these same time periods may also be curtailed with the consent of all the parties interested.[40] If the presiding judge considers it expedient, he may abridge briefs that are too lengthy; ordinarily, the brief of the defense should not exceed twenty

[32] Art. 179, § 2.

[33] Art. 179, § 3.

[34] Cf. arts. 233-235. Doheny (*loc. cit.*) states that the causes heard by the S. R. Rota and the *Signatura Apostolica* are always printed.

[35] Cf. can. 1623; Doheny, *ibid.*, note 19.

[36] Art. 180, § 1.

[37] Art. 180, § 2.

[38] Art. 180, § 3.

[39] Art. 180, § 4.

[40] Art. 181. It is to be noted that this article is more explicit than can. 1862, § 2; it now appears that also the consent of the defender of the bond and of the promoter of justice, if he is engaged in the cause, is necessary.

pages, and the rejoinder should not exceed ten.[41] This ruling is similar to that of the Rota;[41a] hence, by pages are to be understood the printed pages of the large Roman folio size, which are approximately similar to what is known as legal size in this country.[42] The presiding judge should take proper precautions lest copies of the acts of the cause, whether printed or unprinted, fall into the hands of outsiders.[43]

Unless they have previously been designated by the tribunal, the hour and the day for the final decision should be determined by the presiding judge and the parties notified accordingly; a period of at least ten days should intervene between the last defense and the day of the decision.[44] This serves the purpose of offering the parties one last chance in which to propose new proofs or witnesses to the court, and to give the judges time in which to take cognizance of the last written defense in the cause and to write their opinions.[45]

The presiding judge has the right either *ex officio,* or at the request of the defender of the bond or of one of the parties, to permit an oral discussion of the cause.[46] This oral discussion must be requested after the last rejoinder has been submitted and always within seven days preceding the time designated for the final decision of the cause.[47] The party requesting the oral discussion should propose the points and the matter for discussion.[48] The presiding judge should see to it that the oral discussion does not exceed the bounds of a moderate disputation, and that such matters as have already treated both in the defense and in the re-

[41] Art. 182.

[41a] *Lex propria,* Can. 29.—*AAS,* I (1909), 27; *Normae S. Romanae Rotae Tribunalis,* Art. 124.—*AAS,* XXVI (1934), 479.

[42] Doheny, *op. cit.,* I, 445.

[43] Art. 184.

[44] Art. 185.

[45] Doheny, *op. cit.,* I, 447.

[46] Art. 186, § 1.

[47] Art. 186, § 2.

[48] Art. 186, § 3.

joinders be not uselessly repeated.[49] The notary should assist at the oral discussion, so that there may be a record of the points of the discussion, of the confessions, and of the conclusions, if the presiding judge so orders, or if the defender of the bond or the party requests it and the presiding judge accedes to the request.[50]

Scholion I. Incidental Causes

During the course of a trial there frequently can arise questions and matters of varying importance that demand an expeditious settlement. They are incidental, however, to the principal question before the court, but they are so intimately related to the cause that they must ordinarily be settled before the main issue can be decided. An incidental cause is a sort of procedural miniature of a principal cause.[51]

Whenever a party believes that he has a legitimate right to introduce an incidental question, he may request the auditor to admit it; if a party feels aggrieved by the auditor's refusal, he may have recourse to the collegiate tribunal.[52] Once the introduction of an incidental question has been admitted, the situation is taken in hand by the collegiate tribunal, which ascertains whether the proposed question is related to the principal cause and whether it is founded on a probable basis.[53] When these preliminaries have been duly established, the incidental question is introduced with an appropriate joinder of issue *(litis contestatio)* and concordant specification of the point in dispute *(concordatio*

[49] Art. 186, § 4.

[50] Art. 186, § 5; cf. can. 1866. Torre (*Processus Matrimonialis*, p. 120) remarks: "Quoad tamen § 5 evidenter impossible est pro notario, nisi stenographica arte sit ornatus, de disceptatis et admissis referre scripto; optandum e contra est ut permittat Tribunal partium patronis et Vinculi Defensori breviter obiecta praecipua discussionis oralis in scriptis redigere et has allegationes distribuere collegio, praevia concessione 'imprimatur' a praeside apponenda."

[51] Doheny, *op. cit.*, I, 454.

[52] Art. 188.

[53] Art. 189.

dubii).[54] When the public good is actually in jeopardy, e.g., in causes wherein the element of scandal is involved, the intervention of the promoter of justice is mandatory; if such is not the case, and yet the nature or the difficulty of the question indicates that an intervention may be advisable, the intervention of the promoter of justice remains optional and conditioned on the discretion of the tribunal.[55]

After obtaining sufficient information and hearing the principals who are party to the question at issue, the tribunal may determine whether the incidental cause, according to the nature and importance of the matter, is to be settled in a judicial procedure and by way of an interlocutory sentence, or merely by way of a decree and without an observance of the strict formalities of judicial procedure.[56] The tribunal may even decide to define the incidental question together with the principal cause in one and the same sentence.[57]

Before the principal cause is finished, the collegiate tribunal may, for a just reason, correct or revoke its interlocutory sentence,[58] either on its own authority after consulting the parties, or upon the instance of one of the parties, after a hearing has been accorded to the other party; in all such causes, the opinion of the promoter of justice, if he is engaged in the cause, and also of the defender of the bond is required.[59]

Scholion II. The Sentence

When the matrimonial cause has been properly drawn up; when all the evidence is adduced; after the publication of the procedure, and the conclusion; after the briefs of the

[54] Doheny, *op. cit.*, I, 454: Considerable latitude, however, is permitted as to the manner in which the cause is to be settled.

[55] Art. 190, § 2; cf. art. 16, § 1; Doheny, *op. cit.*, I, 459.

[56] Art. 190, § 1, and art. 191; cf. can. 1840 and arts. 192-193.

[57] Art. 194. Cf. also art. 189, § 2. Doheny, *op. cit.*, I, 454.

[58] "Ergo a fortiori, decretum, si quaestionem iudex definivit extraiudicialiter."—Noval, *De Iudiciis*, n. 583.

[59] Art. 195; can. 1841.

advocates and the observations of the defender of the bond are presented; after the discussion of the case has taken place according to law, it becomes the final task of the judges to examine, to appraise, and to evaluate all the judicial evidence, in order that they may obtain the moral certitude that is necessary for a decision.[60] After a thorough and conscientious study, the individual judges are to formulate their written conclusions concerning the cause, which they present at the private meeting of the three judges.[61] It is during this meeting that the final decision is given.[62] Subsequent thereto the sentence is written in Latin[63] and then formally published. The court publishes this sentence in any one of the three ways mentioned in canon 1877.[64]

[60] The discretionary authority of the judges in evaluating judicial evidence is treated in Section III of this work, beginning p. 161.

[61] Art. 198, § 2.

[62] This meeting is arranged by the presiding judge, who sets the hour and the day (art. 198, § 1); for some particular cause, this meeting may be held at a place other than in the hall of the tribunal. Art. 198 does not state who may decide to change the place of the meeting. It appears that the presiding judge, who sets the day and hour, can also determine the place; if any other judge disagrees with him, the matter should be settled by majority vote (cf. can. 1577, § 1, and can. 101, § 1).

[63] Arts. 22, § 1; 200, § 2.

[64] Art. 204, § 1; i.e., 1) by summoning the parties to hear the sentence solemnly read by the judge sitting in court; 2) by notifying the parties that the sentence is at the chancery of the court, and simultaneously granting them permission to read it and request a copy of it; 3) by sending a copy of the sentence by registered mail, wherever this is customary.

CHAPTER XII

JUDICIAL EXPENSES

Art. I. Judicial Expenses in General

The parties ought to be obliged to offer some financial remuneration in view of the judicial expenses incurred unless they are exempted from this obligation by a grant of gratuitous legal assistance.[1] The tribunal should take care:

1) Lest judical expenses be unduly increased in consequence of unnecessary and useless acts;[2]

2) lest the parties be unfairly burdened with the perquisites and expenses due the experts: these fees should be assessed by the presiding judge according to the charge exacted in civil courts for similar services,[3] and

3) lest the procurators and advocates demand fees and expenses other than the perquisites approved by the lists existing in the tribunal,[4] so that, if the party demands it, the presiding judge should determine in his decree the amount of the emoluments to be paid.[5]

The presiding judge may decree that a sufficient sum of money be deposited in the treasury of the court to defray the judicial expenses, the fees of the experts, if there is need of expert assistance, and to serve as indemnity for the witnesses; this deposit of money may be increased during the course of the trial, if such provision appears necessary to the presiding judge.[6] Although this sum is ordinarily deposited by the plaintiff, the presiding judge has the authority to determine whether and in what proportion a deposit should be made by the other party, should the latter inter-

[1] Art. 232; cf. can. 1908.
[2] Art. 234, n. 1.
[3] Art. 234, n. 2.
[4] Cf. art. 233; can. 1909, § 1.
[5] Art. 234, n. 3.
[6] Art. 235, § 1.

vene in the cause.[7] The presiding judge may designate a peremptory period of time for a party who refuses to deposit the money prescribed.[8]

The collegiate tribunal has the right to determine, in the definitive sentence, whether the expenses are to be defrayed by the plaintiff alone or also by the other party, whenever the latter intervenes in the cause; likewise, to determine the proportion of the expenses to be defrayed by both parties.[9] Due note should be taken of the poverty of the party to whom the decision was unfavorable when the fees to be affixed for the payment of expenses are being determined.[10] No distinct appeal is allowed against the decision of the court about expenses; however, a party considering himself aggrieved may lodge an objection within ten days before the same judge, who may examine the matter anew and may adjust and moderate the fees.[11] An appeal from the sentence of the principal question of the cause carries with it an appeal from the decision about expenses.[12]

Art. II. Gratuitous Legal Assistance

The collegiate tribunal is to grant gratuitous legal assistance to a plaintiff if it is certain that he is truly poor and that there exists an indication of a well-founded right, that is, if the party appears to be deserving in view of his present financial condition; in any such circumstance the ad-

[7] Art. 235, § 2.

[8] Art. 235, § 3. It is not clearly indicated whether the tribunal or the presiding judge has the authority to designate the peremptory period of time; in view of the context—nn. 1 and 2 of the same article—it seems that the presiding judge could decide this period of time. Doheny (*Canonical Procedure in Matrimonial Cases,* I, 564) is of the opinion that, in view of the importance of the matter, it appears that this should be decided by the tribunal, rather than by the presiding judge, and even recommends that in difficult cases it might be advisable for the tribunal to consult the Ordinary before designating the peremptory period of time.

[9] Art. 236, § 1.

[10] Art. 236, § 2.

[11] Art. 236, § 3; Can. 1913, § 1.

[12] Art. 236, § 4; can. 1913, § 2.

vocate is designated by the presiding judge.[13] The defendant may be accorded this same privilege of gratuitous legal assistance whenever the tribunal deems this opportune for a very grave reason.[14] These reasons must be present before this is allowed in matrimonial causes, because the defender of the bond has the solemn duty to defend the marriage bond, and hence the rights of the defendant are sufficiently protected by law.[15] If the party is not actually poor, but is unable to defray the ordinary expenses of the trial, he can obtain a reduction of the expenses; but then the advocate must always be designated *ex officio,*[16] i.e., by the presiding judge.

The request of the parties for gratuitous legal assistance or for a reduction in fees should be presented to the court as early as possible, preferably at the time of the introduction of the bill of complaint *(libellus)*.[17] Since the question of the grant of gratuitous legal assistance is ordinarily to be settled by the tribunal before the joinder of issue *(contestatio litis)*, sufficient time should be allowed for the making of any investigations that may be necessary for the ascertainment of the financial status of the person in question.[18]

Before conceding the gratuitous legal assistance or a reduction of expenses, the presiding judge should obtain the opinion of the promoter of justice and the defender of the bond, after having transmitted to them the party's statement and documents.[19] Furthermore, if the presiding judge

[13] Art. 237, § 1.

[14] *Loc. cit.*

[15] Cf. cans. 1587; 1967-1969.

[16] Art. 237, § 2.

[17] Doheny, *op. cit.*, I, 566.

[18] *Loc. cit.*

[19] Art. 238, § 2. Paragraph one of the same article demands from anyone, if he wishes to secure an exemption or a reduction of expenses, a statement and documents by means of which his economic status is clearly demonstrated, together with proof that the party is not introducing a rash or futile cause.

deems it necessary, he can seek other and even secret information.[20]

If, after a total or partial exemption from judicial expenses has been granted, it is ascertained during the course of the trial that the alleged poverty or presumed well-founded right does not exist, the collegiate tribunal should revoke the exemption or the reduction of fees either *ex officio* or upon the instance of the defender of the bond or of the promoter of justice.[21]

Certain expenses may be incurred by the contumacious party. Contumacy may be corrected at any stage of the trial, even up to the time of the pronouncement of the sentence. Having duly exonerated himself, the erstwhile contumacious party must compensate the other party for all the expenses previously incurred, unless he is willing to accept the cause in the stage it has reached at the time.[22] If his participation in the trial at a late date date necessitates the changing of past acts or the gathering of additional testimony from witnesses, he must pay for this additional expense.

ART. III. REIMBURSEMENT OF WITNESSES

A witness has the right to request compensation for the expenses he may have incurred in traveling or by staying at the place where the court is in session. He likewise has the right to equitable reimbursement for the losses entailed through the interruption of his business or work.[23] Such expenses the presiding judge awards in accord with his own good discretion, after hearing the witness and the party and,

[20] Art. 238, § 2.

[21] Art. 239. This ruling of the *Instructio*, similar to that in can. 1915, § 2, appears to presuppose the existence of bad faith. However, one could easily imagine a case wherein a person, poor at the beginning of a trial, suddenly becomes wealthy because of an inheritance, a fortunate investment, the winning of a lottery contest, or the like. Even in such cases, in the complete absence of all bad faith, the court has the right and the duty to revoke the privilege of exemption or reduction of fees. (Doheny, *op. cit.*, I, 570.)

[22] Art. 90.

[23] Can. 1787, § 1.

if necessary, the experts on the question of the amount.[24] Since the amount of compensation is determined by the judge, it would be proper that the payment be made through the agency of the court rather than directly to the witness by the party.[25] Witnesses called at the instance of the defender of the bond, the promoter of justice, and the court are likewise to be given financial reimbursement, if they demand this; these payments should be made out of the sum deposited by the party for the expenses of the trial.[26]

Witnesses, however, must not be paid for the testifying itself; a paid witness is not perfectly free in his testimony. If it is shown that any witness has been suborned by a party there arises a presumption, not only that the testimony of that witness is untrue, but likewise that other witnesses who favor that party have been suborned for the giving of false testimony.[27]

[24] Can. 1787, § 2; art. 127, § 3; cf. art. 68, § 2.
[25] Doheny, *op. cit.*, I, 365.
[26] Cf. can. 1909, § 2; art. 235, § 2.
[27] S.R.R., *Dec.*, V (1913), 497.

SECTION III.

THE DISCRETIONARY AUTHORITY OF THE JUDGE IN EVALUATING THE JUDICIAL EVIDENCE

INTRODUCTION

The term "judge" in this Section refers to any one of the three judges of the collegiate tribunal. These judges issue a joint sentence, arrived at by means of a majority vote,[1] but each arrives at his own conclusion independently, with moral certainty derived from the acts of the process and the incorporated proofs.[2] Consequently, each judge—synodal as well as presiding—has equal discretionary authority in this matter, each evaluating or appraising the evidence according to his own conscience.[3]

Any extensive explanation or consideration of moral certainty is beyond the scope of this work. However, it will not be amiss to repeat some salient points from the Allocution of Pope Pius XII to the Rota in 1942:[4]

> "There is an absolute certainty, in which all possible doubt as to the truth of the fact and the unreality of the contrary is entirely excluded... In contrast to this supreme degree of certitude, common speech often designates as certain a cognition which strictly speaking does not merit to be so called, but should rather be classed as a greater or lesser probability, because it does not exclude all reasonable doubt, but leaves a foundation for the fear of error...
>
> "Between the two extremes of absolute certainty and quasi-certainty, or probability, is that *moral certainty*... of which We principally wish to speak. It is characterized on the positive side by

[1] Can. 1577, § 1.

[2] Can. 1869, §§ 1-2.

[3] Can. 1869, § 3, and can. 1871, § 2- § 5.

[4] *AAS*, XXXIV (1942), 338 ff. English translation from Bouscaren, *Canon Law Digest* (Milwaukee: Bruce Publishing Co., Vol. I, 1934, Vol. II, 1943, Vol. III, 1954), III, pp. 605 ff. Cf. McCarthy, *De Certitudine Morali Quae in Judicis Animo ad Sententiae Pronunciationem Requiritur* (Romae: Officium Libri Catholici, 1948) pp. 66 ff.

the exclusion of well-founded or reasonable doubt and in this respect it is essentially distinguished from the quasi-certainty which has been mentioned; on the negative side, it does admit the absolute possibility of the contrary, and in this it differs from absolute certainty. The certainty of which We are now speaking is necessary and sufficient for the rendering of a judgment, even though in the particular case it would be possible either directly or indirectly to reach absolute certainty . . .

"Sometimes moral certainty is derived only from an aggregate of indications and proofs which, taken singly, do not provide the foundation for true certitude, but which, when taken together, no longer leave room for any reasonable doubt on the part of a man of sound judgment . . . Consequently, if in giving the reasons for his decision, the judge states that the proofs which have been adduced, considered separately, cannot be judged sufficient, but that, taken together and embraced in a survey of the whole situation, they provide the necessary elements for arriving at a safe definitive judgment, it must be acknowledged that such reasoning is in general sound and legitimate.

"In any event, this certainty is understood to be objective, that is, based on objective motives; it is not a purely subjective certitude, founded on sentiment or on this or that merely subjective opinion, perhaps even on personal credulity, lack of consideration, or inexperience . . . To make sure of the objective nature of this certainty, procedural law establishes well defined rules of inquiry and proof."

". . . But since moral certainty, as We have said, admits of various degrees, what degree can or should the judge demand in order to be able to proceed to judgment? In the first place, he must always make sure that there is in reality an objective moral certainty, that is, that all reasonable doubt of the truth is excluded. Once this is assured, he should, as a rule, not require a higher degree of certainty, except where the law prescribes it especially in view of the importance of the case. At times, it is true, even though there be no such express provision of law, it may be prudent for the judge not to be satisfied with a low degree of certitude, in cases of great importance. Yet, if after serious consideration and study, a grade of certitude is attained which corresponds to the requirements of law and the importance of the case, there should not be insistence, to the serious inconvenience of the parties, that new proofs be adduced so as to attain a still higher degree of certitude. To require the highest possible certainty, notwithstanding that a sufficient certainty already exists, is without justification and should be discouraged."

CHAPTER I

ECCLESIASTICAL JURISPRUDENCE CONCERNING THE EVALUATION OF JUDICIAL EVIDENCE

The prescriptions of modern Canon Law which accord considerable discretionary authority to the judge in estimating or evaluating judicial evidence hark back to the rules of classical Roman jurisprudence.[1] Canon Law has never specified exactly the probative value of the various types of judicial evidence, nor on the other hand has the matter been left completely to the discretion of the judge. Rather, Canon Law has prudently maintained a middle course, combining definite probatory rules with the right of the judge to exercise his discretion.[2] There was a tendency among some canonists in the Middle Ages to rely upon a mathematical computation and evaluation of proofs—two half-proofs made a full proof, etc.[3] Reiffenstuel (1642-1703), describing the relationship of the judge to judicial evidence in general, stated that "what proof is here and

[1] Cf. Lega (ed. Bart.), *op. cit.*, II, p. 735. In the *Pandects*, [D. (22.5) (3, 1-2-3)], it is mentioned that the Emperor Hadrian wrote to a certain judge who had inquired concerning the probative value to be assigned to witnesses in a trial: "Tu magis scire potes, quanta fides habenda sit testibus, qui et cuius dignitates, et cuius existimationis sint, et qui simpliciter visi sint dicere, utrum unum eumdemque meditatum sermonem attulerint; an ad ea quae interrogaveras ex tempore verisimilia responderint. Hoc ergo solum tibi rescribere possum summatim, non utique ad unam probationis speciem cognitionem statim alligari debere, sed ex sententia animi tui te aestimare oportere, quid aut credas, aut parum probatum tibi opinaris." Hadrian concluded with this most important observation: "Testibus se, non testimoniis crediturum... Alia est auctoritas praesentium testium, alia testimoniorum quae recitari solent."

[2] Cf. Wernz-Vidal, *Ius Canonicum*, VI, 383; Noval, *De Iudiciis*, p. 308, n. 441.

[3] Cf. Reynes, *La Prueba en el Procedimiento Canónico* (Barcelona, 1943), pp. 11-12.

now full and conclusive is left to the discretion of the judge."[4]

The Code uses the expression "full proof" to denote "*probatio*" in the strict sense—that which carries conviction to the judge; partial proof, on the other hand, simply denotes judicial evidence in general, without any attempt to assign any fractional mathematical value to it.[5] Actually, then, the expression "full proof" can be correctly and concretely applied only in retrospect—this piece or combination of judical evidence *did* convince the judge, therefore it *was* full proof in this particular case. Authors have strongly inveighed against mathematical distinctions.[6]

However, it is to be noted that canon 1869, § 3, indicates certain restraits, when it concludes with the words, "*nisi lex aliquid expresse statuat de efficacia alicuius probationis.*" Thus, the testimony of two or three witnesses above exception[7] and at times the very presumptions of the law itself[8] are ordinarily sufficient to constitute full proof. Likewise,

[4] Reiffenstuel, *Jus Canonicum Universum,* lib. II, tit. XIX, n. 60: "Quaenam probatio hic et nunc sit plena, et concludens, judicis arbitrio relinquitur. Probationes omnes sunt judici arbitrariae. Etenim ad quem modum probandae cuicumque rei argumenta in particularibus casibus adducta sufficiant, nullo certo modo definitum reperitur neque ob infinitatem casuum, diversarumque circumstantiarum definiri potest. Quamquam ejusmodi arbitrium non sit omnino liberum atque absolutum, sed regulatum, ut loquuntur doctores; debet enim regi secundum jura, rationem et aequitatem, non autem pro mera judicis voluntate haec vocari sufficiens probatio, illa veluti insufficiens rejici: quod utique foret absurdum, et iniquissimum."

[5] Cf. *supra,* p. 74.

[6] Cf., e.g., Lega (ed. Bart.), *Commentarius,* II, 630, 631: "Nam non valet, in casu concreto, perpendi et applicari vis istarum subdivisionum. Siquidem unum argumentum, nihil vel parum probans in certa causa, in alia, ob mutata rerum adiuncta, plenissime aliquando probat. Adest, ex adverso, periculum, ne iudicis animus retrahatur a vero, nempe a genuina factorum consideratione per has regulas nimis absolute a canonistis enunciatas legum auctoritate et factorum enarratione firmatas."

[7] Can. 1791, § 2.

[8] Can. 1747, 2°, and can. 1827.

notorious facts do not need to be proved,[9] although what probatory value these facts may have in a given case will depend upon the circumstances.

Pope Pius XII clearly described modern ecclesiastical jurisprudence regarding the factor of moral certainty in his Allocution to the Rota in 1942. The Supreme Pontiff, after having given the true idea of judicial moral certainty, explained that the objective nature of this certainty is assured through the conscientious observance on the part of the judge of the well-defined rules of inquiry and proof as delineated in procedural law. Pope Pius then stated:[10]

> "The conscientious observance of these norms is a matter of duty for the judge; but on the other hand in their application he must remember that they are not ends in themselves, but means to an end, that is, to attain and guarantee a moral certainty with an objective foundation as to the reality of the fact. It should not come about that what the will of the legislator intended as a help and security for discovering the truth, become instead an obstacle to its discovery. If ever the observance of formal rules of law results in injustice or is contrary to equity, there is always a right of recourse to the legislator.
>
> "Hence you see why, in modern, even ecclesiastical, procedure, the first place is given, not to the principle of juridical formalism, but to the maxim of the free weighing of the evidence. The judge must—without prejudice to the aforesaid procedural rules—decide according to his own knowledge and conscience whether the proofs adduced and the investigations undertaken are or are not adequate, that is, sufficient for the required moral certainty regarding the truth and reality of the matter to be decided.
>
> "No doubt there may at times be conflicts between 'juridical formalism' and 'the free weighing of the evidence,' but they will usually be only apparent and hence not difficult to resolve. Now,

[9] Can. 1747, 1°.

[10] *AAS,* XXXIV (1942) 338 ff.; English translation from Bouscaren, *Canon Law Digest,* III, pp. 605 ff.

as the objective truth is one, so too moral certainty objectively determined can be but one. Hence, it is not admissible that a judge declare that personally, from the record of the case, he has moral certainty regarding the truth of the fact at issue, while at the same time, in his capacity as judge, he denies the same objective certainty on the basis of procedural law. Such contradictions should rather induce him to undertake a further and more accurate examination of the case. Not infrequently such conflicts are due to the fact that certain aspects of the case, which attain their full importance and value only when viewed as a whole, have not been properly weighed, or that the juridical-formal rules have been incorrectly understood or have been applied in a manner contrary to the mind and purpose of the legislator."

An examination of Rota decisions yields valuable information on modern ecclesiastical jurisprudence. In a recent decision, the Rota made these pertinent remarks concerning the evaluation of judicial evidence:[11]

"Cuiuslibet causae examen ad quamdam *criticam* pro historica rerum veritate statuenda reducitur, quae, ut in scientia, *externa* et *interna* esse potest; sed erraret, sicut in alio huius generis studio, qui sisteret in *externa* argumentorum ratione solummodo consideranda; si videlicet in iudicando coarctaret robur causae ad numerum sive parvum, sive magnum deponentium, ad attestationes credibilitatis ab iisdem relatas, quae saepe nimis ad formalitatem et opportunitatem traduntur; ad valorem documentorum absque attenta de ipsorum genuinitate et sinceritate disceptatione acceptorum; ex quibus cunctis quis intexeret ineptam demonstrationem, per materialem seriem citationum e quodam summario excerptorum. In *criticam* potius *internam* adsertorum penetrandum atque immorandum erit: sedulo inspiciendo ex dictis et scriptis, ingenium et passiones intervenientium in processibus; verisimilia et inverisimilia perpendendo; in contradictionibus, aestimando quid accidentale prosit credibilitati, quid substantiale obsit. Ita

[11] S.R.R. *Dec.*, XXXV (1943), 196.

tantum recte devenire quis poterit ad scientificam veritatis historicae conclusionem. Hoc est sub cortice res introspicere. Et per hanc tantum methodum saepe causa externe bona, damnanda, mala vero in favorem agentis resolvenda, iuxta obiectivam veritatem, videbitur."

CHAPTER II

THE EVALUATION OF EVIDENCE FROM THE CONSORTS

In addition to applying the norms for the evaluating of testimonial evidence,[1] which are applicable also to the judicial deposition of the parties, *congrua congruis referendo,* special consideration must be given to the confession[2] of the consorts.[3] When made before the judge during the trial, the confession is termed judicial;[4] when made outside the judicial proceedings, either before or during the trial, it is termed extra-judicial.[5]

Statements and admissions made by the consorts play an important part in marriage causes, particularly those which deal with simulated or conditional consent, with fear or coercion, with the impediment of specific criminality as arising from adultery and attempted marriage, and with abduction.[6] In marriage causes which involve impediments, proof of nullity ordinarily is furnished through external facts. But in cases concerning matrimonial consent, the only evidence which is of direct value is that which indicates the actual mind of the parties at the time of the exchange of the consent. Thus, in such cases, the confession of the

[1] Cf. following chapter.

[2] The word is here used in its processual sense: a confession in matrimonial trials is understood as any statement or admission, written or oral, of a consort against himself or against the validity of his marriage. Cf. can. 1750.

[3] The word "consort" is used, since "party" refers to the consorts only after the marriage trial is initiated.

[4] Can. 1750.

[5] Can. 1753.

[6] Cf. Doheny, *Canonical Procedure in Matrimonial Cases*, I, p. 345, n. 6.

consorts[7] and justifiable presumptions[8] form the chief proofs. Since defective consent is an internal act of the will which is contrary to an external and free act, it is most difficult to prove;[9] indeed, no direct proof, in the strict sense, is possible, since only God can see what is in the mind of a man at a particular moment. However, it is possible to secure judicial evidence which has a direct bearing on the alleged defective consent.[10]

[7] Sanchez, *De Sancto Matrimonii Sacramento Disputationum Libri Decem* (3 vols. Venetiis, 1693), Lib. II, disp. 45, n. 13, (hereafter cited *De Matrimonio*) "Caetera impedimenta possunt alia via probari, cum externa sint; dissensus autem, cum corde lateat, non potest alia via probari, nisi per conjugum confessionem, licet conjecturae aliae possint adhiberi." S.R.R. *Dec.*, XIII (1921), 104: "Verum quidem et confessionem coniugis in iudicio, vel etiam ante iudicium post matrimonium factam, vim probandi non habere contra valorem matrimonii; testimonium tamen metum passi, iuramento firmatum, adminiculum summi momenti constituit ad probationem nullitatis matrimonii complendam." S.R.R., *Dec.*, XIII (1921), 266: "At confessio coniugis post matrimonium facta vim probandi non habet contra valorem matrimonii. Quamvis ordinarie adminiculum praebeat ad probationem complendam, id tamen in eo casu solum admitti potest, quo testis ceteroquin fide dignus sit." S.R.R., *Dec.* XXXIII (1941), 435: "Etsi non sit facile eiusmodi simulationem totalem matrimonii probare, tamen haec difficultas non est exaggeranda. Probatio generatim initium capit a *confessione ipsius simulantis*, quae confessio, etsi ipsa non constituat verum argumentum, si tamen desit, probationem reddit difficiliorem; nam contrahens, de cuius consensu inquiritur, semper obiicere posset neminem alium melius ipso iudicare posse de proprio actu interno." S.R.R., *Dec.*, XXXIII (1941), 10: "Ad metus probationem quod attinet, multum profecto attendendum est confessioni personae metum passae, quum agatur de re de se interna, circa quam igitur nemo melius quam ipsa testis exsistere possit."

[8] Cf. *infra*, p. 216.

[9] S.R.R., *Dec.*, IV (1912), 405: "Simulatus consensus in matrimonio difficilis est probatu."

[10] S.R.R., *Dec.*, XX (1928), 343: "Sed haec indirecta probatio non excludit, immo supplet, probationem directam, si haec obtineri possit. Iamvero consensus fictio demonstrari potest directe, si is qui simulavit consensum declaravit ante matrimonii celebrationem se in ineundo coniugio consensum simulaturum esse, ac adiuncta evincunt eum a tali voluntate non recesisse, sed saltem virtualiter in eadem perseverasse: haec tamen omnia idoneis argumentis probari debent."

ART. I. THE EXTRA-JUDICIAL CONFESSION

An extra-judicial confession, according to canon 1753, is a confession made by a party to his adversary or to others outside of the court; when such a confession is referred to the court, the judge is to determine its value in view of all the attendant circumstances. Article 116 of the *Instructio* states that the extra-judicial confession of a consort which impugns the validity of his marriage, and which was made before the wedding, or even after, but at a time that is not suspect, is corroborative evidence which should be properly considered by the judge.

In and of itself a sworn judicial statement is to be preferred to an unsworn extrajudicial statement;[11] however, the contrary is often true in marriage causes, wherein a substantiated extra-judicial confession, if made *tempore non suspecto* can well have more probatory value than a judicial deposition.[12]

An extra-judicial confession may take the form of an oral statement, or it may be made in writing. It may be addressed to the other consort or to relatives, friends, acquaintances and the like. Moreover, the term is not confined to a revelation of intention made in words alone. Any manifestation of the fact—e.g., that a fictitious consent was given—be it only by acts or deeds, may rightly be considered an extra-judicial confession.[13] However, since external acts and conduct can be more suitably treated under presumptions, the present article will be confined to a consideration of the verbal extra-judicial confession.

In evaluating an extra-judicial assertion of a consort, the judge will take into account the following: a) its genuineness; b) its appearance in point of time; c) its perti-

[11] Cf. S.R.R., *Dec.*, XVII (1925), 35.

[12] S.R.R.,*Dec.*, XXXIII (1941), 435: "Confessio vero, quae iam facta est sive ante nutias sive immediate vel brevi post nuptias, magni immo aliquando maximi momenti est; quo fit ut in hoc casu confessioni extraiudiciali maior vis adiudicanda sit quam confessioni iudiciali."

[13] S.R.R., *Dec.*, XXVI (1934), 467; S.R.R., *Dec.*, XXV (1933), 78; S.R.R., *Dec.*, XXV (1933), 443.

nence to the cause at issue; d) the character of the consort who utters it.

A. Genuineness

First of all, it is necessary to establish the fact that the alleged statements were actually made by the person to whom they are attributed. Since extra-judicial assertions of the consorts come to the notice of the court either through documents or testimonial evidence, it will be necessary to properly evaluate these sources of the extra-judicial confession before one can seek to evaluate the confession itself. If the statements are contained in written documents—often in private letters[14]—these documents are presented to the court, and the usual norms for the evaluation of documents are observed.[15] More frequently, statements of this nature are made orally, and thus the principal if not the sole way of establishing the fact is the way of testimonial evidence. The witnesses should declare, in so far as they are able, the actual words spoken by the party, the persons addressed, and the circumstances accompanying the statements.

Usually, at least two reliable witnesses must testify to the extra-judicial confession.[16] In one instance, however, the Rota declared a marriage null in spite of the fact that there had been only one witness who had heard the defendant state that she did not intend to contract a true marriage.[17] In this case, however, the presence of two probable motives, as also her aversion towards the other party both before and after the ceremony, provided very grave indications.

[14] E.g.: S.R.R., *Dec.*, XVII (1925), 77: "Ad haec asserta probanda prostant in actis fragmenta, authentice a Curia dioecesana recognita, epistolarum ab Ida ad Maevium datarum paulo ante matrimonii celebrationem, quibus perversa sponsi voluntas indubitanter affirmatur."

[15] Cf. *infra*, p. 207.

[16] S.R.R., *Dec.*, XXV (1933), 78.

[17] S.R.R., *Dec.*, XI (1919), 36-45.

B. Time

If the extra-judicial statements of the party are to possess true corroborative value, they must have been made at a time that is not suspect—*tempore non suspecto.*[18] Rota decisions frequently emphasize the importance of the element of time in evaluating the extra-judicial statements of the consorts.[19]

The only definition of *tempus non suspectum* in modern canonical legislation is found in the *Regulae Servandae,* issued in 1923 by the Sacred Congregation of the Sacraments for non-consummation causes. Rule 70 states: "Causam enim valde iuvant partium confessiones extraiudiciales tempore non suspecto prolatae; eo nempe tempore, quando de hac quaestione introducenda ne cogitabatur quidem, nec aliae suberant rationes veritatem occultandi aut falsum proferendi."[20] This definition refers specifically to causes which are concerned with the proof of the non-consummation of marriages, but it can also be applied to most nullity causes. Doheny proposes the following definition:[21] "Tempus habetur ut non suspectum quum pars vel ignorabat matrimonium esse irritum vel saltem de eo accusando non cogitabat." Statements made by the consorts or letters written by them *tempore non suspecto* can usually be accepted as representing the truth; on the other hand, all statements, writings and depositions of the consorts and inter-

[18] Art. 116.

[19] E.g., S.R.R., *Dec.,* XVII (1925), 129: "Praesens mulieris inspectio per medicos plane inutilis apparet: verum praetereundum non est quod actrix refert, se duos post annos a matrimonio repertam adhuc virginem fuisse a quodam Carolo et a Ione, qui cum ea pravas relationes habuere: idque eo magis quod fratres illius Furius et Aulus asserant sese idipsum rescivisse a sorore tempore non suspecto." S.R.R., *Dec.,* XXXIII (1941), 10: "Sed, uti patet, confessio ista comprobanda apprime est per alias probationes, sive directas sive saltem indirectas; quarum inter priores adnumeranda sunt testimonia eorum qui tempore non suspecto metum ab ipsa parte patiente vel passa revelatum habuerunt, vel eo magis eorum testimonia qui minas incusserunt aut iisdem adstiterunt."

[20] *AAS,* XV (1923), 389.

[21] *Op. cit.,* I, 336.

ested parties which are made *tempore suspecto* are suspect and as a general rule add little to the available proofs. Yet, if the circumstances are such that it is apparent that no foundation for this suspicion actually exists, then, although the confession made *tempore suspecto* never provides full proof of the fact, it may nevertheless supply corroborative evidence of no little worth.[22] It therefore seems that Cardinal Rauscher (1797-1875) in the well-known and oft-quoted *Instructio Austriaca* was too strict when he stated: "A confession which the consorts make during the progress of the trial itself, or which they made at any earlier time after their contraction of the marriage that is being impugned, lacks all force *(omni vi caret)* when it militates against the validity of the marriage."[23] The Rota itself, in commenting upon this statement, remarked that it is to be observed with certain modifications.[24]

C. Pertinence to the Cause at Issue

The judge must assure himself that the confession was made in connection with the cause at issue, i.e., that the statements here and now offered as judicial evidence in the trial were made concerning this particular marriage, and under the circumstances alleged. Furthermore, it must be ascertained that the alleged statements were uttered seriously, not, for instance, in anger or in jest. In every case, the particular context, circumstances and personalities concerned will have to be considered.[25] A statement made under the influence of anger, for example, is frequently an inaccurate manifestation of a person's true intention.[26] Likewise, apparently fictitious consent may have been uttered merely in jest.[27]

[22] Cf. Wanenmacher, *Canonical Evidence in Marriage Cases*, p. 371.

[23] Instructio pro iudiciis Ecclesiasticis quoad Causas Matrimoniales, § 148—*Collectio Lacensis* V, 1305.

[24] S.R.R., *Dec.*, IV (1912), 441: "Quamvis haec regula vera sit non *absolute* sumpta, sed attentis peculiaribus rerum adiunctis . . .'

[25] S.R.R., *Dec.*, XXIX (1937), 563.

[26] S.R.R., *Dec.*, XXX (1938), 346; S.R.R., *Dec.*, XXVIII (1936), 134.

[27] Cf. S.R.R., *Dec.*, XXVI (1934), 76; S.R.R., *Dec.*, VI (1914), 252.

D. Character of the Consort

Finally, a consort's assertions regarding his own intention may possess very slight probative value because of the unreliability and untrustworthiness of his character.[28] In such a case, the proofs, if any, will have to be drawn in their entirety from the causes of the defective consent, and from the circumstantial evidence.

ART. II. JUDICIAL DEPOSITIONS OF THE CONSORTS

It is a general rule that the judicial depositions of the parties cannot constitute full proof, for a judicial deposition of the consorts is not admissible to constitute proof against the validity of the marriage.[29] However, it is very clear from the jurisprudence of the Rota that the judicial depositions of the parties, while not adequate in themselves to constitute proof against the validity of a marriage, may furnish valuable corroborative evidence which may help in the ascertainment of the entire truth.[30]

Several examples from Rota decisions will illustrate this:

1. In a case where the parties had contracted marriage with a stipulation pending a future event, and had afterwards consummated the marriage without awaiting the outcome of the stipulated event, it was argued that this act was presumably an implicit renewal of unconditional consent, and that hence the marriage was definitely validated. The Rota, however, accepted the judicial deposition of the

[28] Cf. S.R.R., *Dec.*, XXVII (1935), 552; S.R.R., *Dec.*, XXI (1929), 174.

[29] Art. 117. It is to be noted that this article uses the word "proof" in the strict sense of causing conviction in the judge's mind; thus it indicates that the depositions of the parties *can* constitute judicial evidence, for it states that such a deposition *"non est apta ad probationem contra valorem matrimonii constituendam."* If the depositions of the parties were excluded even as partial proof, article 117 would have to be worded, *"non est apta ad probandam nullitatem matrimonii,"* or in similar words.

[30] Doheny, *op. cit.*, I, 339.

parties that the act of coition was not effected with marital intent, and declared the parties free to enter upon new nuptials.[31]

2. In another case, after sixteen years of wedded life, a couple contested their marriage on the ground of impotence and non-consummation, the only proofs being the depositions of the parties supported by the character witnesses. The Rota gave a favorable decision and counselled the Supreme Pontiff to grant a dispensation from a non-consummated marriage.[32]

3. In a case wherein the husband elicited a positive intention *contra bonum prolis,* the depositions of the consorts were divergent. The judicial deposition of the wife could not of itself constitute proof in the case. However, the trustworthiness of her testimony, her character, the concordant testimony of witnesses in contrast to the unreliable, lying tendencies of the husband indicated that her judicial confession might well be considered as corroborative evidence. The Rota decision was favorable.[33]

4. In a case decided by the Rota in 1925, the plaintiff stated that she had been induced to marry under duress. She claimed that she had never given interior consent to the marriage, and being under compulsion to submit to the ceremony she had entered the marriage not of her own will but in a sense of obedience and gratitude. She confessed, however, that at the time of the wedding she had had the intention of establishing a home and of being faithful to her duties as a spouse, hoping that her aversion for the man

[31] S.R.R., *Dec.,* VI (1914), 32: "Hanc copulam non fuisse perfectam ipse etiam Hyginus fatetur implicite... Neque obiiciatur in causa coniugum confessionem utpote pugnantem contra matrimonium contractum esse respuendam, nam id verum est, quando agitur de illo dissolvendo ob impedimentum dirimens, aliud autem in matrimoniis praesumptis obtinet, ut est in praesenti casu in quo ex posita copula vellet praesumi recessus a posita conditione."

[32] S.R.R., *Dec.,* IX (1917), 221.

[33] S.R.R., *Dec.,* VI (1914), 59.

would subsequently disappear. The Rota returned a verdict of *"non constare."*[34]

5. A certain man impugned the validity of his marriage on the ground that his wife had simulated her consent to the marriage. Both total and partial simulation were mentioned in the *libellus*. The woman admitted in court that she had desired to marry the plaintiff solely because the civil status conferred through the marriage would provide her with greater freedom to continue her sinful relations with her lover. She claimed that she had had no intention of obliging herself to the duties of the marriage state. In virtue of this deposition, the Rota determined that this was not a case of total, but rather of partial simulation, and subsequently the marriage was declared null on the ground of the exclusion of the blessing of offspring.[35]

6. In another case, it was alleged that the wife had placed a condition *contra bonum sacramenti*. The consorts testified to this fact, but their judicial depositions lacked full proof, since they impugned the validity of the marriage, and were given *tempore suspecto*, after the union had been contracted. However, the concordant testimony of six witnesses, worthy of credence, indicated the truth of the assertions of the parties. Consequently, the Rota decision was favorable.[36]

7. A certain man asserted that he had placed a condition *sine qua non* to his matrimonial consent, namely by demanding virginity in his spouse. When it subsequently developed that she had not been a virgin, he impugned the validity of his marriage. However, there was no supporting evidence by means of witnesses, documents, or the like. Since the judicial deposition of the consort alone does not constitute proof against the validity of a marriage, the decision of the Rota was *"non constare."*[37]

[34] S.R.R., *Dec.*, XVII (1925), 177; "Quod actrix nec asseruit nec vindicat, quod immo aperte excludit, nequit profecto probari per testes."

[35] S.R.R., *Dec.*, XV (1923), 168.

[36] S.R.R., *Dec.*, VII (1915), 163.

[37] S.R.R., *Dec.*, V (1913), 7.

8. A certain English girl, Agnes, impugned the validity of her marriage on the claim that she had been totally ignorant of the nature of marriage. In view of the fact that her judicial deposition was given *tempore suspecto* and not supported by other evidence of a sufficiently weighty nature, the Rota's decision was a *"non constare."*[38]

Thus it can be seen from the foregoing examples of Rotal jurisprudence, that: a) the judicial depositions of the parties cannot in and of themselves *(per se)* prove the invalidity of a marriage; b) supported by character witnesses, hearsay witnesses, documents, presumptions, and the like, the judicial depositions of the parties can form an important segment of the resultant full proof, and c) without the judicial deposition of the parties it is often impossible to establish the facts, especially in defective consent cases.

The following points should be kept in mind in the evaluating of the judicial depositions of a consort:

1) The party who makes a judicial confession of fictitious consent must reveal by his confession that he is, and always has been, fully aware of this fact. If it becomes apparent that his marital consent had been merely uncertain, or given reluctantly, the truth of the matter may be that he has simulated the confession, and not the consent.[39]

2) The sworn depositions of the parties can be accepted as evidence only when there is a strong personal presumption of veracity which warrants the inference that the parties would not collude or depose falsely even in their own behalf.[40]

3) In the cause wherein a party has refused to answer when lawfully questioned, the judge is to determine the im-

[38] S.R.R., *Dec.*, XVIII (1926), 9: "Adductum proinde argumentum primo per se inefficax est, inspecta eiusdem natura. At est quoque inefficax, admissa patroni opinione, quia quae a coniugibus contra matrimonii validatem asseruntur tempore suspecto, seu post motam litem de eiusdem matrimonii validitate nihil probant."

[39] S.R.R., *Dec.*, XXVIII (1936), 101: "Qui proinde in iudicio sibi adscribit simulationem consensus, is necessario in contrahendo sibi conscius esse debuit suae fictionis; seus nunc fingit, non vero prius."

[40] Wanenmacher, *op. cit.*, n. 568.

plication of the refusal.[41] It is significant that article 112, in quoting canon 1743, § 2, omits these words *"utrum iusta sit, an confessioni aequiparanda, necne."* In private contentious causes, the judge may be more prone to account the disobedience as a confession; in marriage causes he will act with extreme caution. The Instruction of Cardinal Rauscher declared that the contumacy of a party was not to be construed as an argument against the validity of the marriage.[42]

Nevertheless, a cause may arise when it is proper for the judge to view the party's refusal to answer, considered in all its circumstances, as the equivalent of a confession prejudicial to his cause. Thus especially in causes of impotence and non-consummation, the silence of a husband regarding his sexual potentiality, especially when taken in conjunction with the physical inspection or his refusal to allow it, may be viewed as tantamount to an acknowledgment of physical weakness.[43]

Art. III. Partitioned Confessions

The question may be raised whether or not a qualified or complex confession (either judicial or extra-judicial) may be divided, i.e., whether the judge has the discretionary authority to accept only that part of the confession which favors the plaintiff, and reject that part which favors him who made the confession. The canons of the Code are silent about the matter, and the question never was solved by any pre-Code law.[44] Reiffenstuel stated that a qualified confession may not be divided in such a manner that only the part which harms the cause of the one making the confession is accepted; a qualified confession should be considered as an undivided whole, which is either entirely accepted or completely rejected.[45] Cardinal Lega, however, distinguishes

[41] Art. 112.
[42] *Instructio Austriaca,* § 50.
[43] Wanenmacher, *op. cit.,* n. 101.
[44] Lega (ed. Bart.) *Commentarius,* II, 650.
[45] Reiffenstuel, *Jus Canonicum Universum,* lib. II, tit. XVIII, n. 120.

between the right of the plaintiff and the right of the judge: for although the plaintiff does not have the right to divide or split the confession in such a manner that it favors his purpose, nevertheless, the judge may do so if he is certain from the *acta et probata* that the added qualification has no foundation in truth.[46] This consideration applies only to a qualified confession, since a complex confession can ordinarily be considered in each of its statements as a separate confession or assertion.[47]

[46] Lega (ed. Bart.), *op. cit.*, II, 653: "... etiam pro iudice vera est abstracta regula, confessionem utpote quid *individuum* non posse scindi, sed in praxi, verius est dicere, rem pendere in singulis casibus ex recta actorum et probatorum aestimatione, uti concludit De Luca et cui apertissime consentit iurisprudentia nostri fori si hanc desumamus ex decisionibus S.R. Rotae quae constantes sunt in neganda parti facultatem scindendi confessionem qualificatam; plenam probationem sibi desumando ex confessione adversarii, cum hic revera adiiciens qualitatem negat intentionem actoris; sed in merito causae, iudicis est perpendere diligenter omnem actorum et probatorum vim ut deducatur utrum qualitas confessioni apposita probanda sit vel repudianda."

[47] Lega (ed. Bart.), *op. cit.*, II, 654: "... si plura contineat capitula seu diversa facta alleget ... tunc confessio non est proprie qualificata sed complexa et tunc potest pro parte recipi et pro parte respui, quia unum factum asseritur ab alio distinctum."

CHAPTER III

THE EVALUATION OF TESTIMONIAL EVIDENCE

Canons 1789 to 1791 enact the general norms for the evaluation of testimonial evidence in marriage causes.[1] These norms are not mathematical formulas whose use will automatically indicate the value of the evidence, for according to his conscience the judge is prudently to evaluate the evidence proffered.[2] One must bear in mind that these norms are not merely specifications of Church law, but rather are concise summarizations of psychological principles derived from human nature itself, whose worth and truth have been vindicated through centuries of juridical practice in the Church. Obviously, then, even if no canon of the Code prescribed these guides, a judge would *ex natura rei* consider the character of the witness, his manner of testifying, his source of knowledge, etc. In general, then, the judge's discretionary authority in evaluating testimonial evidence is neither enlarged nor restricted by these canons, but rather the judge is given practical guide-posts to follow in rightly exercising his discretionary power. Thus, *salvo meliori iudicio,* it seems erroneous to draw the conclusion that the Code in canons 1789 to 1791 has restricted the wide power of the judge;[3] strictly speaking, the judge has no true discretionary power to go contrary to right reason—which he would be doing, for example, should he ignore the person and consider only the testimony.

In evaluating testimonial evidence, the judge will consider first the evidence in itself (can. 1789), secondly the evidence in relationship to other evidence (can. 1790), and

[1] Art. 136, § 1.

[2] Can. 1869, § 3.

[3] Cf. e.g., Whalen, *The Value of Testimonial Evidence in Matrimonial Procedure*, p. 202; Roberti, *De Processibus*, II, n. 354, p. 74.

thirdly what type of evidence will ordinarily constitute full proof (can. 1791).

ART. I. TESTIMONIAL EVIDENCE CONSIDERED IN ITSELF

The discretionary authority of the judge is first of all guided by the four criteria enumerated in canon 1789 for the evaluation of testimonial evidence taken in itself, apart from a consideration of other evidence. In weighing the depositions of witnesses, the judge should keep in mind the following points:

A. The status of the witness, his reputation for probity, and the position he holds.[4]

B. Whether his testimony is based on personal knowledge, especially sight or hearing, or whether it is based on rumor, public report, or things which the witness heard from others.[5]

C. Whether the testimony is consistent and coherent, or contradictory, uncertain, and vacillating.[6]

D. Whether other witnesses corroborate the testimony, or whether it is unsupported.[7]

A. The Status of the Witness as a Criterion

In estimating the value of testimony, the judge should consider the character and reputation, as well as the dignity and position, (ecclesiastical or civil) of the witness.[8] This criterion is rather self-evident and needs little demonstration.[9]

However, the judge is not to rely solely upon the examination of the witness to judge the credibility of the witness.

[4] Can. 1789, n. 1.

[5] Can. 1789, n. 2.

[6] Can. 1789, n. 3.

[7] Can. 1789, n. 4.

[8] Cf. can. 1789, n. 1.

[9] Lega (ed. Bart.), *op. cit.*, II, p. 736, n. 3: "Hoc est ita perspectum ut non vacet ulterius explicare, sed tantum advertam, inde patere, maxime interesse ut interrogationes *generales* solerter fiant ad omnimode cognoscendam conditionem, civilem, religiosam, moralem, politicam et domesticam testis."

The judge should demand evidence from other sources of the religious character, the probity and credibility of *all* witnesses; for the stronger the evidence of the requisite qualities of good character, the greater the credence to be given to the witness.[10] Moreover, when the testimony of the witness has an important bearing upon the validity of a marriage, his veracity is to be examined even more diligently than would ordinarily be the case.[11] For instance, the fact that the parties do not take exception to a witness does not of itself support the fact that his deposition, directed agains the validity of the marriage, is worthy of credence.[12]

B. The Source of the Witness's Knowledge as a Criterion

Canon 1789, n. 2, distinguishes four types of witnesses according to the source of their knowledge: 1) *de scientia propria,* 2) *de credulitate,* 3) *de fama,* and 4) *de auditu ab aliis.*

1) Witnesses who testify from their own knowledge *(de scientia propria)* are those who make an attestation about a thing which they perceived with their own senses; only such are witnesses in the proper sense of the word.[13] Such witnesses are called witnesses *de visu vel de auditu proprio* when they testify to what they have personally seen or heard. Besides ascertaining the objective source of the witness's knowledge, it is particularly important to note *at what definite time* the witness acquired his knowledge,[14] for two reasons: first, the reliability of the source of the knowledge depends to a great extent upon its relationship to the time of the marriage: whether or not the information has its origin *tempore suspecto;*[15] and secondly, the memory of the witness will generally be less reliable when the fact witnessed happened at some remote time.

[10] Art. 138, § 1; cf. *supra,* p. 126, for methods of obtaining this information.

[11] Art. 136, § 2.

[12] Art. 136, § 3.

[13] Reiffenstuel, *op. cit.,* lib. II, tit. XX, nn. 342, 343.

[14] Cf. art. 100.

[15] Cf. *supra,* p. 173.

2) Witnesses testifying *"de credulitate"* are not witnesses properly so, but their testimony at times can be of great value. The expression *"de credulitate"* is generally interpreted by canonists to be synonymous with *"ex coniecturis"*;[16] consequently, it seems incorrect to identify *"de credulitate"* with *"de credibilitate"*; there is a real distinction between the two, although it is quite possible that a witness *de credibilitate* would derive his opinion from conjectures; however, character witnesses are preferably witnesses *de scientia*, not indeed of the object of the trial, but precisely of the character of the person in question, about whom they have formed an opinion from their own personal knowledge and observation.

Witnesses who state their opinion of an event do not thereby beget full proof of the fact, but rather an indication of, and an aid to, proof; and this indication or aid is stronger or weaker according as the opinion is more or less directly derived from what the witnesses have perceived with their own senses.[17]

3) A witness *de fama* is one who testifies concerning another's reputation or to the notoriety of a fact, as it exists in a community, city, or nation.[18] When witnesses testify that an event is reputed to have taken place, the value of this testimony will increase according as the persons named as authors of this repute are grave and reliable, and as the causes are probable and proportionate, through which the people have come by the repute. When the repute is thus well substantiated, the testimony may form part proof, or even full proof of the case,[19] particularly in causes involving non-consummation and duress.[20]

[16] Reiffenstuel, *op. cit.*, lib. II, tit. XX, n. 344; Roberti, *De Processibus,*, II, p. 74; Noval, *De Iudiciis*, n. 510, p. 351.

[17] Wanenmacher, *Canonical Evidence in Marriage Cases*, n. 263.

[18] Lega (ed. Bart.), *op. cit.*, II, 737; Noval (*op. cit.*, n. 510) stated: "... id est, testificatur non de facto controverso, sed de pervulgata populi opinione circa factum et eius auctores, et circumstantias."

[19] Wanenmacher, *op. cit.*, n. 262, p. 162.

[20] Cf. S.R.R., *Dec.*, VIII (1916), 371.

When it is not established that the authors of a public repute are grave and reliable sources, or that the causes of it are probable and proportionate, the judge will consider the current talk rather as a rumor than as genuine repute.[21]

4) Hearsay witnesses, *de auditu ab aliis*, relate what they have heard from others.[22] *Septimae manus* witnesses are often hearsay witnesses to the fact of non-consummation,[23] but they are witnesses *de scientia* concerning their own primary object as witnesses *de credibilitate*. Witnesses testifying to what they heard a party say *tempore non suspecto* are hearsay witnesses to the direct object itself of the trial, but are witnesses *de scientia* to the extra-judicial confession itself of the party. It is plain that hearsay testimony is to be appraised by the source from which it originates.

Direct hearsay testimony may be of great value and weight, especially when the witnesses testify to what they heard *tempore non suspecto*. When a witness offers indirect hearsay testimony, it gives the judge an opportunity to inquire into the names and addresses of those persons who are the sources of the hearsay, and are themselves at least directly hearsay witnesses. If these direct hearsay witnesses are alive and can be heard, the indirect hearsay testimony is inadmissible as proof, because it is not the best obtainable pertinent evidence. If these direct hearsay witnesses are not alive or cannot be heard, the indirect hearsay testimony may be accepted as a more or less weighty support to other evidence, at the discretion of the judge.[24]

[21] Cf. Lega (ed. Bart.) *op. cit.*, III 737.

[22] These are *direct* hearsay witnesses if they have heard of the event from those who saw it or otherwise experienced it; they are *indirect* hearsay witnesses (*de auditu auditus, de auditu alieno,* etc.) if they heard of the event only from those who in turn merely heard of it.

[23] Reg. 60, § 2, *Regulae Servandae*: "Habendi sunt autem quasi testes *de scientia*, et hinc maximam faciunt fidem, cum referunt se ex coniugibus aut ex proximioribus parentibus, tempore non suspecto ..., didicisse matrimonium mansisse inconsummatum."—*AAS*, XV (1923), 404.

[24] Wanenmacher, *op. cit.*, n. 261.

C. The Consistency and Coherency of the Testimony as a Criterion

This criterion depends upon whether the testimony of the witness is in itself consistent and coherent, or is contradictory, variable, or uncertain.[25] This is a most important consideration. Roman law embodied it in the expression, *non testimoniis sed testibus credere.*[26] Reiffenstuel repeated this admonition.[27] It is quite commonly said in this country: "It's not *what* you say, but *the way* you say it, that counts!" Thus, the conduct of a witness during the examination frequently indicates his emotions. The judge, then, will be further guided in his evaluation of the testimony by the constancy or inconstancy, the coherence or contradiction, the certainty or uncertainty of the witness and his answers. A consistent, logical witness furnishes better proof than another who is uncertain, vaccillating and at variance with himself. However, a witness who frankly and spontaneously corrects one or another of his statements just after the testimony has been given need not be considered untrustworthy.[28]

Reiffenstuel's discussion of this particular aspect of the

[25] Can. 1789, n. 3. Reiffenstuel (*op. cit.*, lib. II, tit. XX, nn. 313-316) offered these definitions: "Testis contrarius dicitur, qui deponit duo vel plura inter se repugnantia: ut si quis interceptus per diversas interrogationes sibi factas talia asserat quae prorsus inter se repugnant, et simul esse non possunt . . . Testis varius, seu varians censetur: qui varia loquitur; hoc est, qui non stat firmus in dicto suo: puta, quia in uno iudicio sic, in altero autem, sive iterum examinatus, diverso modo loquitur super eodem facto . . . Differt autem testis varius a contrario: quia hic in eodem examine dicit contraria, seu inter se repugnantia; testis varius autem successive, seu in diversis instantiis, aut examinibus; ille testis proprie dicatur variare, qui non deponit contraria, sed qui diverso modo dicit . . . Testis vacillans dicitur, qui timendo, titubando, vel dubitando testimonium dicit. Unde, ut testis censeatur vacillans, sufficit, quod dubitando, timendo, aut titubando deponat, etsi non loquatur contraria . . ."

[26] Cf. *supra*, p. 164.

[27] *Op. cit.*, lib. II, tit. XX, n. 320.

[28] Wanenmacher, *op. cit.*, n. 264.

evaluation of testimonial evidence is so masterfully done that it is quoted here at some length:

"Si deponit vere dubitando, fidem non meretur. Et quidem testis vacillans, quando deponit vere dubitando, fidem non meretur: quia hoc ipso, quod vere dubitet, in neutram inclinat partem; sicque incertum est ejus testimonium: nec est ratio, cur uni potius quam alteri parti assensus praebeatur, ac proinde tollitur fides ejus in totum ...[29]

"Et quid, si deponat titubando, timendo, sudando? Quod si vero sit tantummodo vacillans, quatenus deponit titubando, timendo, sive sudando, tunc probatio ejus non tollitur in totum, bene tamen de fide ejus diminuitur. Et merito, quia non obstante tali timore, aut sudore, vel pallore vultus, qui vel ex periculi magnitudine, vel ob cordis debilitatem, aut pusillanimitatem saepius oriri solet, testis duntaxat titubando, vacillans vere in favorem unius partis, et quidem sub juramenti religione deponit; sicque non destituitur omni fide, sed meretur aliquam, majorem tamen, vel minorem, pro qualitate suae vacillationis, formidinis, seu palloris, aliarumque circumstantiarum, prudenti judicis arbitrio dimetiendam.[30]

"Judex debet vacillationem testis, et causam ipsius in actis ponere—et per quem modum vacillavit; debeatque ipsam vacillationem scribi facere in actis, ipso deponente intelligente, et tunc quando deponit.[31] Certum est, si unus idemque testis sibimet ipsi expresse contradicat in sua depositione judiciali, non valere ejus testimonium, nisi forsan hoc fecerit in continenti corrigendo dictum suum, nam tunc statur dicto posteriori, utpote prius corrigenti.[32] Accedit, quod non sit major ratio, cur uni potius quam alteri dicto talis testis sibi contrarii credatur. Imo ex manifesta illa contrarietate redditur testis suspectus, atque perjurus; cum juraverit dicere veritatem, et contraria non possint esse vera.[33]

[29] Reiffenstuel, *op. cit.*, lib. II, tit. XX, n. 317.
[30] Reiffenstuel, *ibid.*, n. 318.
[31] Reiffenstuel, *ibid.*, n. 319.
[32] Cf. can. 1752.
[33] Reiffenstuel, *ibid.*, n. 326.

> "Certe juxta Hostiensem et Glossam marginalem ibid. id arbitrio judicis erit relinquendum, ut considerata qualitate personae, quantitate intervalli, colloquio partium, et reliquis circumstantiis correctionem admittat, vel non.[34] Quando testis in diversis judiciis (puta summario et ordinario), vel in diversis instantiis ejusdem judicii, super eodem facto contraria deponit, *ordinarie* statur primae ejus depositioni juratae.[35] Licet prima depositio ... per secundam contrariam totaliter revocari non possit ... nihilominus prima depositio per secundam judicialem contrariam debilitatur, ac redditur plurimum suspecta; et judex ex circumstantiis, aliisque indiciis discernere debebit, an, et quanta ei fides sit adhibenda."[36]

There are many other indications which will warn the judge of the possible untruthfulness of a witness. Whalen lists the following as among the more important indications:[37] a) a defensive smile and a nervous laugh unwarranted by circumstances, but apparently used unconsciously, with a desire to cover deceit; b) avoidance of looking at the judge, except for an occasional quick glance, and keeping the eyes fixed in an unnatural manner on a distant object; c) an almost inaudible voice, indicating a desire possibly to be elsewhere, or trying to cover the mouth or face while testifying; d) repetition of plain and audible questions in what appears to be an unconscious effort to recall testimony and frame a good reply; e) unnecessary and minute accuracy to show that the whole truth is being told; f) repeated avowal of a desire to tell the truth; g) unnatural emphasis on one point with a reluctance to be questioned regarding the source of information and the logical result of premises.

However, it must be borne in mind that these are only indications which must be evaluated along with all other circumstances of the examination and the character

[34] Reiffenstuel, *ibid.*, n. 327.
[35] Reiffenstuel, *ibid.*, n. 330.
[36] Reiffenstuel, *ibid.*, n. 340.
[37] Whalen, *op. cit.*, p. 233.

testimony concerning the person examined, for in themselves they may simply indicate uneasiness in the presence of church officials, etc.

D. The Numerical Criterion

The number of witnesses who agree in their assertions has a logical bearing on the probative value of the testimony; however, not only the number of the witnesses, but also the quality of the witnesses should be considered.[38] This particular consideration of whether or not witnesses have other agreeing witnesses chiefly concerns witnesses produced by the *same* party.[39]

Ciprotti recommends,[40] in order to avoid the non-Latin word "*contestes*" and to complete logically the norms of canon 1789, that n. 4 be understood as if written, "*utrum testimonium confirmetur, ex toto vel ex parte, aliis probationibus necne;*" i.e., "whether or not the testimony is confirmed, in whole or in part, by other proofs."

However, even corroborative testimony may be overdone, and when the judge perceives that several witnesses render testimony in the same words, the judge may have reason to suspect collusion with or coaching of the witnesses.[41]

[38] S.R.R. *Dec.*, XXV (1933), 528.

[39] Lega (ed. Bart.), *op. cit.*, II, p. 738, n. 7: "Nam testes, respective, ab adversis partibus inductis ut plurimum, sunt ad invicem contrarii; et cum iudex examinat omnia acta et probata, respective, a partibus litigantibus, facit quoque attestationum hinc inde deductarum examen, sed sub alio respectu, magis generali et cumulativo, habita nempe ratione omnigenarum probationum exhibitarum; dum intentio nostri articuli ... potissimum eo tendit ut iudici suppeditentur regulae quibus testium fides aestimatur. Nihilominus nemo non percipit, regulas heic positas valere quoque, congrua congruis referendo, ad aestimandam fidem testimoniorum ab adversis partibus ab unaquaque in suam defensionem productorum. Sed tunc valet alia regula, scilicet, quod omnibus perpensis, in dubio est pro reo respondendum."

[40] *Observaciones al Texto del Codex Iuris Canonici* (translated from 1st. Italian edition [1944] by Tomás García Baberena; Salamanca, 1950), p. 90.

[41] Wanenmacher, *op.cit.*, n. 270.

Art. II. Testimonial Evidence Considered Relatively

Testimonial evidence is to be evaluated not only in itself, but also in relationship to that of other witnesses. Thus, if the witnesses are at variance, the judge is to consider whether their depositions are mutually contradictory, whether they merely cover different facts or circumstances of a case, or actually supplement each other.[42] A classic illustration of this principle is found in the Biblical story of Susanna (*Dan.*, XIII, 54-58), who was accused of adultery by two old men, one of whom alleged that the crime was committed under a mastic tree, whereas the other declared that it had taken place under a holm tree. Because of their divergent testimony, their accusation was discredited.

Witnesses can be at variance in three different ways: a) their testimony can be contradictory, e.g., as when one witness testifies that a person was baptized, another that this person was never baptized; b) it can be contrary, e.g., as when one witness states that a man died in Europe, another that he died in America; c) it can simply be diversative, i.e., witnesses may refer to various disconnected events, as when several witnesses testify to various occasions when each separately heard a person give a promise of marriage, but not two witnesses testify to the same event.[43]

Contrary and contradictory testimonies destroy rather than furnish proof. Nevertheless, it is for the judge to seek to effect a concordance between the apparently discrepant testimonies,[44] or to decide, from the character, position, and manner of speaking of the witnesses, whether one group must be believed rather than the other. If two groups of witnesses contradict each other, an internal discrepancy among the witnesses of one group discredits their testimony in favor of the other coherent group.[45] Witnesses cannot

[42] Can. 1790: "Si testes inter se discrepent, iudex perpendat utrum edita ab eis testimonia sibi invicem adversentur, an sint dumtaxat diversa vel adminiculativa."

[43] Wanenmacher, *op. cit.*, n. 186.

[44] S.R.R. *Dec.*, III (1911), 517.

[45] Cf. S.R.R. *Dec.*, I (1909), 55.

be expected to agree so perfectly, however, that no discrepancies can be detected in their testimony. Hence, minor discrepancies are not usually to be given any profound attention.[46] The date of betrothal, marriage, time and circumstances of the marriage ceremony, etc., are oftentimes such unimportant details upon which a discrepancy among the witnesses will not devaluate the testimony.[47] Such discrepancies are in fact rather a sign that there was no collusion among the varying witnesses.[48]

Reiffenstuel's comments on the varying testimony of several witnesses are of considerable assistance to the judge in evaluating such testimony:

> "Si testes ... videntur inter se contrarii, tunc pro possibili debet judex eorum dicta interpretari, ut non contradicant, etc. Ratio est quia 'dubia in meliorem partem interpretari debent.' ... Simulque quia nemo praesumitur esse perjurus, si verba ipsius quoquo modo in partem meliorem trahi possunt; ergo, si testes prima fronte contrarii appareant, prius judex, si fieri poterit, eos concordare studebit, ne alioquin quidam eorum perjuri esse convincantur.[49]
>
> "Si duo duntaxat testes ex una parte producti fuerint; et sibi manifeste contradicant, certum est eos nihil probare: quia unus enervat dictum alterius, nec constat, quis eorum veritatem dixerit. Se-

[46] S.R.R., *Dec.*, V (1913), 327: "Ceterum meminisse, iuvat, quae, circa accidentales testimoniorum circumstantias, habet divus Thomas: 'Si vero sit discordia testimoniis in aliquibus circumstantiis non pertinentibus ad substantiam facti ..., talis discordia non praeiudicat testimonio ... quin immo aliqua discordia in talibus facit testimonium credibilius, ut Chrysostomus dicit super Mattaeum.' ... Cui plene adhaeret Benedictus XIV, qui ita scribit: 'Expedit enim aliquando, ut aliqua adsit discordia inter testes, non in substantialibus, sed in accidentalibus; concordia siquidem in omnibus, hoc est tum in substantialibus tum in accidentalibus, tantum abest ut fidem conciliet, ut eam potius testibus minuat' ... Et hoc magis verum est, quando testes de his quae tempore remoto evenerunt, reddere debent testimonium ..."

[47] S.R.R. *Dec.*, VI (1914), 147; S.R.R. *Dec.*, VII (1916), 211.

[48] S.R.R., *Dec.*, IV (1912), 474; S.R.R. *Dec.*, V (1913), 189.

[49] Reiffenstuel, *op. cit.*, lib. II, tit. XX, n. 321.

cus est, quando multi ab eadem parte testes producuntur, quorum plures inter se concordant; aliqui vero, sed pauciores, ab eis discordant: valet enim, caeteris paribus, testimonium plurium inter se concordantium; quamvis negari non possit, ex tali quorundam contradictione, si fiat circa substantiam negotii, seu qualitates intrinsecas, aliorum testium concordantium fidem debilitari, ita ut minus probent... Quia non ad solam testium multitudinem respicere oportet, sed etiam, an caetera sint paria, considerando videlicet eorum qualitatem, et quorum dictis potius affulgeat lux veritatis, seu qui verisimiliora deponant.[50]

"Et conformiter dictis resolvendum est illud dubium, quid videlicet agendum sit, si duo testes contestes ab eadem parte producti allegent tertium contestem, iste tertius vero neget se interfuisse, vel aliquid scire, au recordari talis facti. Standum quippe est testimonio duorum testium concordantium, ceteroquin tamen habilium: tum quia sunt numero plures, sicque procedunt proxime dicta. Tum quia magis credendum est duobus testibus affirmantibus, quam centum negantibus... Addita ea ratione, quia possibile est, quod ubi etiam plures sunt praesentes, duo tantum ad id, quod agitur, sint attenti, caeteris non advertentibus, vel non curantibus, aut postea non amplius recordantibus; et hinc aptius et naturalius est testimonium affirmantium, praesertim si plures sint bonaeque fidei quam negantium.[51]

"Quod si manifesta contrarietas sit inter testes hinc inde productos, ex parte actoris videlicet ac rei, tunc si testes utrinque producti ejusdem sint honestatis, atque existimationis, praeferuntur numero plures; si vero testes ex una parte producti tantae praeeminentiae fuerint, quod eorum auctoritas merito sit praeferenda aliorum numero, tunc praevalet digniores, et verisimiliora deponentes... Non semper judex debeat se referre ad multitudinem testium, sed potius ad eorum honestatem et opinionem, et qui verisimiliora dicant; puta, juri consona, vel aptiora negotia.[52]

[50] Reiffenstuel, *ibid.*, n. 322.
[51] Reiffenstuel, *ibid.*, n. 323.
[52] Reiffenstuel, *ibid.*, n. 324.

> "Si vero testes ex utraque parte producti omnino pares existant, et deponant contraria, tunc pro reo fertur sententia: nisi forsan actor foveat causam favorabilem, stantem videlicet pro matrimonio, libertate, dote, aut testamento . . ."[53]

Diversative testimonies can generally be reconciled, and then each witness furnishes partial proof of what is asserted, and together the testimonies may be so conclusive as to approach, even though they alone do not attain to it, full proof.[54] When, however, the testimony of a single witness is diversative from that of a party and favors nullity, it is not usually given much value.[55]

Complementary testimonies taken separately, generally furnish partial proof of the various assertions, and taken together have an added cumulative value, which may amount to full proof of the cause.[56] This is especially so in causes of nullity by reason of the insanity of a party.[57]

The practice of the Sacred Roman Rota requires that a lack of conformity between the statements of witnesses must be proved and not merely stated. The attestations of witnesses should be reconciled with one another, and in as far as it is possible, one should not call the good faith of witnesses into question.[58]

[53] Reiffenstuel, *ibid.*, n. 325. [54] Wanenmacher, *op. cit.*, n. 272.

[55] Wanenmacher, *loc. cit.;* S.R.R. *Dec.*, IX (1917), 136: "Assertio vero alterius testis, Josephi Chappuis, de minis eiectionis filiae e domo paterna, reiicienda est, non solum quia unius testis est, sed etiam quia plane contradicit testimonio reae conventae, quae de aliis minis, praeter illas exhaereditationis, se nihil scire declarat."

[56] S.R.R. *Dec.*, III (1911), 169: "Hi testes videntur prima fronte singulares, sed non sunt stricte singulares sed potius contestes, quia referunt facta relativa ad eundem finem, seu referunt adminicula tendentia ad probandum factum secutae copulae. Iamvero hi testes singulares non singularitate obstativa sed tantum adminiculativa plene probant in iudicio."

[57] S.R.R. *Dec.*, XV (1923), 129.

[58] S.R.R., *Dec.*, V (1913), 496: "Si vero . . . hactenus adlaboravimus, quasi inter se conciliare discordantes attestationes, distinguendo varia tempora et variam intentionem minarum (semper enim adnitendum esse ut testium dicta inter se concilientur, constans docuit H.S.O. iurisprudentia), et quantum fieri poterat non in discrimen adducenda

ART. III. EVALUATION OF FULL PROOF BASED ON TESTIMONIAL EVIDENCE

Canon Law recognizes that the probative value of the testimony of witnesses is utterly incapable of being measured by mathematical formulas. The personal element behind an attestation is a vital one, which cannot be appraised exactly by rules. Nevertheless, canon 1791 offers certain norms by means of which the judge can estimate that full proof is normally acquired.

A. The Value of the Testimony of One Witness

According to canon 1791, § 1, the deposition of one witness does not constitute full proof, unless he is an officially qualified witness who testifies regarding things done in his official capacity. It is a general rule, then, that the testimony of one witness, although admissible as evidence, is not sufficient alone to form the basis of a decision or a verdict. The well-known principle, *unus testis, nullus testis,* is not found in the Mode, thus modifying the old rule that one witness is no witness by stating that one witness *alone* does not suffice to provide full proof. Thus, the testimony of one witness who is above all suspicion forms partial proof of that which he affirms or denies.[59] This partial proof, when joined with other partial proofs, such as justifiable presumptions, may amount to sufficient evidence so that the case may be favorably decided, especially in the event that more witnesses cannot be had.[60] Thus, when a parent confesses that he has coerced his daughter into marriage, and there are other indications that this is the objective truth, it may amount to full proof.[61]

erat testium bona fides, hoc factum est quia testes, etiam qui validitati adversantur, exhibentur ut probi et honesti."

[59] S.R.R. *Dec.,* III (1911), 327: "At dato etiam quod unicus sit testis, certissima doctrina est, unum testem, etsi plenam probationem non exhibeat, inducere tamen iuridicam veritatis praesumptionem, si omni exceptione testis maior sit."

[60] S.C.C., 29 iul. 1854.—Pallottini, XIII, 428.

[61] S.R.R., *Dec.,* VIII (1916), 136; S.R.R., *Dec.,* IX (1917), 65; S.R.R., *Dec.,* IX (1917), 423.

However, at times even full proof can be engendered by one witness, if that witness is a *testis qualificatus* testifying to what has been done in his official capacity. Thus, a pastor is a *testis qualificatus* in those matters that strictly belong to or are intimately bound up with his pastoral office, such as the administering of baptism, the witnessing of marriage, etc.; a notary of an ecclesiastical tribunal in matter concerning his office; a police officer in the discharge of his duty, and the like.[62] There seems to be a lack of sharp distinctions concerning a *testis qualificatus* among many authors. According to Noval,[63] a *testis qualificatus* is a person in a public office who has sworn to fulfill his duties. The fact that he holds a public office and is sworn to fulfill his duties is the foundation of the presumption of law that he is to be believed. Furthermore, he must be above all exception, such as being unfit, suspect, or disqualified, and he must testify *de scientia,* not *de credulitate.* Noval therefore excludes experts as *testes qualificati.*[64]

B. The Value of the Testimony of Two or More Witnesses

According to canon 1791, § 2, if two or three absolutely trustworthy witnesses testify in court under oath on some affair or fact, doing so of their own personal knowledge, and their testimony is strictly concordant, such joint testimony is considered sufficient proof. If, however, in view of the very serious nature of an affair or because of indications which create doubt as to the truth of things asserted, the judge believes that further evidence is necessary, he may demand more complete proofs. The dictum that two or three witnesses as a rule produce complete proof must, however, by no means be considered as a prohibition to admit many witnesses. It merely specifies that ordinarily at least two witnesses are required to produce full credibility,

[62] Doheny, *op. cit.,* I, 379.

[63] *De Iudiciis,* n. 512.

[64] *Loc. cit.* However, a physician, duly appointed and sworn, would be a *testis qualificatus* concerning the physical facts observed in a corporal examination.

in causes namely wherein no other adminicular proofs are available.[65]

In view of all the factors involved in testimonial evidence, full proof is ordinarily present where the following conditions exist concomitantly:[66]

1. Testimony of two or three persons;
2. Testimony under oath;
3. Testimony *de scientia;*
4. Persons testifying are absolutely worthy of credence;
5. Persons testifying are in strict agreement with one another.

However, the judge may demand further evidence, if he estimates that fuller proof is necessary, in two situations: a) when the case is of a very serious nature *(ob maximam negotii gravitatem)*,[67] and b), because of indications[68] that engender some doubt about the truth of the assertion.

The following valuable remarks form the conclusion of Cardinal Lega's commentary on the evaluation of testimonial evidence:[69]

> "Cum edicatur aliquando attestationes non plenam facere probationem, aliquando *plenam, pleniorem* non semel requiri, induci posset conclusio, revera canones ponere *etiam mensuram legalem* in probationibus ... Non diffiteor canonistas et maxime pragmaticos nimis instantes in regulis quibus fides testimoniorum et probationum in genere aestimari quasi mathematice contendebatur, potuisse iudices in errorem inducere et corrupisse genui-

[65] Cf. Whalen, *op. cit.*, p. 251.

[66] Doheny, *op. cit.*, I, 379.

[67] Noval (*op. cit.*, n. 512) stated: "... non igitur *quamqunque* gravitatem, nec quidem *notabilem*, sed *maxima*. Equidem iudicis est aestimare utrum gravitas sit maxima, aut notabilis aut simplex; sed, posito quod reputet negotium non esse maximae gravitatis, non est in eius arbitrio nec potest absque gravi conscientiae offensione abstinere a sententia pronuntianda iuxta probata coram se, nisi in casu qui statim a legislatore exprimitur."

[68] Noval (*loc. cit.*) stated: "*ob indicia*: non talia quae sint sibi soli privatim nota, sed quae innotescant et indigitari possint in actis ..."

[69] Lega (ed. Bart.), *op. cit.*, II, p. 744, n. 11.

na legis dictamina; sed hodie canonies, uti clarissime patet, etiam errandi occasionem repulerunt; bene determinatis elemento *subiectivo* et *objectivo* moralis certitudinis in iudice. —Quamobrem dum canon praecipit ex. g. *unum testem plenam fidem non facere,* vult prohibere ne iudex, tantum unius testimonio nitatur in definitione causarum, asserendo, se inde hausisse certitudinem moralem; nam in communi hominum aestimatione unius attestatio non sufficit ad definiendam inter duos contendentes litem. Sed si iudex in sua sententia demonstrare posset unius attestationem esse vallatam praesumptionibus, indiciis ex actis promanantibus et aliis probationibus, nemo inficiatur sententiam esse legitimam, quia subiectiva aestimatio elementis obiectivis corroboratur.

"Mens enim nostrae legis est, ponere certos limites subiectivae aestimationi probationum; et adigere iudicem ut rationem reddens in sententia demonstret argumenta suae persuasionis esse obiectiva seu innixa in actis et probatis: quare non habetur probatio legalis sed *cautio legalis* de elementis a iudice assumendis ut suam concipiat et demonstret atque probet certitudinem moralem."

Scholion. Evaluation of Unsworn or Unsigned Depositions

According to article 96, § 1, if the summoned person refuses to testify under oath, and if the presiding judge or auditor nevertheless considers that the testimony will be of value to ascertain the truth, he may receive the testimony; but mention should be made in the acts of the fact of the refusal to take the oath and the reason for it. This latter procedure is particularly important for the evaluation, for the judges of the tribunal will often have to depend upon the information set down by the auditor in order to arrive at the probative value of the unsworn deposition. All the considerations as discussed in the foregoing chapter should be taken into account; but specifically the probative value of an unsworn deposition will depend to a large extent upon the motive or reason for the person's refusal to swear.[70]

[70] Cf. *supra*, p. 86.

The probative value of unsworn depositions as such will be the greater, then, as the motive for not swearing is the more grave and sincere. Thus, the taking of an oath, which has for its essence the invocation of God to witness the truth, would be empty and meaningless in the case of atheists, pantheists, or materialists who either allegedly have no belief in a personal God, or adore false gods.[71] A solemn promise from such persons upon their honor to tell the truth can in many instances be considered the equivalent to an oath in assuring that the deposition is truthful. Likewise, depositions given by those who, like the Quakers and Mennonites, refuse to take an oath on religious grounds can often have considerable probatory value.[72]

If a God-fearing non-Catholic or Jew, however, would refuse to take the oath, but is otherwise willing to testify, there would seem to be grounds for viewing their depositions with suspicion, and, consequntly, considerably less probatory value could be attached to such depositions. If a Catholic would refuse to take an oath, and perchance the auditor would nevertheless, have allowed his deposition very little probatory value could be given his statements. Practically considered, the only value inherent in such testimony would be the fact that it gives an indication as to where other and more valuable evidence might be secured, and serves to corroborate such evidence.

Schmalzgrueber[73] and Reiffenstuel[74] stated that unsworn testimonies do not furnish even partial proof, but do beget presumptions. Such a presumption has this practical application that, if the evidence furnished by both parties is about equal, the judge would decide in favor of the party who has the greater number of unsworn witnesses.[75] This statement, of course, is subject to many qualifications. In brief, one may say that the unsworn depositions of parties,

[71] Moriarity, *Oaths in Eclesiastical Courts*, p. 53.
[72] Cf. Moriarity, *loc. cit.*
[73] *Ius Ecclesiasticum Universum*, lib. II, tit. XX, n. 89.
[74] *Ius Canonicum Universum*, lib. II, tit. XX, n. 479.
[75] Moriarity, *op. cit.*, p. 55.

witnesses, and experts will have greater or lesser value according to the character and motives of the person. No specific rule of measurement can be given: each deposition will have to be evaluated in the light of accompanying circumstances and conditions.

As in unsworn testimony, it is left to the discretion of the judge to evaluate testimony to which the deponent refuses to affix his signature. This refusal would rarely happen when the person has consented to appear before the court; it occurs not infrequently when the rogatory commission is used, or under similar circumstances in the same diocese. In any case, it can happen that the person will answer the questions, perhaps even swear to the truthfulness of his answers, but for personal reasons will refuse to sign the deposition. The judge must prudently estimate the reason, and indicate the facts and his conclusions for the evaluation of the tribunal.

This writer can recall two such cases, in which the testimony was actually of considerable probative value. In the first, the witness was a bookkeeper who absolutely refused to sign his deposition, although he was otherwise quite cooperative; his reason was that he knew too many people "who got into trouble by signing things." In the other case, the witness belonged to a religious sect deeply opposed to things Catholic; he answered the questions, unsworn, with some reluctance, but refused to sign. In all such cases the judges will have to consider the circumstances surrounding the refusal to sign, before they reach a final conclusion as to the value of the testimony rendered.

CHAPTER IV

THE EVALUATION OF EXPERT OPINION

ART. I. THE DIFFERENCE BETWEEN CANONICAL AND MEDICAL CONCEPTS

In his evaluation of the testimony of experts, a knowledge of the physiological and psychological phenomena involved will be of considerable help to the judge. While it is beyond the scope of this study to enter into any extensive discussion of impotence and insanity, it may properly be pointed out that the two terms stand for different concepts in ecclesiastical jurisprudence and in medical science. For this reason it is very important that the experts should possess proper instruction beforehand as to the meaning and import of these terms in the ecclesiastical forum.

The words "impotence" and "consummation" are accepted with various meanings among different groups of men. The essence of potency or of consummation as the Church understands them will have to be carefully explained and acknowledged.[1] Causes involving the impediment of impotence occur not infrequently in matrimonial tribunals; it

[1] S.R.R., *Dec.*, V (1913), 31-32: "Praeprimis notandum venit, potentiam coeundi alio sensu sumi a medicis peritis et alio a iuris canonici interpretibus. Iuxta peritos ... potentia coeundi ex parte viri idem est ac potentia ad copulam imperfectam, quae per se non sit apta ad generationem ex defectu veri seminis; et ideo eam distinguunt a potentia generandi, quae est potentia ad copulam perfectam, seu de se aptam ad prolis generationem; e contra, sacri iuris interpretes potentiam coeundi non distinguunt a potentia generandi. Et ideo utraque impotentia, sive coeundi, sive generandi, eo sensu quo sumitur a medicis peritis, constituit impedimentum, quod iure naturae dirimit matrimonium; at eo sensu quo ea definitur a canonistis, hoc impedimentum constituitur tantum ab impotentia coeundi, quia pro istis impotentia generandi est mera sterilitas, quae nec dirimit nec impedit matrimonium."

is absolutely imperative, therefore, that the judges and other officials of the Church's courts have very clear and definite notions of the distinctions necessary for the proper understanding of this impediment, particularly of the difference between impotence and sterility, and between relative and absolute impotence.[2]

ART. II. CASES CHANGED FROM IMPOTENCE TO NON-CONSUMMATION

If, while the evidence for impotence is being weighed, it becomes evident that proof of non-consummation rather than of impotence has been established in the judgment of the collegiate tribunal, the acts of the cause together with the tribunal's opinion must be sent to the Sacred Congregation of the Sacraments.[3] The permission to prepare and draw up a non-consummation cause, as it is ordinarily demanded by the Sacred Congregation,[4] need not be secured in such a circumstance. The published volumes of the S. R. Rota clearly indicate that quite a few cases involving the impediment of impotence are eventually solved on the basis of non-consummation.[5] If the inability to establish proof of impotence becomes evident, but the concomitantly indicated non-consummation is still not sufficiently proved, the tribunal has immediate authority to commit the case to the presiding judge or to the auditor for the completing of the proofs. Only thereafter need the case be forwarded to the Holy See.[6] The same procedure obtains when probable non-consummation appears in a cause originally presented on the grounds of lack of consent, coercion and fear, etc., but without sufficient proof.[7]

[2] Doheny, *Canonical Procedure in Matrimonial Cases*, I, 591.

[3] Art. 206, § 1.

[4] Reg. 2, *Regulae Servandae*—*AAS*, XV (1923), 392. If one of the parties is a non-Catholic, the acts are sent to the Holy Office. (*AAS*, XX (1928), 75.)

[5] Doheny, *loc. cit.*

[6] Cf. art. 206, § 1.

[7] Art. 206, § 2.

ART. III. DIVERGENCE OF TERMINOLOGY CONCERNING INSANITY

Concerning insanity, there is a decided divergence, and even a contradiction, existing between the terminology adopted by canonists and that accepted by psychological and psychiatric authorities. The Code and the canonists use the word *amentia* as a general term to signify any kind of mental ailment causing an incapacity of responsible action and correct thought; *dementia* is synonymous with monomania —i.e., the having of fixed ideas concerning certain spheres of thought, though otherwise the person remains apparently rational.[8] Judges must form their conclusions and make their decisions according to Canon Law and the norms of ecclesiastical jurisprudence, based on the principles of rational psychology integrated with the findings of clinical psychology and psychiatry, thus avoiding the tenets of pseudo-scientific hypotheses.[9]

So much attention is frequently given to the opinions of experts in matrimonial causes of insanity that the judges sometimes fail to evaluate properly the usual and common indications of insanity, as they are known to everyone. For this reason, witnesses are to be summoned and questioned about the ordinary habits of the person, whose sanity is doubtful. The daily actions of such a person, his conversation, his tone of voice, his manners, his idiosyncrasies, his manner of dress, the measure of his regard for others, his conduct in company, and similar indications furnish invaluable norms for forming correct judgments as to the sanity of the person.[10]

Another point of importance is that the proper distinctions must be clearly made between those actions which a person performs in consequence of an acquired habit in

[8] Pickett, *Mental Affliction and Church Law,* p. 147.

[9] Cf. Doheny, *op. cit.,* I, 792; Nuttin, *Psychoanalysis and Personality* (New York: Sheed and Ward, 1953), pp. VI-VII; 162-163.

[10] S.R.R., *Dec.,* VII (1916), 211; Doheny, *op. cit.,* I, 794.

[11] S.R.R., *Dec.,* XIV (1922), 320; Doheny, *loc. cit.*

his daily life and those which proceed from deliberate decisions. The former are almost automatic or mechanical actions and do not require a great deal of sanity; the latter reflect the powers of the mind and will of the person.[11]

Art. IV. Probative Value of Expert Opinion

The direct findings of experts have a greater value as proof than the conclusions drawn from their findings. When the report of an expert contains merely the recountal of what he has observed in the course of his inspection, his testimony to these facts has at least the same value as the testimony of any direct witness. Thus, an expert's report on the condition in which he has found the hymen, or on the condition in which he has found the mental conditions of a person, must not be easily set aside.[12] However, when the expert's report goes on to draw inferences from the observations made, these inferences must be accorded such deference as the ability and logic of the expert rightly demand from the judge, but they are not necessarily conclusive, for the expert is not the judge of the cause.[13] The same holds true with regard to expert inspection of documents.[14]

As in the case of witnesses, the concordant reports and testimonies of several experts are of stronger probative value than the single testimony. When two or more experts agree upon facts witnessed during their expert examination, their testimony, like that of other witnesses, is generally conclusive.[15] The testimony of one expert may be conclusive when it is added to the deposition of the parties or to other personal presumptions, but it does not of itself constitute full proof, for the experts ordinarily are not *testes qualificati*.[16]

[12] S.C.C., 18 iun. 1831—Pallottini, XIII, p. 396, nn. 76, 77; S.R.R., *Dec.*, I (1909), 87; S.R.R., *Dec.*, VII (1915), 219.

[13] S.C.C., 29 maii, 1852—Pallottini, XIII, 47; S.R.R., *Dec.*, XII (1920), 209; S.R.R., *Dec.*, X (1918), 3.

[14] Bassibey, *Le Mariage*, n. 473.

[15] *Instructio Austriaca*, § 174—*Collectio Lacensis*, V, 1307.

[16] S.R.R., *Dec.*, II (1910), 285; cf. *supra*, p. 195.

When two or more experts are in agreement on an inference immediately and legitimately derived from the known facts, there arises a strong argument in favor of their conclusions, and in some causes this argument is tantamount to conclusive proof.[17]

The conclusions, inferences and opinions of the experts should be based upon facts judicially proved—i.e., documentated, properly witnessed in court, or discovered by the experts appointed by the judge in the course of official inspection.[18] If they are founded on facts not judicially proved, they are not strictly to be classified as an expert's proofs.[19] Thus, the Rota in a cause involving impotence rejected the expert opinion that was founded on the extraneous medical history relating to the cause.[20] There is, however, a greater leniency observable in cases involving lack of consent because of insanity.[21]

Informal inspections made by experts not appointed by the judge, but rather consulted by the parties, do not strictly serve to establish an expert's proof in the canonical sense. Nevertheless, it has been the practice of the Roman Curia to ratify such informal inspections when the making of a new inspection has become impossible or very difficult.[22] According to article 143 of the *Instructio,* those persons who in causes of impotence or insanity examined the consort privately are debarred from acting in the capacity of a

[17] *Instructio Austriaca,* § 174—*Collectio Lacensis,* V, 1307.

[18] Wanenmacher, *Canonical Evidence in Marriage Cases,* n. 325.

[19] Wanenmacher, *loc. cit.*

[20] S.R.R., *Dec.,* V (1913), 673: "Primo notandum est iudicium Medicorum fundari non solum in repertis ex peracta inspectione corporis, sed etiam in factis ab aliis extraiudicialiter et sine iuramento relatis, quae iuxta peritos constituit 'criterium historicum' . . . Iamvero excedit competentiam medici iudicare in causa matrimoniali de veritate vel secus huiusmodi factorum extraiudicialiter relatorum, unde cadit fundamentum 'historici critici.' "

[21] S.R.R., *Dec.,* VII (1916), 211: "Ceterum in praesenti specie, peritia non omnino defuit; medici quidem sententiam suam de morbo Mariae ore proprio coram iudice non expresserunt, sed eorum dicta pluribus testibus relata sunt."

[22] S.R.R., *Dec.,* XII (1920), 75; S.R.R., *Dec.,* V (1913), 23-24.

canonical expert; however, in a cause of impotence, they *may* be introduced as witnesses, and in the cause of insanity they *must* be.

ART. V. OBLIGATION TO FOLLOW EXPERT OPINION

The judges must therefore not only weigh well the reports and the testimonies of the experts, but they must also consider carefully all the circumstances attending the cause.[24] The tribunal is not bound to follow the opinions of the experts, even if their conclusions are concordant, but should carefully weigh also any other attendant circumstances.[25] Even the opinions and conclusions of the one who reflects a superior skill *(peritior)* need not be followed by the judges.[26] The tribunal, in giving the reasons for its decision, must indicate upon which arguments it admitted or rejected the conclusions of the experts.[27]

An example of the rejection of the opinion of the experts is given in a Rota decision handed down in 1937.[28] A certain Galla declared that as the result of an excessive use of drugs she was habitually deprived of the use of reason for some time previous to her marriage. Some witnesses corroborated this assertion, but the majority of them denied it. Two experts had been called by the diocesan tribunal; they had tried to prove that Galla did not have sufficient power of mind and will to give a matrimonial consent. In examining the events preceding the marriage, the Rota learned from the testimony of the pastor, the relatives, and the friends that Galla apparently enjoyed sufficient powers of mind and will to enable her to perform a truly human act and to enter upon a marriage contract. There was every indication that Galla had freely and voluntarily given consent, that she had truly loved her husband, and that she desired the

[23] Cf. cans. 1978; 1982.
[24] Can. 1804, § 1.
[25] Art. 154, § 1; S.R.R., *Dec.*, III (1911), 453 ff.
[26] S.R.R., *Dec.*, X (1918), 3; S.R.R., *Dec.*, XX (1928), 80.
[27] Art. 154, § 2; cf. can. 1804, § 2.
[28] S.R.R., *Dec.*, XXIX (1937), 195-196.

marriage. The Rota called upon a person of profounder skill *(peritior)* to study the case in great detail; however, even some of his opinions and conclusions were rejected by the judges of the Rota:

> "Iam dictum est peritiorem errasse, quia ad valide contrahendum quoad *intellectum* asserit usum rationis non sufficere, sed insuper requiri sanam criticam, prudentiam, consilium, iudicium, etc. Etiam *quoad voluntatem* plus postulat quam necessarium est. Dato siquidem, non concesso, quod actrix sine iniectione morphinae consensum suum non dedisset, id in casu non obstaret valido matrimonio. Nam indifferens est, *quomodo* quis ad volendum perveniat, utrum nempe tantum ab intrinseco, an etiam ab incitamento extrinseco: requiritur scilicet et sufficit ad valide contrahendum, ut contrahens ponat positivum actum voluntatis, legitime manifestatum. Iamvero non est demonstratum actricem ad talem actum ponendum fuisse incapacem; patet potius contrarium, *Superata* enim *resistentia consanguineorum, victa incertitudine subiectiva,* Galla reapse sibi proposuit nuptias inire, omnia ad hunc finem praeparavit, ad ecclesiam ivit ibique consensum suum dedit; quomodo peritior ex antecedenti incertitudine actricis consensum eiusdem non valere iudicet, non intelligitur. Hae proinde sunt rationes, ob quas Patres de turno neque dicta testium intentioni actricis favorabilia, neque vota peritorum in favorem actricis pronuntiata, acceptare possint."

The final decision therefore was a "*non constare.*"

CHAPTER V

THE EVALUATION OF DOCUMENTARY EVIDENCE

Proof by means of documents, both public and private, is admitted in every kind of trial.[1] As implicit in the very term, a public document is one that emanates from public authority, while a private document is one that depends upon private authority for its efficacy. Canon Law has always considered documentary proof or written evidence as one of the most cogent forms of proof.[2] It is important to note, however, that a mere document does not constitute proof until it has been properly scrutinized and adjudged genuine.[3] Even then the contents must be examined carefully before a determination can be reached by the court regarding the measure of credence to be given, and the store of value to be attached to the facts set forth in the document.[4] Documents do not have probative force in court and therefore cannot be admitted unless they are originals or are presented in a duly authenticated copy and consigned to the chancery of the tribunal.[5]

The tribunal, i.e., either the presiding judge or the auditor, is to search diligently upon its own authority for documents of both kinds, unless the parties submit them voluntarily, and should interrogate the parties and witnesses about them in the examination.[6] The party, the defender of

[1] Can. 1812; art. 155.

[2] Cf. Doheny, *Canonical Procedure in Matrimonial Cases*, I, 399.

[3] Cf. cans. 1814-1817; 1820; art. 160, 161.

[4] S.R.R., *Dec.*, IX (1917), 135.

[5] Art. 159, § 1; can. 1819. Art. 159, § 2, goes on to state that in order that a copy be considered authentic, "oportet sit manuscriptum . . ." It is obvious from the practice of the Holy See that this need not be restricted to handwritten copies, but includes typed, printed, or even photostatic copies, when duly signed and attested.—cf. Doheny, *op. cit.*, I, 403.

[6] Art. 158.

the bond, or the examining judge *ex officio* has the right to demand that the complete document, either the original or an authentic copy, be submitted to the court whenever only an excerpt of the document has been presented, even though it has been transcribed in an authentic form.[7]

Whenever a party refuses to submit a document which he is alleged to possess, and which is presumed to have some important bearing on the cause, the presiding judge or the auditor, at the request of the party, or *ex officio,* is to determine by means of a decree whether and in what way the document is to be exhibited.[8] If the party persists in his refusal even after this decree, the collegiate tribunal is to decide what significance to attach to the refusal.[9] If the party, however, denies that he possesses the document, the examining judge can invite him to confirm this denial by means of an oath, if he deem this expedient.[10]

Art. I. Public Documents

Canon Law presumes that public documents—civil or ecclesiastical—are genuine,[11] i.e., that they have emanated from public officials, while acting within the limits of their competent authority, who have set down in such documents the true facts.[12] This presumption of law results in the fact that public documents provide full proof in court.[13] However, a distinction must be made between the document itself as a written attestation of a contract or transaction, and the juridical force itself of the recorded act. Thus, the parochial marriage records will not provide full proof of the validity of a marriage, but only of its canonical celebration,

[7] Art. 166.
[8] Art. 167, § 1; cf. can. 1824, § 1.
[9] Art. 167, § 2.
[10] Art. 167, § 3; cf. can. 1824, § 3.
[11] Can. 1814.
[12] Cf. Lega (ed. Bart.), *Commentarius,* II, p. 790, n. 1.
[13] Can. 1816; S.R.R., *Dec.,* XXXV (1943), 437: "Adversus huiusmodi probationem, probatio contraria difficillima est . . . aequivalent nempe plenae probationi."

which latter fact of course gives rise to the presumption of validity as honored in canon 1014.[14]

Furthermore, it is not the intention of the law that public documents should furnish full proof concerning all their parts; they furnish this proof only concerning those facts which are the direct and principal object of the document.[15] It is important, therefore, for the judge to determine which facts are thus asserted, before he can properly estimate the probative value of any document. Any facts which are merely incidentally and accessorily affirmed are not included among those parts of a public document which furnish full probative value.[16] However, the mention of these incidental and accessory facts does give rise to a strong personal presumption *(praesumptio hominis)* as to their truth, and can constitute full proof in conjunction with other judicial evidence.[17] Thus, a baptismal record fully proves only the fact of the baptism conferred upon the individual named, the date of the baptism, the identity of the god-parents, and also that of the minister who conferred the sacrament; the marriage record, likewise, is conclusive proof only that the parties named gave the external matrimonial consent, that the marriage ceremony took place on the recorded date, and that the persons named as witnesses assisted in

[14] Lega (ed. Bart.), *op. cit.*, II, p. 791, n. 4: "... publicum habetur documentum publicam obtinens fidem de secuto coniugio. Dein movetur quaestio de valore matrimonii ex capite liberi consensus; contendit enim uxor se metu gravi fuisse compulsam; obstat ne introductioni actionis documentum paroeciale, matrimonium fuisse legitime celebratum? Minime sane, quia ex hoc documento evincitur factum legitimae celebrationis ad normam ss. canonum, et de hoc facto publicam facit fidem attestatio libri paroecialis; sed impraeiudicata manet quaestio de valore intrinseco coniugii ex aliquo obstante impedimento. Eadem conclusio valet pro quocumque publico documento seu ecclesiastico seu civili."

[15] Can. 1816; cf. S.R.R., *Dec.*, X (1918), 83.

[16] Noval, *De Iudiciis*, n. 550; Roberti, *De Processibus*, II, n. 370.

[17] Coronata, *Institutiones*, III, n. 1347; Muñiz, *Procedimientos Eclésiasticos*, III, n. 378; Willett, *The Probative Value of Documents in Ecclesiastical Trials*, p. 76.

that capacity.[18] But the accessory information, such as that of the date of birth, of the qualities and conditions of the persons or of their domiciles, etc., is not fully proved by the fact of being recorded in such public registers.[19]

Art. II. Affidavits and Notary Public

Affidavits are frequently resorted to as a means of documentary proof or evidence in English-speaking countries. These affidavits are written declarations or statements confirmed either by oath or by a solemn affirmation made before a notary public or other public official authorized for such purpose. Since they are oftentimes presented in ecclesiastical courts, the judge should be careful not to ascribe to them more probative force than they may canonically be permitted to carry. An affidavit merely certifies that a specific person made a solemn affirmation confirmed by oath before a duly qualified notary public at a certain time. Obviously, such a statement in itself, even though it was made under oath, does not constitute full proof[20] of the question at issue before the ecclesiastical tribunal; indeed, such an affidavit provides full proof of only one thing—that the person did make an affidavit.[21] However, declarations and affirmations contained in affidavits can give corroborative force to extant proof.[22]

If a non-Catholic refuses to appear in court to testify, but is willing to make a deposition before a notary public, this sworn statement should be secured. Such a statement is to be evaluated as an extra-judicial deposition of the person;

[18] Willett, *op. cit.*, p. 76.

[19] S.R.R., *Dec.*, VIII (1916), 71.

[20] Willett, *op. cit.*, p. 85; Doheny, *op. cit.*, I, 400.

[21] Cf.can. 1816.

[22] S.R.R., *Dec.*, XVIII (1926), 195: "Depositiones coram iudice ecclesiastico factae plene confirmantur ab iis quae coram notario civili sub iuramento declaraverunt. Hae declarationes enim, etsi perfectam probationem efficere nequeant, cum non constituant iudiciales testificationes iuxta can. 1754 et seqq., eoque magis quod in iis conficiendis defuerat vinculi defensor, cuius praesentia requiritur ad normam canonis 1587, valorem tamen adminiculativum habent."

however, it does have the added value of being a sworn statement.[23]

If the civil bond of marriage has been dissolved by divorce, or declared null, the presiding judge or the auditor should see to it that the parties submit the petition presented to the civil court as well as the sentence given by the magistrate; should the case demand it, even the acts of the civil suit may be requested.[24]

ART. III. PRIVATE DOCUMENTS

Letters, contracts, last wills, and testaments as well as all other writings drawn up by a private individual in his private capacity are included among the number of private documents.[25] Documents issued by non-Catholic churches may also be brought into court, but they constitute proof only in the quality and with the limitations of private documents.[26] Private documents, as in the case of public documents, furnish proof only concerning those facts which are the direct and principal object of the document.[27]

The Code admits all private writings as proof only if and when they are produced in court and appear to the judge to be plainly of value.[28] Thus, depending upon its individual nature, a private document may furnish complete proof, partial proof, or be destitute of all probative value, against its author or signatory, according to the discretion of the

[23] S.R.R., *Dec.*, XVIII (1926), 195: "Prout enim a notario publico rite confectae fuerunt secundum Statuum Foederatorum Americae Septentrionalis leges, documenta publica constituunt, ideoque ex can. 1816 'fidem faciunt de iis quae directe et principaliter in eisdem affirmantur.' "

[24] Art.168.

[25] Can. 1813, § 3; art. 156, § 3.

[26] Wanenmacher, *Canonical Evidence in Marriage Cases*, n. 378.

[27] Cf. Lega (ed. Bart.) *op. cit.*, II, 793. There, by way of commentary on can 1816, the following is stated: "... canon respicit documenta publica; sed suapte vi, regula privata quoque complectitur documenta; quia documentum ex sua intentione ordinatur ad probationem *faciendam* de aliquo facto iuridico apud notarium secuto et veluti circumscribitur ad eiusdem facti relationem et attestationem."

[28] Willett, *op. cit.*, p. 101.

judge when the latter has considered all the circumstances attending the case.[29]

Letters are usually of particular importance in matrimonial trials, since through them often an extra-judicial confession can be established.[30] The parties frequently express their sentiments and convictions more fully and intimately in letters than in any other documents. Consequently, special scrutiny should be made of the envelope and postmark, the handwriting, the phrases employed, and the like; even the watermark of the paper may furnish important clues as to the genuineness of the letters.[31]

Letters that the parties wrote to each other or to other persons before or after the marriage, but *tempore non suspecto*,[32] can be private documents of no little probative weight, particularly in cases of fear and conditional consent, provided their genuineness[33] and the time when they were written are clearly certain.[34] The presiding judge or the auditor should seek out these letters in good time, warning the parties and the witnesses that they should present to the tribunal any such letters which they may have; however, the letters submitted as evidence by one party must always be formally acknowledged by the other party as to the genuinity of their authorship.[35] If the other consort is contumacious and refuses to make such acknowledgment, the court must take proper measures to assure itself of their genuineness.

Letters, like other private documents, have that weight which must be accorded them in view of the circumstances

[29] Willett, *loc. cit.*

[30] Cf. *supra*, p. 171.

[31] Doheny, *op. cit.*, I, 401.

[32] Cf. *infra*, p. 173, for discussion of *tempus non suspectus*.

[33] Art. 163, § 1, here uses the word "authenticity," but it is evident that it refers to and means the genuineness of the authorship of the writings.—Willett, *op. cit.*, p. 102.

[34] Art. 163.

[35] Art. 163, § 2. Cf. Willett, *op. cit.*, pp. 88-90; Doheny, *op. cit.*, I, 407-408.

and particularly the time when they were written.[36] Through a reading of the decisions of the Rota, it becomes quite obvious in many cases that without the evidence supplied by letters the true facts would have been very difficult if not impossible to prove.[37]

Anonymous letters and all other kinds of anonymous documents cannot, of themselves, be considered even as an indication of proof except in so far as they refer to facts that may be otherwise proved.[38] This ruling is in accord with canon 1645, § 4, which states that anonymous letters which add nothing to the merits of a case are to be destroyed after the cause is finished. Anonymous letters may be used at the prudent discretion of the judge, for they may give a hint as to the way of inquiry into the truth.[39]

ART. IV. DEFECTIVE DOCUMENTS

In the case of defective documents—namely, those which show erasures, corrections, interpolations, or other defects —it is left to the discretion of the judge to determine whether and how far they prove anything.[40] A written instrument is invalidated by alteration if the following conditions concur: 1) if the alteration is material; 2) if it was made intentionally; 3) if it was made by the grantee or promisee; 4) if it was made without the consent of the grantor or promisor, and was made after the execution of the instrument.[41] An erasure, interpolation, correction or any other defect appearing in either a public or a private instrument may or may not affect its probative value; the judge has the discretionary authority, after carefully examining the document,

[36] Art. 164.

[37] Willett (*op. cit.*, p. 103) cites a long list of Rota decisions illustrating the value of letters as evidence.

[38] Art. 165.

[39] S.R.R., *Dec.*, III (1911), 274; S.R.R., *Dec.*, IV (1912), 112.

[40] Can. 1818.

[41] Woywod-Smith, *A Practical Commentary on the Code of Canon Law* (7. printing, 2 vols., New York: Joseph F. Wagner, Inc., 1943), II, 287.

to determine what degree of credibility, if any, is to be accorded to the defective document.

Willett recounts an interesting example of a public document which retained its probative force despite a false date.[42] A priest had falsely dated a marriage record in order to make two children, born out of wedlock, appear as legitimate. In the trial regarding the nullity of the parents' marriage it was argued that, since the date was proved false, the entire document was to be considered false and useless as evidence. But the Rota decided otherwise. Its contention was that there had been a motive for falsifying the date, but to suppose in addition that the priest had drawn up a document without performing the marriage was absurd.[43]

On the other hand, the date can be the determining factor of the usefulness of the document. In such a case any doubt concerning the dates will have to be settled before the judge can ascribe any probatory force to the document.

The absence of the proper signature on entries made in public registers does not change their nature, for such entries, when once made, are regarded as public documents furnishing juridical credibility.[44] Even if the records appear on papers detached from their proper books, they may still be considered as parts of the register, and hence do not thereby lose their value as public instruments, provided that they have the proper marks of authenticity.[45]

An erasure, interpolation, correction or any other defect found in a public or private document does not destroy the probative value which the instrument has by its nature, unless these defects occur in a notable or substantial part of the said instrument, e.g., regarding the filled-in date and place indicative of the time and locality attending the draft-

[42] Willett, *op. cit.*, p. 104.
[43] S.R.R., *Dec.*, I (1909), 158.
[44] S.R.R., *Dec.*, II (1910), 221.
[45] S.R.R., *Dec.*, I (1909), 198.

ing of the instrument, or regarding the name of the one who drafted the instrument.[46]

In a similar way, any defects which occur in that part of the document which directly bears upon the matter at issue will destroy the probative force of the document only in so far as they render doubtful the juridical import or meaning of the document.[47] Judges should not lightly discard documents in which there are erasures or corrections, if despite such defects the proper and original import and meaning of such written instruments can nevertheless be ascertained and certified.[48]

[46] Willett, *op. cit.*, p. 106.
[47] Willett, *loc. cit.*
[48] Cf. c. 9, X, *de crimine falsi*, V, 20.

CHAPTER VI

THE USE OF PRESUMPTIONS IN EVALUATING EVIDENCE

A presumption, in the probative sense, is defined as a probable conjecture on an uncertain issue,[1] and serves as an indirect source of proof. Circumstantial evidence, adjuncts, and indications form the basis for presumptions. Presumptions which are stated in the law itself *(praesumptio iuris)* constitute full proof[2] until the contrary is shown. A full explanation of the presumptions of law is beyond the scope of this dissertation; it is to the point, however, to enumerate the presumptions of law pertaining to marriage cases. Furthermore, the judge in evaluating the judicial evidence and in drawing conclusions from the acts of the process and the proofs incorporated therein *(acta et probata)*, has the discretionary authority to deduce personal presumptions *(praesumptiones hominis)*,[3] which in turn may be of help to him in the reaching of moral certainty.

ART. I. PRESUMPTIONS OF LAW *(praesumptiones iuris)*

A. The Nature and Effects of a Presumption of Law

The real nature of the *praesumptio iuris* consists in this that the law sets down some abstract situation as a premise, which may be simply one fact or also a collection of facts and circumstances. Whenever this abstract situation materializes in a certain case, the law states the result which, as experience has shown, will ordinarily occur. Obviously, then, it may be demonstrated that in some particular case

[1] Can. 1825, § 1.
[2] Can. 1747, 2°; can. 1827.
[3] Can. 1828.

the effect did not follow; however, the presumption enacted in the law still remains in general force.[4]

A presumption of law has two striking effects: a) it constitutes full proof until the contrary becomes established, and b) the entire burden of proof is shifted onto the one who challenges the presumption. In the latter case, however, some obligation rests on the party who claims the support of a presumption of law: he must establish in a judicial manner, the facts upon which the presumption rests, during the process of the trial.[5]

To overthrow this presumption of law, the opponent challenges either the presumption itself or the facts upon which it rests. In the first case, he attacks the presumption directly by attempting to prove that, while a foundation for the presumption does indeed exist, it is in fact the contrary of the presumption that evinces the evident truth; in the second case, he attacks the presumption indirectly by attempting to show that the very foundation for a presumption is lacking inasmuch as there are wanting any and all facts or constitutive parts that could serve to form a real foundation.[6]

B. Presumptions of Law Applicable to Marriage Causes

Presumptions of law applicable to marriage causes are:

1) Marriage once contracted is presumed valid until proof of its invalidity becomes established.[7]

2) Once a married couple have lived together, consummation is presumed.[8]

3) A baptism whose invalidity would nullify a marriage is presumed to be a valid baptism until the contrary is proved.[9]

[4] Cf. Manning, *Presumptions of Law in Marriage Cases*, The Catholic University of America Canon Law Studies, no. 94 (Washington, D.C.: The Catholic University of America, 1935), p. 15.

[5] Cf. Manning, *op. cit.*, p. 17.

[6] Manning, *loc. cit.*

[7] Can. 1014.

[8] Can. 1015, § 2.

[9] Can. 1070, § 2.

4) Persons after the age of puberty are presumed to have sufficient knowledge about marriage to give a valid consent.[10]

5) Internal consent is presumed to be present when there is a manifestation of consent through external signs in the marriage ceremony.[11]

6) Although a marriage has been contracted invalidly because of an impediment, consent once given is presumed to persevere until its revocation is proved.[12]

7) The child's father is presumed to be he whom legitimate wedlock points out as such, unless the contrary is proved by way of conclusive arguments.[13]

8) Children born at least six months after the celebration of the marriage, or within ten months of the dissolution of conjugal life, are presumed to be legitimate in their very conception.[14]

9) Condonation by the innocent party is presumed when within six months upon gaining knowledge of the guilty partner's act of adultery, the former has neither expelled nor deserted the latter, nor raised any legally warranted accusation.[15]

10) A marriage which during the lifetime of the parties remained uncontested is upon the death of either or both of the parties to be presumed as valid in such a manner that no proof to the contrary is tolerated unless it serve in vindication of some incidental question, such as the claims of legitimacy or succession in behalf of the children.[16]

11) Public documents are presumed to be genuine until the contrary is proved by way of conclusive arguments.[17]

It was the opinion of some scholars that all compelling *(violentae)* presumptions were presumptions of law. This opinion does not obtain in the legislation of today. Likewise results in nature or the matters of necessary cause and effect are not to be regarded as presumptions of law, e.g.,

[10] Can. 1082, § 2.
[11] Can. 1086, § 1.
[12] Can. 1093.
[13] Can. 1115, § 1.
[14] Can. 1115, § 2.
[15] Can. 1129, § 2.
[16] Can. 1972.
[17] Can. 1814.

smoke from a chimney means fire below, *"coisse quae peperit,"* etc. These are not conjectures, for there is no underlying possible doubt.[18]

A unique type of *praesumptio iuris* mentioned in the Code is the *praesumptio iuris et de iure;* the only canon which in the entire Code reflects this type is canon 1904, § 1, which ordains that an adjudicated issue *(res iudicata)* is by reason of the *praesumptio iuris et de iure* to be held as true, so that it cannot be directly impugned.[19]

Art. II. Personal Presumptions *(praesumptiones hominis)*

Personal presumptions *(praesumptiones hominis)* of the judge are of particular value for his arriving at the truth in causes involving questions of consent,[20] fear,[21] and non-consummation.[22]

A. Probatory Value of Personal Presumption

According to the degree of directness with which they are drawn from certain and determinate facts connected with the cause, and consequently also according to the degree of force with which they compel the mind, personal presumptions are known as light, grave, or dominant.[23] These degrees of value are not the result of any arbitrary classification. Experience, national customs, and such norms in general as influence the estimation of human conduct determine their weight.[24] Consequently, degrees of probability are to be admitted as well as degrees in the signs that lead up to these probabilities.

If the judge entertains personal presumptions which are light, weak, or rash, and which do not spring from certain

[18] Manning, *op. cit.*, p. 18.
[19] Manning, *op. cit.*, pp. 24-25.
[20] Art. 174; cf. S.R.R., *Dec.*, XXXIII (1941), 887.
[21] Cf. S.R.R., *Dec.*, XXXIII (1941), 10.
[22] Reg. 81, *Regulae Servandae—AAS,* XV (1923), 408.
[23] Cf. Reg. 81, *Regulae Servandae—AAS,* XV (1923), 408.
[24] Manning, *op. cit.*, p. 11.

and definite facts directly connected with the case, or which are unduly extended in their scope, he cannot utilize such presumptions as offering judicial evidence.[25] Thus he cannot allowably presume the nullity of a marriage in view of the contempt of court on the part of the respondent. Nor can he allowably draw up presumptions for whole classes of marriages. The Rota in 1909 forbade missionaries in Oceania and America both to presume that, because certain Methodists and pagans held a frivolous view of marriage and readily obtained divorces, such marriages were invalid, and as a result thereof to settle marriage causes on this presumption.[26] Similarly, when the Holy Office was asked whether in deciding marriage causes one could presume that the baptisms in certain sects, viz., of the Disciples of Christ, the Presbyterians, the Congregationalists, the Baptists, and Methodists, were invalid for lack of intention of the part of the minister, it answered, in 1949, that the baptisms in said sects must be presumed valid on this score until the contrary is proved.[27] A valid *praesumptio hominis,* based on Rotal jurisprudence, is the presumption of the existence of insanity at the time of the marriage ceremony, when the fact of insanity both before and after the marriage is sufficiently established.[28]

Grave, and even dominant, personal presumptions have not as a general rule the value of full proof, and alone will ordinarily not be sufficient to offset the effect of the legal presumption for the validity of a marriage; but they may have the value of partial proof, even against presumptions of law.[29] The Rota in a recent decision clearly sets forth the relationship between presumptions of law and personal presumptions:[30]

[25] Cf. can. 1828.

[26] S.R.R., *Dec.,* I, (1909), 158.

[27] S.C.S.Off., 28 dec. 1949—*AAS,* 41 (1949), 650.

[28] S.R.R., *Dec.,* V (1913), 565; cf. S.R.R., *Dec.* XIV (1922), 312-320.

[29] S.R.R., *Dec.,* IV (1912), 87; S.R.R., *Dec.,* IV (1912), 240; S.R.R., *Dec.,* XIII (1921), 265.

[30] S.R.R., *Dec.,* XXXIII (1941), 370. It is interesting to note that

"Haec tamen 'disputatio iuris' concludi non potest, quin dicantur quaedam verba etiam circa 'praesumptiones hominis,' ne scilicet Patres Turni praesentis suo silentio approbare videantur quae hac de re in sententia Turni antecedentis inveniuntur. Patres appellati, qui adeo contrarii sunt praesumptionibus hominis, sub influxu fuisse videntur alicuius libelli cui titulus *Incipit lamentatio Vinculi,* auctoris anonymi, ubi inter alia sub n. 64 proclamatur falsum principium: 'Contra iuris praesumptionem praesumptio hominis vix admittitur.' Si hoc principium esset verum, tunc in re matrimoniali, in qua plures habentur praesumptiones iuris in favorem validitatis matrimonii, non intelligeretur, curnam tantum praesumptio hominis et non etiam aliae probationes contrariae excludi deberent. E contra, nulla praesumptio iuris—non confundenda cum praesumptione iuris et de iure—praetendit se esse normam generalem pro omni casu, sed potius semper admittit probationem contrariam. Ultro conceditur quod apud Wernz-Vidal dicitur: 'Quemadmodum in aliis probationum generibus contrarietas quaedam exsistere potest, cum v. gr. testis testi contradicat, ita in praesumptionibus conflictus non raro vitari nequit' (Vol. VI, n. 521). Et si duae praesumptiones inter se contrariae secum comparantur, norma generalis est quod 'fortior praesumptio vincat necesse est minorem. Hinc cum praesumptio iuris fortior sit praesumptione facti, generi per speciem derogetur' (loc. cit.). Sed '*si praesumptio hominis validior et verisimilior est, contra iuris etiam praesumptionem praevalet*' (Schmalzgrueber, in lib. II, tit. 23, *De praesumpt.*, n. 38); nam omnis praesumptio iuris per se est generalis et superari potest per quamlibet certam probationem contrariam, in specie, per praesumptionem hominis violentam, 'quae ex multis vel uno valde efficaci, et veritati proximo indicio formatur, et vehementer movet cogitque ad credulitatem, ita ut moraliter non relinquat dubium' (Schmalzgrueber, l.c., n. 5). Audiatur adhuc Lega, qui docet: 'Si vero praesumptio (scilicet hominis) est gravissima seu vehemens, tunc ipsa

this decision was given by a special *turnus* of five judges, who decided for nullity, overthrowing a previous Rota decision.

sufficit ad causam definiendam in foro ecclesiastico. In Decretalibus habentur textus, quibus statuitur vehementem praesumptionem efficere plenam probationem; uti vehementi praesumptioni innixus processit Salomon ad sententiam in suo celebri iudicio. In nostro iure canone 1869 ponitur regula, iudicem debere rem definire iuxta moralem certitudinem ex actis et probatis desumptam; quocirca si ex actis iudex hauriat vehementem praesumptionem, huic sententiam suam plane conformare valet. *Hoc etiam pro causis gravioribus, quales sunt matrimoniales, vim habet,* maxima tamen cum cautela et dummodo quodlibet positivum dubium ex adverso sit eliminatum' (*Commentarius in Iudicia ecclesiastica iuxta* Codicem I. C., cura Bartoccetti editus, Romae 1939, vol. II, pag. 821."

It is the part of the judge alone to determine whether the personal presumption be light, grave, or dominant, what force of proof it possesses, and what degree of certainty is derivable from it.[31]

Circumstantial evidence which gives rise to justifiable personal presumptions, especially in defective consent and non-consummation causes, is deduced from the circumstances in existence before, during, and after the marriage.[32] It is left to the discretionary authority of the judge to estimate what conjectures suffice for the begetting of moral certitude in each cause,[33] although it is evident that greater force is to be attributed to indications according as their proximity to the act is greater.[34]

A legitimate presumption in favor of the nullity of a marriage in a particular case is usually based on more than one of the sources of judicial evidence which have been established.[35] Since in their import the circumstances are

[31] S.R.R., *Dec.*, V (1913), 18; S.R.R., *Dec.*, VII (1915), 125.

[32] Art. 174; cf. S.R.R., *Dec.*, XXXIII (1941), 887; S.R.R., *Dec.*, XXXV (1943), 625.

[33] S.R.R., *Dec.*, XXVII (1935), 79; cf. Sanchez, *De Matrimonio*, lib. II, disp. XLV, n. 5.

[34] S.R.R., *Dec.*, XV (1923), 167.

[35] Cf. Roberti, *Schemata*, B, Can. 135: "Quando agitur de probando aliquo facto interno, ut puta metu, ficto consensu, aut aliis eiusmodi,

never identical from case to case, it would be rash to attribute in all cases a similar probative value to the presence of a particular circumstance.[36]

B. Examples from the Jurisprudence of the Rota

1. The following circumstances gave rise to the presumption that a true consent had been given: The fact of a friendship and affection before marriage usually outweighs the claim that the ceremony was submitted to only because of parental urging, the fear of scandal, the loss of reputation, etc.[37] The usual tokens, such as love-letters and frequent visits, serve to establish the existence of such a friendship.[38] Similarly, when the party declared before the ceremony that he desired to marry, there is an indication that his marital consent was not feigned.[39] Hesitation and reluctance in consenting, or the shedding of tears in so doing, more frequently indicate a genuine rather than a fictitious consent.[40] This behavior may be explained in certain cases by the natural hesitancy or timidity of the party, by the gravity of the moment, by fear of the parent's displeasure, or by many other reasons.[41] Yet these same facts may also indicate true fear when joined with other indications and evidence.[42]

ita effectus externos, indicia, praesumptiones, adminicula ponderet et cumulet iudex, ut quid sit verum assequi possit."

[36] S.R.R., *Dec.*, I (1909), 59: "... resolutiones S. Congregationis non facile esse trahendas de casu ad casum..." The Sacred Congregation of the Council handled matrimonial causes prior to 1908, when the Rota was re-established.

[37] S.R.R., *Dec.*, XXX (1938), 346; S.R.R., *Dec.*, XXIX (1937), 670; S.R.R., *Dec.*, XXVIII (1936), 11; S.R.R., *Dec.*, XXIII (1931), 197.

[38] S.R.R., *Dec.*, XV (1933), 80; S.R.R., *Dec.*, XXV (1933), 246.

[39] S.R.R., *Dec.*, XXIX (1937), 739; S.R.R., *Dec.*, XXVIII (1936), 99.

[40] S.R.R., *Dec.*, XXVIII (1936), 134; S.R.R., *Dec.*, XXVI (1934), 171.

[41] S.R.R., *Dec.*, XXIX (1937), 318; S.R.R., *Dec.* XXIX (1937), 736; S.R.R., *Dec.*, XXVI (1934), 171; S.R.R., *Dec.*, XXV (1933), 248.

[42] Cf. S.R.R., *Dec.*, XXX (1938), 345; S.R.R., *Dec.*, XVIII (1926), 260.

Save in the case wherein the simulation was motivated by lust, any display of affection for the other consort at the beginning of conjugal life supplies a basis for a presumption that the marital consent was not merely fictitious.[43] The natural and principal means of manifesting such an affection is in the marriage act itself; thus, the consummation of the marriage, especially when it has been prompt and frequent, furnishes a weighty indication in favor of the presence of a true marital consent.[44] Moreover, an argument for the presence of true consent is had when the cohabitation of the consorts has endured for a lengthy period of time.[45]

2. The following circumstances gave rise to presumption that a true consent had *not* been given: When it is shown that until the moment of the marriage the party continually expressed his desire to marry someone else, then it is to be presumed that he lacked the necessary matrimonial consent.[46] When a man has simulated consent in order to possess the woman carnally, the circumstances of the case will usually reveal that he had previously attempted to seduce her but was unsuccessful in the attempt,[47] and his deception of the woman regarding his intention was accompanied with other falsehoods.[48]

The fact that the marriage was never consummated at any time may well indicate that the consent of one party was feigned, especially when fear was the cause alleged for the nullity.[49] When one of the consorts has deserted the

[43] Cf. S.R.R., *Dec.*, XXX (1938), 587; S.R.R. *Dec.*, XXVIII (1936), 11; S.R.R., *Dec.*, XXV (1933), 249; S.R.R., *Dec.*, XXI (1929), 210.

[44] Cf. S.R.R., *Dec.*, XXX (1938), 348; S.R.R., *Dec.*, XXVIII (1936), 11; S.R.R. *Dec.*, XXV (1933), 447.

[45] Cf. S.R.R., *Dec.*, XXVIII (1936), 11; S.R.R., *Dec.*, XXV (1933), 249; S.R.R., *Dec.*, XXI (1929), 210.

[46] S.R.R., *Dec.*, XXI (1929), 238; S.R.R., *Dec.*, V (1913), 213; S.R.R., *Dec.*, XVII (1925), 69.

[47] Cf. S.R.R., *Dec.*, XVIII (1926), 37.

[48] Cf. S.R.R., *Dec.*, XXI (1929), 237.

[49] Cf. S.R.R., *Dec.* XX (1928), 396; S.R.R., *Dec.*, XVII (1925), 73; S.R.R., *Dec.*, XVI (1924), 72.

other immediately or almost immediately after the ceremony there is a grave indication that his consent to the marriage was merely fictitious.[50]

If the conjugal life of the consorts was extremely brief, there may be a good indication that it was not properly instituted inasmuch as it was so quickly dissolved.[51] This presumption will naturally be less compelling than in the case wherein there had been no cohabitation whatsoever, yet the Rota has frequently considered the early cessation of cohabitation as an indication of simulation in particular cases.[52] Marital infidelity on the part of one of the spouses in the early days of the marriage, though usually of greater probative value in cases of partial simulation, may likewise provide adminicular proof that the consent was totally simulated.[53]

[50] S.R.R., *Dec.*, XXV (1933), 465; S.R.R., *Dec.*, XVII (1925), 49.

[51] S.R.R., *Dec.* XX (1928), 83.

[52] Cf. S.R.R., *Dec.*, XVIII (1926), 39; S.R.R., *Dec.*, XV (1923), 166.

[53] Cf. S.R.R., *Dec.*, XX (1928), 396; S.R.R., *Dec.*, XV (1923), 165-173.

CONCLUSIONS

1. The discretionary authority of the judge in marriage causes is indeed wide in scope, but it is circumscribed by the demands which derive from reason and the positive law; it is the result of a combination of elements of Roman law and Germanic law, leavened by the wisdom and experience of the Church.[1]

2. The ultimate purpose of the discretionary authority of the judge in conducting the trial is the reducing of all but likewise only the necessary judicial evidence to the written acts of the process and incorporated proofs *(acta et probata)*, for the final decision must be based solely on these *acta et probata*.[2]

3. The object of a marriage trial is not that of proving the plaintiff right or wrong, but that of arriving at the truth; in achieving this end, the judge has the discretionary authority to limit or augment the judicial evidence as he deems necessary, in accordance with justice and equity.[3]

4. Every judicial examination must follow the same general pattern in the pronouncing of the oath, in the identification of the deponent, and in the method of interrogation, regardless of whether it is an initial examination, a re-examination, or a confrontation.[4]

5. While the depositions or confessions of the parties themselves are incapable of alone forming full proof, they are of the utmost importance in arriving at the truth, particularly in marriage causes involving defective consent, impotence, and non-consummation; unsworn, extra-judicial confessions of the parties, given *tempore non suspecto*, generally have more probative value than sworn judicial depositions.[5]

[1] Cf. *supra*, pp. 1, 9, 14.

[2] Cf. *supra*, pp. 74, 161.

[3] Cf. *supra*, p. 78.

[4] Cf. *supra*, pp. 85, 93, 137.

[5] Cf. *supra*, p. 171.

6. Perhaps the widest field for the discretionary authority of the judge is found in his evaluation of the judicial evidence presented in the trial; he is limited only by his conscience and certain directives, such as those formed by presumptions of the law.[6]

7. The conscience of the judge should be based not only on a thorough knowledge of the substantive law, but also on a careful study of ecclesiastical jurisprudence, chiefly to be found in the decisions of the Sacred Roman Rota.[7]

8. There are no mathematical formulas by which the judge can arrive at his final decision; all the evidence must be carefully weighed, as a whole. And it is the total force of the judicial evidence which will convince, or fail to convince, the judge. Thus, no piece of evidence should be evaluated in itself, independently of the other evidence.[8]

9. Personal presumptions *(praesumptiones hominis)* are of great value to the judge in finally arriving at moral certainty, especially such as are based upon circumstantial evidence derived *tempore non suspecto.* Indeed, strong personal presumptions may at times suffice for dislodging a contrary legal presumption.[9]

[6] Cf. *supra,* p. 164.
[7] Cf. *supra,* p. 167.
[8] Cf. *supra,* pp. 74, 165.
[9] Cf. *supra,* p. 219 ff.

BIBLIOGRAPHY

Sources

Acta Apostolicae Sedis, Commentarium Officiale, Romae, 1909-1929; Civitate Vaticana, 1929-

Acta Conciliorum et Epistolae Decretales ac Constitutiones Summorum Ponticum, ed. Jean Hardouin, 12 vols., Parisiis, 1714-1715.

Acta et Decreta Sacrorum Conciliorum Recentiorum, Collectio Lacensis, 7 vols., Friburgi Brisgoviae, 1870-1892.

Acta Sanctae Sedis, 41 vols., Romae, 1865-1908.

Bruns. H. Th., *Canones Apostolorum et Conciliorum Saeculorum IV-VII*, 2 vols., Berolini, 1839.

Canon Law Digest, The, edited by T. Lincoln Bouscaren, 3 vols., Milwaukee: Bruce Publishing Co., Vol. I, 1934, Vol. II, 1943, Vol. III, 1954.

Codex Iuris Canonici, Pii X Pontificis Maximi Iussu Diguestus, Benedicti Papae XV Auctoritate Promulgatus, Romae, Typis Polyglottis Vaticanis, 1917.

Codicis Iuris Canonici Fontes, cura Em̃i Petri Card. Gasparri editi, 9 vols., Romae (postea Civitate Vaticana): Typis Polyglottis Vaticanis, 1923-1939. (Vols. VII-IX ed. cura et studio Em̃i Iustiniani Card. Serédi.)

Collectio Omnium Conclusionum et Resolutionum S. C. Concilii ab anno 1564 ad annum 1860, ed. S. Pallottini, 17 vols., Romae, 1868-1893.

Concilium Tridentinum, Diariorum, Actorum, Epistularum, Tractatum, Nova Collectio. Edidit Societas Goerresiana, 13 vols., Friburgi Brisgoviae: B. Herder, 1901-

Corpus Iuris Canonici, ed. Lipsien. 2. post Aemilii Ludovici Richteri curas . . . instruxit Aemilius Friedberg, 2 vols., Lipsiae: Tauchnitz, 1879-1881. Editio anastatice repetita, Lipsiae: Tauchnitz, 1928.

Decretales D. Gregorii Papae IX, suae integritati, una cum glossis restitutae, cum privilegio Gregorii XIII, Pontif. max., et aliorum Principum, Romae, 1582.

Decretum Gratiani, emendatum et notationibus illustratum, una cum glossis, 2 vols., Romae, 1582.

Didascalia et Constitutiones Apostolorum, ed. F. X. Funk, Paderborn, 1905.

Hinschius, *Decretales Pseudo-Isidorianae et Capitula Angilramni* Lipsiae, 1863.

Jaffé, Phillipus, *Regesta Pontificum Romanorum ab condita Ecclesia ad annum post Christum natum MCXCVIII*, 2. ed., correctam at auctam auspiciis Gulielmi Wattenbach, curaverunt S. Löwenfeld, F. Kaltenbrunner, P. Ewald, 2 vols., Lipsiae, 1885-1888.

Mansi, J., *Sacrorum Conciliorum Nova et Amplissima Collectio,* 53 vols. in 60, Parisiis, 1901-1927.

Migne, P. J., *Patrologiae Cursus Completus, Series Latina,* 221 vols., Parisiis, 1844-1855.

Monumenta Germaniae Historica, Hanoverae, 1826—Legum Sectio III, Concilia Tom. I, Concilia Aevi Merovingia, ed., F. Maassen, 1893; Tom. II, Concilia Aevi Karolini I, ed. A. Werminghoff, 1904; *Epistolae,* ed. L. M. Hartmann, Berolini, 1899.

Potthast, Augustus, *Regesta Pontificum Romanorum inde ab anno post Christum* natum MCXCVIII ad annum MCCCIV, 2 vols., Berolini, 1874-1875.

Sacrae Romanae Rotae Decisiones seu Sententiae quae . . . prodierunt anno 1909- , Romae, Typis Vaticanis, 1912- .

Schroeder, H. J., *Canons and Decrees of the Council of Trent,* Original Text with English translation, St. Louis: B. Herder Co., 1941.

Thesaurus Resolutionum Sacrae Congregationis Concilii, 1718-1908, 167 vols., Vols. I-V, Urbini, 1739-1740; Vols. VI-CLXVII, Romae, 1741-1909.

AUTHORS

Abbo, John A.-Hannan, Jerome D., *The Sacred Canons,* B. Herder Co.: St. Louis, 1952.

Amos, Sheldon, *The History and Principles of the Civil Law of Rome,* London, 1883.

Ayrinhac, H. A.,-Lydon, P. J., *Penal Legislation in the New Code of Canon Law,* New York: Benziger Brothers, 1936.

Bassibey, R., *Le Mariage devant les Tribunaux Ecclésiastiques; Procédure Matrimoniale Générale,* Paris, 1899.

Benedetti, Ivo, *Ordo Iudicialis Processus Canonici Super Nullitate Matrimonii Instruendi,* 2. ed., Taurini: Marietti, 1938.

Benedictus XIV, *De Synodo Dioecesana—Opera omnia,*—Tom. XI, Prati, 1844.

Blat, A., *Commentarium Textus Codicis Iuris Canonici,* 5 vols. in 6, Romae: Institutum Pontificium Internationale "Angelicum," Vol. V, *De Processibus* 1927.

Bouix, D., *Tractatus de Judiciis Ecclesiasticis,* 2 vols., Parisiis, 1855.

Buckland, W. W., *A Textbook of Roman Law from Augustus to Justinian,* 2. ed., Cambridge: University Press, 1932.

Burdick, William L., *The Principles of Roman Law and their Relation to Modern Law,* Rochester, N. Y.: The Lawyers Coöperative Pub. Co., 1938.

Cappello, Felix M., *Summa Iuris Canonici,* Apud Aedes Universitatis Gregorianae, 3 vols., Romae: 1928-36.

Cavanagh, John R.,-McGoldrick, James B., *Fundamental Psychiatry*, Milwaukee: Bruce Pub. Co., 1953.

Cicero, M. T., *Opera Omnia*, ex recensione Christ. Godofr. Schützii, Augustae Taurinorum, 1823.

Cicognani, Amleto G., *Canon Law*, 2. ed., authorized English version by J. O'Hara and F. Brennan, Philadelphia: Dolphin Press, 1935.

Ciprotti, Pio, *Observationes al Texto del Codex Iuris Canonici*, translated from 1st. Italian ed. [1944], by Tomás García Baberena, Salamanca, 1950.

Claeys-Bouuaert, F.-Simenon, G., *Manuale Juris Canonici*, 3 vols., Vols. I, III, 4. ed.; Vol. II, 2. ed., Ghent-Liège, 1934-1935.

Clune, Robert B., *The Judicial Interrogation of the Parties*, The Catholic University of America Canon Law Studies, n. 269, Washington, D.C.: The Catholic University of America Press, 1948.

Cocchi, Guidus, *Commentarium in Codicem Iuris Canonici ad Usum Scholarum*, 8 vols., Taurinorum Augustae: Marietti, 1920-1930.

Conran, Edward J., *The Interdict*, The Catholic University of America Canon Law Studies, n. 56, Washington, D.C.: The Catholic University of America, 1930.

Coronata, Matthaeus Conte a, *Institutiones Iuris Canonici*, 2. ed., 5 vols., Vol. III, *De Processibus* 3. ed., 1948, Taurini: Marietti.

De Becker, Julius, *De Sponsalibus et Matrimonio Praelectiones Canonicae*, 2. ed., Lovanii, 1913.

Devoti, Ioannes, *Institutionum Canonicarum Libri IV*, 4. ed. Romana, Leodii, 1874.

Doheny, William J., *Canonical Procedure in Matrimonial Cases*, 2 vols. Vol. I, *Formal Judical Procedure* 2. ed., 1948; Vol. II, *Informal Procedure*, 1944; Milwaukee, Bruce Pub. Co.

———, *Practical Manual for Marriage Cases*, Milwaukee, Bruce Pub. Co., 1938.

Duerr, Charles J., *The Judicial Notary*, The Catholic University of America Canon Law Studies, n. 312, Washington, D.C.: The Catholic University of America Press, 1951.

Dugan, Henry F., *The Judiciary Department of the Diocesan Curia*, The Catholic University of America Canon Law Studies, n. 26, Washington, D.C.: The Catholic University of America, 1925.

Durandus, Gulielmus, *Speculum Iuris*, Venetiis, 1566.

Ferrari, Iosephus C., *Summa Institutionum Canonicarum*, 4. ed., 2 vols., Genuae, 1889.

Fournier, Edouard, *Les Origines du Vicaire Général*, Paris, 1922.

Fulton, Thomas B., *The Prenuptial Investigation*, The Catholic University of America Canon Law Studies, n. 274, Washington, D. C.: The Catholic University of America Press, 1948.

Gasparri, Petrus Card., *Tractatus Canonicus de Matrimonio*, ed. nova ad mentem Codicis Iuris Canonici, Romae: Typis Polyglottis Vaticanis, 1932.

Glasson, E., *Histoire du Droit et des Instuiions de la France*, Paris, 1889.

Hanssen, Antonius, *De Sanctione Nullitatis in Processu Canonico*, Romae: Apollinaris, 1939.

Hogan, James, *Judicial Advocates and Procurators*, The Catholic University of America Canon Law Studies, n. 133, Washington, D.C.: The Catholic University of America Press, 1941.

Jolowicz, H. F., *Historical Introduction to the Study of Roman Law*, Cambridge: University Press, 1932.

Kealy, John, *The Introductory Libellus in Church Court Procedure*, The Catholic University of America Canon Law Studies, n. 108, Washington, D.C.: The Catholic University of America, 1937.

Lega, Michaelis, *Praelectiones in Textum Iuris Canonici de Iudiciis Ecclesiasticis: De Iudiciis Ecclesiasticis Civilibus*, 2. ed., 2 vols., Romae, 1905.

———, *Commentarius in Iudicia Ecclesiastica*, curante V. Bartoccetti, 2. ed., 3 vols., Romae: Anonima Libraria Cattolica Italiana, 1950.

Lyons, Avitus E., *The Collegiate Tribunal of First Instance*, The Catholic University of America Canon Law Studies, n. 78, Washington, D.C.: The Catholic University of America, 1932.

Manning, John J., *Presumptions of Law in Marriage Cases*, The Catholic University of America Canon Law Studies, n. 94, Washington, D.C.: The Catholic University of America, 1935.

Mansella, Iosephus, *De Impedimentis Matrimonium Dirimentibus ac de Processu Iudiciali in Causis Matrimonialibus*, Romae, 1881.

Mascardus, Josephus, *De Probationibus*, Frankfurt, 1684.

McCarthy, Eduardus A., *De Certitudine Morali Quae in Judicis Animo ad Sententiae Pronuntiationem Requiritur*, Romae, Officium Libri Catholici, 1948.

Metz, John E., *The Recording Judge in the Ecclesiastical Collegiate Tribunal*, The Catholic University of America Canon Law Studies, n. 287, Washington, D.C.: The Catholic University of America Press, 1949.

Moriarity, Eugene J., *Oaths in Ecclesiastical Courts*, The Catholic University of America Canon Law Studies, n. 110, Washington, D.C.: The Catholic University of America, 1937.

Muirhead, J.-Goudy, H.-Grant, A., *Historical Introduction to the Private Law of Rome*, 3. ed., London, 1916.

Muñiz, T., *Procedimientos Eclesiásticos*, 2 ed., 3 vols., Sevilla, Imp. y Lib. de Sobrino de Izquierdo, 1925.

Noldin, H.-Schmitt, A., *Summa Theologiae Moralis*, 23. ed., 3 vols., Oeniponte: Rauch, 1935.

Noone, John J., *Nullity in Judicial Acts*, The Catholic University of America Canon Law Studies, n. 297, Washington, D.C.: The Catholic University of America Press, 1950.

Noval, J., *Commentarium Codicis Iuris Canonici*, Liber IV, *De Processibus*, Pars. I, *De Iudiciis*, Augustae Taurinorum-Romae: Marietti, 1920.

Nuttin, Joseph, *Psychoanalysis and Personality*, New York: Sheed & Ward, 1953.

Panormitanus, Abbas (Nicholaus de Tudeschis), *Commentaria in Quinque Libros Decretalium*, 5 vols. in 7, Venetiis, 1588.

Perrone, Ioannes, *De Matrimonio Christiano*, 3 vols., Romae: Typis S. Congr. de Prop. Fide, 1858.

Pickett, R. Colin, *Mental Affliction and Church Law*, Universitas Catholica Ottaviensis, series canonica, tom. 25, Ottawa, Ontario: The University of Ottawa Press, 1952.

Pirhing, Ernricus, *Ius Canonicum*, Venetiis, 1759.

Prince, John E., *The Diocesan Chancellor*, The Catholic University of America Canon Law Studies, n. 167, Washington, D.C.: The Catholic University of America Press, 1942.

Reiffenstuel, Anacletus, *Jus Canonicum Universum*, 5 vols. in 7, Parisiis, 1864-1870.

Reynes, Lorenzo Quintana, *La Prueba en el Procedimiento Canónico*, Barcelona, 1943.

Roberti, Franciscus, *De Processibus*, 2 vols., Romae: Vol. I, 2. ed., 1941; Vol. II, 1926.

———, *Codicis Iuris Canonici Schemata, Lib. IV, De Processibus, I, De Iudiciis in Genere*, Romae: Typis Polyglottis Vaticanis, 1940.

Sägmüller, J. B., *Lehrbuch des katolischen Kirchenrechts*, 2. ed., 2 vols., Freiburg im Breisgau, 1909.

Sanchez, Thomas, *De Sancto Matrimonii Sacramento Disputationum Libri Decem*, 3 vols., Venetiis, 1693.

Schmalzgrueber, Franciscus, *Ius Ecclesiasticum Universum*, 5 vols. in 12, Romae, 1843-1845.

Smith, S. B., *Elements of Ecclesiastical Law*, 3 vols., Vol. II, 2. ed., New York, 1887.

Thomassinus, Ludovicus, *Vetus et Nova Ecclesiae Disciplina circa Beneficia et Beneficiarios*, Lucae, 1728.

Tobin, Thomas Joseph, *De Officiali Curiae Dioecesanae*, Romae: Apud Aedes Pontificiae Universitatis Gregorianae, 1936.

Toliusis, Casimir T., *De Notario Curiae Dioecesanae*, Romae, 1951.

Torre, Joannes, *Processus Matrimonialis*, Neapoli: M. D'Auria, 1947.

Van Hove, A., *Commentarium Lovaniense in Codicem Iuris Canonici,* Vol. I, tom. I, *Prolegomena,* 2. ed., Mechliniae-Romae, H. Dessain, 1945.

Vaughan, William E., *Constitutions for Diocesan Courts,* The Catholic University of America Canon Law Studies, n. 210, Washington, D.C.: The Catholic University of America Press, 1944.

Vermeersch, A.,-Creusen, J., *Epitome Iuris Canonici,* 3 vols., Vols. I-II, 5 ed., 1933-34; Vol. III, 4 ed., 1931, Romae-Mechlinae: H. Dessain.

Wanenmacher, Francis, *Canonical Evidence in Marriage Cases,* Philadelphia: Dolphin Press, 1935.

Wenger, Leopold, *Institutes of the Roman Law of Civil Procedure,* rev. ed., translated by O. H. Fish, New York: Veritas Press, 1940.

Wernz, F. X., *Ius Decretalium,* 6 vols., Vol V, *De Judiciis Ecclesiasticis,* Prati, 1914.

Wernz, F. X.,-Vidal, P., *Ius Canonicum,* 7 vols., in 8, Vol VI, *De Processibus,* Romae: Apud Aedes Universitatis Gregorianae, 1927/8.

Whalen, Donald W., *The Value of Testimonial Evidence in Matrimonial Procedure,* The Catholic University of America Canon Law Studies, n. 99, Washington, D.C.: The Catholic University of America, 1935.

Wigmore, John H., *The Principles of Judicial Proof as Given by Logic, Psychology and General Experience and Illustrated in Judicial Trials,* Boston: Little, Brown & Co., 1913.

Willett, Robert A., *The Probative Value of Documents in Ecclesiastical Trials,* The Catholic University of America Canon Law Studies, n. 171, Washington, D.C.: The Catholic University of America Press, 1942.

Wohlhaupter, Eugen, *Aequitas Canonica: Eine Studie aus dem kanonischen Recht,* Paderborn, 1931.

Woywod, Stanislaus-Smith, Callistus, *A Practical Commentary on the Code of Canon Law,* 7. printing, 2 vols. New York: Joseph F. Wagner, Inc., 1943.

Article

Schmidt, John Rogg, "The Juridic Value of the INSTRUCTIO provided by the *Motu Proprio "Cum Iuris Canonici," The Jurist,* I (1941), 289-316.

Periodical

Jurist, The, Washington, D.C., 1941-

ABBREVIATIONS

AAS—*Acta Apostolicae Sedis.*
Art.—Article of the *Instructio of* the S. Congregation of the Sacraments, 1936.
ASS—*Acta Sanctae Sedis.*
Can.—Canon of the *Codex Iuris Canonici.*
Fontes—*Codicis Iuris Canonici Fontes.*
S.R.R., *Dec.*—S. Romanae Rotae, *Decisiones seu Sententiae.*

CHRONOLOGICAL INDEX OF THE CITED ROTA CASES

matrimonii, 7 augusti, coram R.P.D. Quattrocolo, 224, 225

XXI (1929), *S. Romanae Rotae Decisiones seu Sententiae:*

Dec. XXI 171-184 *Marianopolitana,* Nullitatis matrimonii, 5 aprilis, coram R.P.D. Guglielmi, 175

Dec. XXV, 206-217 *Parisien.,* Nullitatis matrimonii, 5 iunii, coram R.P.D. Jullien, 224

Dec. XXVII 232-239—Nullitatis Matrimonii, 1 iulii, coram Revm̃o P.D. Massimi, Decano, 224

XXIII (1931), *S. Romanae Rotae Decisiones seu Sententiae:*

Dec. XXIV, 194-202—Nullitatis matrimonii, 2 iunii, coram R. P.D. Quattrocolo, 223

XXV (1933), *S. Romanae Rotae Decisiones seu Sententiae:*

Dec. X, 77-86—Nullitatis matrimonii, 16 februarii, coram R.P. D. Grazioli, 171, 172, 223

Dec. XXVII, 241-253—*Lugdunen.,* Nullitatis matrimonii, 21 aprilis, coram R.P.D. Guglielmi, 223, 224

Dec. LII, 442-450—Nullitatis matrimonii, 11 iulii, coram Excm̃o P.D. Massimi, Decano, 171, 224

Dec. LV, 461-480—Nullitatis matrimonii, 17 iulii, coram R. P.D. Grazioli, 225

Dec. LXII, 526-535—Nullitatis matrimonii, 8 augusti, coram R.P.D. Wynen, 189

XXVI (1934), *S. Romanae Rotae Decisiones seu Sententiae:*

Dec. VII, 71-70—*Meliten.,* Nullitatis matrimonii, 1 martii, coram R.P.D. Wynen, 174

Dec. XVI, 166-173—Nullitatis matrimonii, 9 aprilis, coram Excm̃o P.D. Massimi, Decano, 223

Dec. LIV, 465-473—*Liburnen.,* Nullitatis matrimonii, 2 iulii, coram R.P.D. Grazioli, 171

XXVII (1935), *S. Romanae Rotae Decisiones seu Sententiae:*

Dec. X, 76-91—*Beryten. Maronitarum,* Nullitatis matrimonii, 23 februarii, coram R.P.D. Jullien, 222

Dec. LXVI, 551-556—Nullitatis matrimonii, 8 augusti, coram R.P.D. Grazioli, 175

XXVIII (1936), *S. Romanae Rotae Decisiones seu Sententiae:*

Dec. I, 1-14—*Parisien.,* Nullitatis matrimonii, 6 februarii, coram R.P.D. Jullien, 223, 224

Dec. XI, 99-114—*Matriten.,* Nullitatis matrimonii, 6 februarii, coram R.P.D. Wynen, 178, 223

Dec. XIV, 129-133—Nullitatis matrimonii et dispensationis super rato, 18 februarii, coram R.P.D. Quattrocolo, 174, 223

XXIX (1937), *S. Romanae Rotae Decisiones seu Sententiae:*

Dec. XVII, 169-197—*Matriten.,* Nullitatis matrimonii, 27 februarii, coram R.P.D. Wynen, 205

Dec. XXX, 314-319—*Varsavien.,* Nullitatis matrimonii, 27 februarii, coram R.P.D. Wynen, 223

Dec. LVI, 556-568—*Parisien.,* Nullitatis matrimonii, 30 iulii, coram Excmo P.D. Grazioli, 174

Dec. LXVIII, 663-674—*Rapidopolitana,* Nullitatis matrimonii, 16 novembris, coram R.P.D. Quattrocolo, 223

Dec. LXXIV, 733-741—*Czesto-*

INDEX OF AUTHORS

(Principal authors who are cited more than once)

GENERAL INDEX

INDEX OF CANONS

INDEX OF ARTICLES OF THE *INSTRUCTIO*, S. C. SACRAM., AUGUST 15, 1936

BIOGRAPHICAL NOTES

A brief biographical sketch of Archibald M. Bottoms follows:

1. Born in Wichita Falls, Texas, October 12, 1916.
2. Attended Catholic grade and high schools in Amarillo, Texas.
3. Made seminary studies at the Pontifical College Josephinum, Worthington, O.
4. Ordained priest, May 30, 1942, by the Most Reverend Amleto G. Cicognani, D.D., Apostolic Delegate in the United States of America.
5. Served as assistant in parish and chancery in Amarillo for three years.
6. Enrolled in the School of Canon Law, the Catholic University of America, Washington, D.C., in September, 1945.
7. Received degrees of J.C.B. in June, 1946, and J.C.L. in June, 1947.
8. Appointed chancellor, Diocese of Amarillo, July, 1947.
9. Returned to the Catholic University of America in September, 1953, to complete the third year of study in Canon Law.

CANON LAW STUDIES*

349. Bottoms, Rev. Archibald M., J.C.L., The Discretionary Au-Authority of the Ecclesiastical Judge in Matrimonial Trials of the First Instance.
350. Kekumano, Rev. Charles A., A.B., J.C.L., The Secret Archives of the Diocesan Curia.
351. McGrath, Rev. Robert E., O.M.I., J.C.L., The Local Superior in Non-exempt Clerical Congregations.
352. McManus, Rev. Frederick R., A.B., J.C.L., The Congregation of Sacred Rites.
353. Rodimer, Rev. Frank J., A.B., S.T.L., J.C.L., The Canonical Effects of Infamy of Fact.
354. Rouillard, Rev. Jacques, A.B., Ph.B., J.C.L., Une étude comparée du droit canonique et du droit civil paroissal de la Province de Québec dans l'administration des biens paroissaux.
355. Ryan, Rev. Thomas C., J.C.L., The Juridical Effects of the *Sanatio in Radice.*
356. Sullivan, Rev. Bernard Owens, J.C.L., Legislation and Requirements for Permissible Cohabiation in Invalid Marriages.
357. Tatarczuk, Rev. Vincent A., A.B., S.T.L., J.C.L., Infamy of Law.

* For a complete list of the available numbers of Canon Law Studies apply to the Catholic University of America Press, 620 Michigan Ave., N.E., Washington 17, D.C., for a general catalogue.

www.ingramcontent.com/pod-product-compliance
Lightning Source LLC
LaVergne TN
LVHW041116090826
844660LV00060B/636